FX TRADING

A GUIDE TO TRADING FOREIGN EXCHANGE

FX TRADING

A GUIDE TO TRADING FOREIGN EXCHANGE

ALEX DOUGLAS ■ LARRY LOVRENCIC ■ PETER PONTIKIS

First published in 2012 by Wrightbooks
an imprint of John Wiley & Sons Australia, Ltd
42 McDougall St, Milton Qld 4064

Office also in Melbourne

Typeset in Chaparral Pro Regular 12/13.5 pt

National Library of Australia Cataloguing-in-Publication data:

Author:	Pontikis, Peter.
Title:	FX trading : a guide to trading foreign exchange / Peter Pontikis, Alex Douglas and Larry Lovrencic.
Edition:	2nd ed.
ISBN:	9780730376521 (pbk.)
Notes:	Includes index.
Subjects:	Foreign exchange.
	Foreign exchange market.
	Foreign exchange futures.
Other Authors/Contributors:	Douglas, Alex.
	Lovrencic, Larry.
Dewey Number:	332.45

Cover design by Punch Bowl Design

Cover image: © kentoh/Shutterstock.com

Photograph of Alex Douglas Courtesy IBFX Australia Pty Ltd

Figures 2.1, 3.1, 3.2, 3.3, 8.23 and 9.7 Microsoft Excel charts reproduced by permission from Microsoft Corporation

Printed in China by Printplus Limited

10 9 8 7 6 5 4 3 2 1

Contents

Preface *vii*
About the authors *xi*

1 Money management — an overview 1
2 What is foreign exchange? 3
3 Show me the money! 23
4 Talking the talk 31
5 Who's who at the FX marketplace 51
6 Trading platforms for retail traders 69
7 Factors influencing FX markets 89
8 Technical analysis for traders 115
9 FX fundamental analysis for traders 159
10 FX trading at the big end of town 181
11 Introduction to FX trading strategy 201
12 Money management — the fundamentals 231
13 (Your) Wealth on the global stage 241
14 New technology 253

Conclusion and next steps *261*
Appendix: World currency codes *263*
Index *267*

Preface

Since my first introduction to the foreign exchange market in 1983, there have been many, many changes. For a start, we no longer have to plot price movements on hand-drawn charts! The exponential and ongoing advances in technology have completely transformed the trading landscape. Even in the six years since the first edition of this book was written, in 2005, a new generation of trading platforms has evolved, offering faster and more advanced trade execution with improved functionality and ease of use.

The environment in which we trade has also undergone enormous change. Many countries around the world have either introduced or tightened regulations relating to retail foreign exchange trading. This has dramatically improved the integrity of the market for all participants.

Some of the changes that have taken place have rendered information in the first edition of this book obsolete or even erroneous. In writing this second edition of *FX Trading*, we have taken the opportunity to amend outdated information, expand on areas of specific interest and add new sections that will strengthen the reader's command of the subject.

While there have been numerous changes specific to the foreign exchange market and retail traders in particular, there have been just as many changes in the macroeconomic arena, many with a global impact. Back in 2005 we were yet to hear of the US mortgage crisis and the ensuing global financial crisis (GFC) that engulfed the world in 2008 and 2009. Massive spending programs by the US government and bouts of quantitative easing (QEI and QEII) have significantly weakened the US dollar and played a part in the downgrading of the US credit rating by Standard & Poor's. There have been threats to the dominance of the US dollar in global trade as some countries experiment with trading oil in EUR instead of USD. Even the role of the US dollar as the world's reserve currency has been questioned as numerous countries have been seen diversifying their holdings to include more EUR, JPY, AUD and even BRL.

However, the prime contender to challenge the supremacy of the US dollar is also looking shaky. Major debt problems in Europe have called into question the long-term viability of the euro.

In the meantime, the so called BRIC countries — Brazil, Russia, India and China — have seen their fortunes improve as the world turns to these emerging markets to provide the engine needed to revive growth.

Strong growth in China has sometimes been linked to what many regard as an artificially weak currency, thus giving their exports an advantage over those from other countries. On 21 July 2005, Chinese authorities relaxed the fixed peg of CNY against the USD, which had been in place since 1994. The USD/CNY rate initially fell from 8.28 to 8.11. A gradual, managed firming of the CNY paused around 6.83 during the GFC, but the path to a firmer CNY has resumed in recent times, with the USD/CNY currently around 6.38.

Although the massive boom in commodities has had the odd stumble, prices remain elevated and 'commodity currencies', such as the Australian dollar, have benefited enormously. The sustained push above parity with the US dollar is being blamed on, or credited with, driving changes in the makeup of the Australian industrial landscape. A strong currency is also having an impact in Japan where a surging yen is damaging the competitiveness of major export-driven companies.

Amid all this turmoil, the price of gold has posted dramatic gains. With faith in fiat currencies shaken and the US dollar losing value, gold has recently traded above US$1900 per ounce. This is some four times higher than when we wrote the first edition of this book in 2005.

While global economies and their currencies advance and decline, technology remains on a sustained path of advancement. Traders are no longer tethered to their desks. Thanks to wireless internet access, smart-phones and tablet computers, the dream of being able to trade from anywhere has finally arrived.

Advances in technology have also influenced trading techniques. There has been phenomenal growth in the use of algorithmic, or robotic, trading tools by retail traders in the last few years. General consensus is that this will only increase in the years ahead.

Of all the changes associated with foreign exchange trading that have occurred in recent years, the rise in the retail segment of the market has been one of the most interesting. In January 2011 a conference was held in Singapore catering primarily to institutional foreign exchange traders and fund managers. On the second day of the conference, after lunch, I was part of a panel discussion about retail currency trading. Given the timing of this session and the predominance of institutional representatives at the conference, I feared that this session would not be particularly well attended. To my astonishment, the panel discussion on retail trading drew one of the largest audiences of the two-day event. With retail traders reportedly contributing as much as 8 per cent of the daily turnover in the global foreign exchange market, it seems that even the institutional crowd now acknowledges the significance of this slice of the market.

Of course, not everything has changed. The underlying concepts remain the same. As with any trading, the main goal remains to sell at a higher price than the price at which you buy. And, as always, the key determinant of likely trading success remains your ability to develop and adhere to a sound strategy for money management.

Good luck and good trading!

Alex Douglas
<www.alexdouglas.com>
September 2011

About the authors

Alex Douglas drew his first currency chart by hand in 1983. This opened the door to a career in the financial markets that has included being an FX voice broker, a trader on the floor of the Sydney Futures Exchange and a director of global FX and derivative trading firms. He has been a director and president of several technical analyst associations around the world and has established a solid media reputation for his lucid comments on markets. Alex is currently the managing director of IBFX Australia.

Views and opinions expressed in this book are not necessarily those of IBFX. Visit Alex's website <www.alexdouglas.com> and follow him on Twitter: @AlexDouglasFX

Larry Lovrencic GDipAppFin (FINSIA), Dip TA (ATAA), CFTe, SF Fin has extensive experience trading financial markets and teaching technical analysis.

He is Vice President of Australian Professional Technical Analysts (APTA), a member of the Market Technicians Association (MTA), a Senior Fellow of the Financial Services Institute of Australasia (FINSIA) and was a Director of the International Federation of Technical Analysts (IFTA) and the Australian Technical Analysts Association (ATAA).

Larry is Executive Director of First Pacific Securities and IchimokuCharts.com, which provide research and educational services.

He is co-author of *Charting for Dummies* and FX *Trading: An Australian Guide to Trading Foreign Exchange*.

Peter Pontikis is a capital markets and private wealth management specialist for high net and ultra net worth families. He has more than 30 years of institutional and corporate experience in Australia and South-East Asia. Peter is past director and treasurer of the International Federation of Technical Analysts (IFTA) and Australian Technical Analysts Association (ATAA). He is an accredited dealer with AFMA, and is a Fellow of CPA Australia as well as a Senior Fellow of FINSIA, and sits on their financial markets and national advisory councils. Peter has several degrees in finance and economics as well as a master of arts.

Chapter 1

Money management—an overview

The more things change, the more they stay the same.

There is no doubt that the environment in which we trade is evolving rapidly. Since the first edition of this book was published in 2005 we have seen the rise of high-frequency trading, the adoption of algorithmic trading robots by retail traders, an explosion in the use of social networking and a significant increase in both the number and quality of brokers catering to retail foreign exchange traders.

No matter how much the trading environment changes and technology advances, the ultimate goal remains the same: to make a profit.

Over the years, in various locations around the world, we have encountered dozens of trading experts who have shared their knowledge through seminars, conferences, workshops, books, software, websites and blogs. In all probability you have also encountered some of the same people. Many claim to have discovered or created a special secret or tool that has helped them achieve phenomenal trading success, while others have diligently studied the methods of successful traders of days gone by. Some are willing to share this information for a token fee, while others attempt to charge truly eye-popping amounts of money based on the promise of untold fortunes to be made. As you would expect, some are worth every cent and some are not (even some of the free ones!).

As we look back over the methods and techniques presented by these traders, analysts and commentators, one point has become startlingly clear — and it is not just that some techniques 'work' and others don't. On the surface of it, all the market experts we have come across have different techniques for deciding when to enter and when to exit the market, but of those who have been demonstrably successful in the markets, there is one thing—and only one thing—that they *all* have in common: they all have a stringent method of money management and they all follow it unfailingly.

Although the journey taken by each trader is unique and will be influenced by changes in technology and the trading environment, the need for sound money management remains constant. To my mind, then, if there is a 'Holy Grail' in trading, money management must be it.

First things first: money management is by no means exclusive to the field of foreign exchange trading. It is used by traders in all markets. Those who are most diligent in its application tend to have the longest and most successful trading careers. At its core are the goals of protecting capital and maximising profits through appropriate trade selection, position sizing and exit strategies, with an overall focus on the discipline of adhering to the money management plan. Hence, money management is more about the process than the tactic to achieve the result; perhaps it could be described as the oyster shell that encases the growing pearl that is your trading methodology. Fingers crossed that with the discipline of iron-clad money management your wealth will grow steadily and surely for you to reap its eventual rewards.

But now we come to a considerable structural challenge for this book: we believe that the first chapter of any trading book should be on the topic of money management. However, beyond the briefest outline it is difficult to provide any kind of instruction or explanation of money management if the ground upon which it is set is yet to be explained or set out in detail. The overriding purpose of this book is to introduce you to the characteristics and jargon that are unique to the foreign exchange market, so it makes sense to leave the rest of this chapter until the end of the book. But in so doing, please do not let this lead you to believe it is any less important. Once more for the record: effective money management is *absolutely crucial* to your long-term trading success.

Now, let's find out what foreign exchange is ...

Chapter 2

What is foreign exchange?

The abbreviations and words 'FX', 'forex' and 'foreign exchange' are all interchangeable terms used to describe the market in which the currency of one country is exchanged for that of another country. Foreign exchange transactions may be as simple as those encountered by a tourist when visiting a local money changer to conduct a physical exchange of one currency for another, or as complex as multi-legged option strategies executed between global investment banks over electronic trading platforms with multiple settlement dates in multiple currencies. Each transaction forms a part of the foreign exchange market.

An important concept to understand from the beginning is that, unlike the equities and futures markets, the foreign exchange market does not have a physical 'exchange' in which transactions are conducted. Nor is there a single electronic platform for the execution of FX trades. Foreign exchange is what is known as an 'over-the-counter' (OTC) market. In basic terms, this means that any two parties that come together and exchange currencies between one another on agreed terms are participating in the foreign exchange market. Unlike an 'exchange-traded market', like that which operates through the Australian Securities Exchange (ASX), with an OTC market there is no need for either party to report a trade to a central exchange, or for any other third party to ever know of the existence of the trade.

While it is possible for every foreign exchange transaction to have a unique set of characteristics agreed to by each party, for the sake of simplicity and efficiency certain market conventions have emerged that allow for trading to take place within a framework of standard rules and conditions. These FX market conventions cover issues such as quoting methodology, terminology, and settlement dates and procedures. Because foreign exchange trading follows these conventions, we can view trades executed via many different methods as all forming a part of the one market. Don't worry, we'll get to explanations of the different methods of FX trading over the next few chapters.

Market segments: wholesale, clients (of wholesale) and brokers

Chapter 5 covers the three main groups of players and forums for FX trading, but let's have a quick look. Without doubt the biggest players in foreign exchange are the major international investment banks and fund managers. The activities of this section of the wholesale market drive the majority of moves in the market, influencing the levels at which one currency may be exchanged for another. Despite the OTC nature of the forex market, most trading that takes place around the world will be executed at prices that are very close to replicating those rates that are currently being used by these major players in what is known as the 'inter-bank' market. Any notable difference between the rates on the retail market and the inter-bank market would quickly be arbitraged out of existence (arbitrage is seeking to profit from price differences by buying or selling from one party for immediate resale or purchase to another). Traders would notice the difference and move to profit from the gap, buying in the underpriced market and selling in the overpriced market, quickly bringing the two back into line.

Importantly, the vast majority of transactions in the foreign exchange market take place between major institutional players in the inter-bank market. Corporations and small to mid-sized financial institutions generally use one of the major trading banks as their intermediary to the foreign exchange market. While some sophisticated and wealthy private traders are also able to participate in the forex market via an intermediary trading bank, it is becoming much more common for private retail traders to make use of the services of online margin FX providers as their bridge to the global foreign exchange market. (See chapter 6 for more on retail broking platforms through margin FX providers.)

Other than a small difference in the bid/ask spread and the amount of capital required, the key difference between participating in the forex market as a major trading bank in the inter-bank market and as a private trader using a margin FX provider is the nature of the counterparty. In the inter-bank market, the counterparty is the bank or institution on the other side of a deal. This counterparty may be different for each trade (though there are in-house limits and various rules that determine which counterparties may be traded with and how much may be traded with each of them). In contrast, a trader using an online margin FX provider will invariably have the same counterparty on each and every trade; namely, the margin FX provider that he or she has chosen to hold an account with. We will discuss the characteristics of the various market participants in a later chapter.

Why different sources quote different highs and lows

In the equities and futures markets there is rarely any dispute regarding the absolute high or low of trading activity on any particular day. It is a simple matter of checking the record of trades that have been registered with, or executed through, the exchange in question and determining the highest or lowest price achieved on the day. In such exchange-traded markets there is a single source of information, which is recorded by the relevant exchange and the ultimate high or low cannot really be disputed.

But in the OTC world of foreign exchange trading there are many different methods by which trades may be executed, including through traditional voice brokers (which have now been almost entirely replaced by electronic brokers), direct party-to-party deals, and online FX trading facilitators. Although the levels of the exchange rates used by participants in each of these areas will be very close to one another, they will not necessarily move in 100 per cent lock-step.

For example, if a trader using the EBS platform (an electronic broking platform for the inter-bank market) is desperate to buy EUR/USD, they may choose to pay slightly more than participants using the other trading methods. As a result, EBS may report a slightly higher high for EUR/USD than is seen elsewhere. No central authority has the final word on the absolute high or low of the market, so a situation will often exist where different platforms or brokers quote different levels for the highs and lows.

The existence of different trading platforms and brokers and the different supply and demand profiles of their individual clients at any particular point in time will not only affect absolute highs and lows, it will also result in slight differences in the bid and offer quotes. As mentioned, these variations will only ever be small because the foreign exchange market is extremely efficient and transparent, and any significant difference will be arbitraged out of existence very quickly.

Volume of data

Because of the lack of a central authority to collect data on each and every trade, it is impossible for anybody to acquire accurate figures for volume, or the exact number and value of FX transactions that take place each day. Traders can certainly tell reasonably well whether the market is busy or quiet (especially if they sit on an inter-bank trading desk), and those who have access to the tightly controlled data of the major electronic trading platforms will also have a good idea of the broad level of activity in the market, but there is no single authoritative agency that brings all this information together in one place. Nor is there likely to be — the companies that control the major trading platforms would be very reluctant to give out such information.

Although we lack day-to-day volume data for the foreign exchange market, a major international survey is conducted every three years by the Bank for International Settlements (BIS). This is an international body charged with the promotion of cooperation between the central banks and monetary authorities of the world with an aim of achieving monetary and financial stability. A central bank is a nation's principal monetary authority, responsible for monetary policy (interest rates) and stability of the financial system. Where required, this is the body that will intervene in the markets to influence the exchange rate of its currency. In Australia, the central bank is the Reserve Bank of Australia. The results of the BIS survey are published in the *Triennial Central Bank Survey*, which is on its website <www.bis.org>.

The results of the latest survey, conducted in April 2010 and published in December 2010, show that average daily turnover in the traditional (inter-bank) market was estimated at US$3981 billion (US$3.981 trillion), up significantly from a daily average of US$3210 billion in April 2007.

By comparison, data from the World Federation of Exchanges <www.world-exchanges.org> suggests that during May 2011, average daily turnover of all of the world's 52 associated equity exchanges combined (that is, the Australian Securities Exchange, Tokyo Stock Exchange, New York Stock Exchange, London Stock Exchange, and the many other exchanges) was in the vicinity of approximately US$241 billion. These figures for both the equities markets and foreign exchange markets fluctuate from day to day, depending on current events in each market, but in broad terms we can say that the foreign exchange market is roughly 10 times larger than the equities market, as shown in figure 2.1. By any measure, then, the FX market is the biggest market on earth by a very long way.

Figure 2.1: average daily turnover comparison

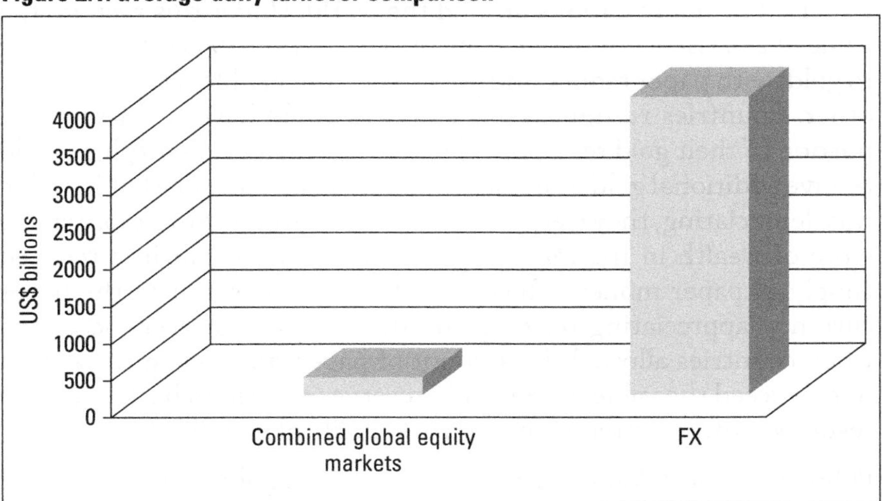

Brief history of the FX market

Merchants and travellers who trekked along the Silk Road through Asia selling and transporting their precious wares and traders in ancient Babylonian marketplaces may not have a great deal of relevance to your life today, but they were among the earliest participants in the foreign exchange markets. Any time that these border-hopping, business-savvy people wanted to exchange the currency unit of one country or region for that of another, the two parties involved in the transaction would have to settle on an acceptable rate of exchange in order for the transaction to take place. By doing so, traders from the Far East were able to trade successfully with traders from Mediterranean countries and vice versa. The ability to conduct foreign exchange transactions has always been of great significance in facilitating international trade. And in the absence of a common currency the world over, this situation is just as true today as it was hundreds of years ago.

In modern-day markets, most of the major currencies of the world are allowed to float relatively freely, with a myriad market forces that affect supply and demand determining the rates at which one currency may be exchanged for another. But this has not always been the case ...

In the decades prior to World War I, an international gold standard was used by many nations around the world. Under this system, the value of a particular unit of currency of each country was tied directly to gold, with paper money and gold freely convertible from one to the other. Countries running a trade deficit would have to surrender a portion of their gold reserves, while those with a trade surplus would receive additional gold. If holders of a particular currency felt its value was depreciating, they were able to shift their funds into a more stable store of wealth in the form of gold. This would result in a reduced supply of paper money, which would eventually result in the paper currency appreciating once again. There were, however, occasions when countries allowed the amount of paper currency in circulation to far exceed the value of their gold reserves needed to back it up. The result was often extreme inflation and political instability.

Following World War I, a revised version of the gold standard, known as the gold bullion standard, was put into place and accepted by many countries. The main difference from the gold specie standard that was in place prior to World War I was that banks were allowed to issue paper currency in excess of the value of the gold bullion they held. Eventually though, wide disparities in balance of payment positions between countries arose due to significant overvaluation and undervaluation of currencies. Before the outbreak of World War II, this version of the gold standard had collapsed.

Bretton Woods Accord

In July 1944, while World War II was still in progress, delegates of the 44 Allied nations met in Bretton Woods, in the US state of New Hampshire, to discuss plans to help the world rebuild in a climate of economic stability that would aid growth and prosperity in postwar years. The plan they constructed became known as the Bretton Woods Accord. The key feature of this accord was the gold exchange standard in which the United States dollar (US$ or USD) would become the defining yardstick, pegged to gold at US$35/oz. Other currencies were subsequently pegged to the US dollar (and therefore gold) with a band of 1 per cent either side to allow for minor currency fluctuations. The Bretton Woods Accord also saw the creation of the World Bank and the International Monetary Fund (IMF).

However, over the years the 1 per cent band for fluctuations proved too constrictive and with gold fixed at US$35/oz there was a drain on US gold reserves that weighed on market sentiment and the level of confidence in the US dollar. By 1971 it was abundantly clear to world markets that the Bretton Woods Accord had failed. At first there was an attempt to improve the situation by widening the fluctuation bands for other currencies against the US dollar from 1 per cent to 4.5 per cent under the Smithsonian Agreement of 1971, but this too had failed by 1973. Subsequently, countries began to move towards 'free-floating' currencies, in which the market forces of supply and demand were left largely unimpeded to determine the rate of exchange between currencies.

Free-floating currencies

Since 1973 most of the world's major currencies have moved toward this free-floating model, with governments mostly agreeing to refrain from attempts to keep their currency pegged at some artificial level against another currency or basket of currencies. The Australian dollar (A$ or AUD) was allowed to float freely in December 1983, after spending the years from 1974 to 1983 pegged to a basket of currencies known as the Trade Weighted Index (TWI), with a 'crawling peg' in place from 1976 (a crawling peg is a currency peg subject to frequent small adjustments). The TWI was created from a basket of currencies of Australia's trading partners, with the Australian dollar then pegged against the TWI rather than the US dollar. In November 1976 there was a significant devaluation of 17.5 per cent of the Australian dollar against the TWI. After this, it was decided that the value of the Australian dollar against the TWI should be subject to frequent small adjustments rather than larger, infrequent adjustments. The New Zealand dollar was also pegged against a trade-weighted basket of currencies from July 1973 through to March 1985; since then it too has been allowed to float freely.

Although currencies may be 'free floating', this doesn't mean that they are immune from official attempts to influence rates. For example, the central bank of a particular country may deem it necessary to take certain steps to influence the exchange rate in order to meet their obligations to achieve particular monetary goals, or simply to ensure a smooth and orderly market. Thus, while the Reserve Bank of Australia (RBA) does not have a preferred price level for the A$, it will intervene if it deems that movements in the market have become disorderly, or potentially destabilising. Occasional intervention is seen in almost all currencies, including the United States dollar, the European euro (EUR), the Great British pound (GBP) and the Japanese yen (JPY), to name a few (we'll look at these and other currencies in the next chapter). Of these major currencies, intervention has been seen most often in the JPY, undertaken by the Bank of Japan (BoJ) with occasional assistance from other central banks acting on behalf of the BoJ. In situations in which a government, through its central bank, regularly attempts to influence the value of its currency through active participation in the open market, the terms 'dirty float' or 'managed float' are often seen to be more appropriate than 'free float'.

Towards international cooperation

As any regular news observer will be aware, global economic stability has not been left entirely in the hands of market forces. Indeed, regular meetings are held between senior ministers and heads of state of countries (and indeed central bankers) that make up the Group of Eight (G8) and Group of Twenty (G20) countries. The idea behind such meetings is to foster global economic and financial harmonisation, promoting trade and reforming regulations to provide incentives for growth and trade to encourage good governance and risk management practices the world over (of course, whether they succeed in these endeavours is open to debate!). Their regular meetings are strategically important to economic global happenings and the influence they exert on currencies and currency trading cannot be overstated, even if it is not always immediately apparent.

The powerful G20 has its roots in the G8, which came about through the invitation for Russia to join what was previously considered the G7. Not surprisingly, the G7 can be traced back to its predecessor, the G6, and its origins in the recession that followed the 1973 oil crisis. In 1975, a meeting was held in Rambouillet, France, between the heads of state of France, West Germany, Italy, Japan, the United Kingdom and the United States, and the G6 was born. The following year the G6 was expanded to include Canada. The fall of communism in Russia in the early 1990s witnessed its entry into the global grouping, creating what is now called the G8.

To make things even more complicated for the uninitiated, in 1999 the G20 was established as a forum specifically for discussion, consultation and cooperation on all matters relating to the international financial system. Members of the G20 include the finance ministries and central banks of the G8 countries, plus those of Argentina, Australia, Brazil, China, India, Indonesia, South Korea, Mexico, Saudi Arabia, South Africa and Turkey. In addition, the European Union is represented by the council president and the European Central Bank. At meetings of the G20, those world-governing institutions that were created out of the original Bretton Woods meeting are also represented by the World Bank's president and IMF's managing director.

The G20 played a crucial part in the stabilisation of the world economy when it faced its most important financial challenge in 80 years in 2008, something we discuss a little later.

Bringing Europe together and the birth of the euro

The efforts of the G20, G8 and the various incarnations and manifestations that have been created since 1944 have all been to promote a global sense of financial security, prosperity and transferability. This cooperative inter-governmental spirit can also be found at the more localised level of European countries. Indeed, cross-border financial cooperation and stability has been high on the agenda in post–World War II Western Europe. Decades of efforts aimed at creating closer economic cooperation has culminated in the formation of the European Union (EU) and its common currency, the euro.

The origins of the euro can be traced to the Treaty of Rome (March 1957), which saw the founding of the European Economic Community (or 'Common Market'), which was formally brought to life on 1 January 1958. This body was created with the express aim of achieving economic and political union of its members, which at the time consisted of Belgium, France, Italy, Luxembourg, the Netherlands and West Germany. Other goals included moving towards more unified policies on trade, transport, agriculture and the free movement of labour. The importance of the European Economic Community (EEC) eventually saw the word 'economic' dropped from its name, so that it became simply the European Community. This, in turn, has become what we now know as the European Union (EU), with 25 member states.

In 1978 the European Community established the European Monetary System (EMS), which involved the member states linking their currencies to one another to avoid large fluctuations. Under the stated exchange rate mechanism (ERM), movements in member state currencies were restricted to just 2.25 per cent either side of bilateral 'parity grid' rates (although 6 per cent movement was allowed for the Italian lira). These rates were based on the newly created European currency unit (ECU), a unit of account based on the weighted average of the currencies of the European Community. The ECU can then be seen as the direct precursor to the euro.

The European Community became the European Union as a result of the 1992 Maastricht Treaty, with the aim of establishing an economic and monetary union. The treaty also saw the creation of the European Central Bank (ECB) and the intention to fix the exchange rates of participating countries and replace their sovereign currencies with a single new currency, the euro (EUD).

Eleven currencies were replaced by the euro, which officially came into existence in a non-physical form on 1 January 1999, although it wasn't until Monday 4 January 1999 that trading in the new currency actually began. The conversion rates for the legacy currencies were based upon market rates on Thursday 31 December 1998. The rates were as shown in table 2.1.

Table 2.1: conversion rates for legacy currencies, 31 December 1998

Country	Currency	Code	Rate
Germany	German mark	DEM	1.95583
France	French franc	FRF	6.55957
Italy	Italian lire	ITL	1936.27
Spain	Spanish peseta	ESP	166.386
Portugal	Portuguese escudo	PTE	200.482
Finland	Finnish markka	FIM	5.94573
Ireland	Irish punt	IEP	0.787564
Netherlands	Dutch guilder	NLG	2.20371
Austria	Austrian schilling	ATS	13.7603
Belgium	Belgian (Flemish) franc	BEF	40.3399
Luxembourg	Luxembourg (Flemish) franc	LUF	40.3399

These conversion rates were irrevocably fixed from 1 January 1999 and remained in force until the legacy currencies were finally replaced by euro notes and coins, which were first issued on 1 January 2002.

Subsequent to the first 11 nations joining the currency union, Greece joined in 2000, followed by Slovenia in 2006. In 2007 Cyprus and

Malta joined. In 2009 Slovakia joined after qualifying the previous year, with the seventeenth country, Estonia, joining in 2011.

Monetary and interest rate policy of all countries in the euro zone is now managed by the European Central Bank (ECB). The euro system now comprises the ECB together with the central banks of the EU states who have joined the euro zone.

When talking about the euro zone it is important to distinguish it from the European Union (EU). The reason is that, in some cases, the euro is the official currency of countries not in the EU. For example, Monaco, San Marino and Vatican City, while not part of the EU, have formal agreements to use the euro and to mint coins.

Some countries in the EU have chosen not to use the euro (or are not yet eligible to), the most famous being Great Britain, which still uses its pound (GBP). Great Britain and Denmark are legally exempt from the euro zone unless their domestic governments decide otherwise. Other non-EU countries such as Andorra, Kosovo and Montenegro formally use the euro but have no issuing rights.

Regardless of whether a country is in the EU or has euro issuing rights, it is generally accepted that countries that use the euro as their standard currency of transaction are deemed to be part of the euro zone.

The euro is important because it is the currency of the world's largest trading bloc, Europe, which has a larger population than the US, with a population of more than 326 million users. The euro's significance also extends into other foreign exchanges because it is used as a benchmark currency to which many other currencies are pegged and they may or may not be allowed to fluctuate in bands around a central point.

While it is obvious EU members and European countries outside the euro zone (that is, those that still have their own currencies) need to peg their currencies against the euro as a precondition to entry into the euro zone, other non-European countries use the euro for their FX markets. For instance, the Moroccan dirham, the West African franc, the South Pacific franc and the Central African franc are all formally pegged to the euro. More than 20 African and

South Pacific countries have ties to the European currency, making the euro a serious contender with the US dollar as the pre-eminent world currency. According to the Bank for International Settlements (BIS), approximately 28 per cent of the world's currency trades are EUD/USD transactions, twice that of its nearest traded currency pair, the USD/JPY. The euro features in 39 per cent of all currency transactions, still well behind the 85 per cent that feature the US dollar.

The US dollar still dominates the trade in currency markets, but as the second decade of the 21st century rolls on and the US economy struggles with its post-GFC hangover, the US dollar's role in the international financial system is under challenge in a way not seen since the late 1970s, when it was decoupled from gold, if not since World War II. We discuss the US dollar's prospects and its potential rivals and their problems in the next few sections.

The rise of the Chinese yuan

China's economy achieved two important milestones in 2010. In the first quarter it overtook Germany as the world's largest trading nation; in the third quarter it became the second largest economy in the world, surpassing Japan. China also made significant gains on the US, as the size of GDP relative to the US in pure dollar terms was 40 per cent the size of the US economy. In purchasing parity (PPP) terms, the Chinese economy rose to 68.60 per cent, up from 57.25 per cent in 2008.

This acceleration of China's involvement in the global economy has also given rise to an important change in foreign exchange markets. The Chinese government has attempted to internationalise the domestic currency, the Chinese renminbi or yuan, which is coded CNY (short for Chinese 'new' yuan) per international standards.

From the foundation of the People's Republic of China in 1948 until about 1978, under China's planned economy the exchange rate was relatively stable. The Central Bank of China (PBoC) enforced a strict exchange rate policy of keeping the currency overvalued to discourage international trade, foreign debt and investment. However, from 1978 all that began to change.

In 1978, China started to open up its economy. The domestic regulator of Chinese foreign exchange dealings, the State Administration of Foreign Exchange (SAFE), was established and authorised to manage the country's foreign exchange reserves. The official US dollar/ CNY rate was set around 1.5 and hurt the development of China's external trade, so a parallel trade-related rate was established with a more favourable 2.8 rate (favouring Chinese exporters). The dual system was ended in 1984 when the rates were unified at 2.8, but in 1988 a dual system was reintroduced and until the early 1990s the market-related rate rose to highs of 8.72 CNY to the US dollar by late 1993.

In 1994 the dual currency system was again unified, accompanied by a pegging of the currency at 8.26 yuan to the US dollar on the eve of the Asian financial crisis of 1997–98. It was a rate maintained until July 2005, when Chinese authorities announced a one-off 2 per cent revaluation and that the currency would be managed against a basket of currencies that saw the CNY appreciate 20 per cent in nominal terms into 2008.

The subsequent global financial crisis of late 2008 saw the USD/CNY rate steady through into later 2010 by the temporary imposition of a peg to the US dollar. This stability has given rise to accusations that the CNY is fundamentally undervalued, making China's exchange rate policy a point of significant political and market discussion.

Those who feel the currency is undervalued suggest this delivers a subsidy to Chinese exporters to the detriment of other countries' exporters and take their domestic market share away. What cannot be argued is that China's overall trade surplus jumped to 8 per cent of GDP in 2007 from 1.7 per cent in 2004. That said, the story of China's export success is in fact a mixed one. While it enjoys significant trade surpluses with the EU and the US, it runs large trade deficits with Australasia's larger economies such as Japan, Taiwan, South Korea and Australia. China's apparent success relates to its processing trade sector that functionally imports and assembles intermediary products for re-export.

Since the middle of 2010, the PBoC has relinquished the 23-month, post-financial crisis peg to the US dollar and instituted a 0.5 per cent trading band around a trading partner-related currency basket.

At around the same time as this occurred, new relaxed currency regulations were announced that greatly expanded the ability of both Chinese and foreign businesses and people to transact and settle CNY denominated trade deals outside mainland China. The PBoC did this by promoting close cooperation with the Hong Kong central bank (the Hong Kong Monetary Authority or HKMA) as the preferred location for offshore CNY transactions, otherwise coded CNH; that is, CNY or Chinese renminbi yuan transactions settled in Hong Kong bank accounts.

This is accelerating a trend in the use of the CNY in international trade and by the end of 2010 the amounts of CNY on deposit outside China amounted to $48 billion USD or CNY 315 billion. While a small amount when compared with the current daily turnover of more than $3 trillion of global currency markets, it nonetheless is a part of the continuing process of internationalising the currency of the world's largest trading country and goes some way towards closing the gap in economic scale between it and the US.

The long-term significance of the growing Chinese economy, paralleled by its rapid currency liberalisation and circulation in trade and investment flows of the future, demands closer analysis. It will be necessary in calibrations of Asian and more global currency trading strategies. The growth in the Chinese economy cannot be ignored, and is a story that will get bigger and even more important in the background, if not the main game in the Pacific Ocean FX markets.

The global financial crisis of 2008 and the currency markets

The build-up to the global financial crisis of late 2008 had its genesis in the US mortgage market. Throughout the first decade of the 21st century, the US mortgage market enjoyed a boom powered by then low interest rates. This boom morphed into a bubble that led to an underestimation of risks, which happens with many markets that enjoy a long and sustained one-way trend. When the US mortgage market bubble finally burst in 2007 it precipitated a domino effect with the failure of US mortgage lenders, followed by banks exposed to these types of financial institutions.

Unfortunately for the US and global financial systems, investors and banks around the world began to hoard cash as a precaution, as well as tightening lending to borrowers and other banks, beginning the so-called 'credit crunch' in mid 2007. The resultant lack of lending quickly led to a collapse in equity markets as fear overtook precaution and a general run for cash was seen as other assets (principally equities) were sold aggressively. The collapse of equity values of between 25 and 90 per cent was seen across the globe in the space of a few weeks in September–October of 2008.

Specific to the currency markets and as a direct result of the lack of inter-bank lending of US dollars, the Reserve Bank of Australia, together with the US Federal Reserve and other major central banks, established so-called swap lines of credit whereby the US central bank lent large amounts of US dollars to other central banks in exchange for their currencies to provide liquidity to the global markets as an interim measure to stabilise markets.

The crisis culminated on 11 October 2008 with the heads of G20 countries hammering out a plan to confront the financial crisis. The plan involved hundreds of billions of US dollars of new spending designed to avoid a global depression, coupled with coordinated and sharp reductions in official interest rates around the world.

Despite the unified support of the world's central banks and governments, many non-major currencies collapsed as a general aversion to 'risky' and periphery currencies saw money drain back to main financial centres. The AUD/USD rate, for instance, was not immune to this financial market volatility and fell 40 per cent along with other second and third tier currencies in the space of three months on the back of general risk aversion seen around the world.

The global financial crisis of late 2008 resulted in a temporary reversal of the rapid growth in global foreign exchange turnover seen since the start of the decade, with some estimates by the Reserve Bank of Australia suggesting a decline of 25 per cent from late 2008 to early 2009. This decline in foreign exchange turnover coincided with the sharp decrease in cross-border investment flows in 2008 as, internationally, banks had heightened and mutual concerns of counterparty risk; that is, of going broke and not honouring their commitments. Coupled with continued de-leveraging by hedge funds, non-US banks had difficulty finding US dollar funds in view of the sub-prime debt problems besetting the US banking system at the time.

The unwinding of leveraged positions and international exposures led to one-sided markets as the extent of falls in equity markets both here and overseas meant these flows were larger than usual, creating price 'gaps' in the market when large deals were being digested by the inter-bank market.

This lower turnover and more volatile exchange rate action in the foreign exchange market does not appear to be linked to any problems with its market function (as a place to buy and sell currency). Indeed, throughout the financial crisis this market tended to function better than most other markets. But one thing was apparent—the risk aversion of the main banks and financial institutions reduced liquidity and saw inter-bank bid/ask spreads increase two to three times, with markets prone to episodes of illiquidity, prompting central banks (like the RBA) to intervene several times to test and smooth their respective FX markets.

It is important to accept the role that central banks play in the FX markets. While some participants look at them as often intrusive, in this case they played the stabilising role of confirming market prices and providing liquidity when markets become one-sided.

An important postscript is that since the stresses of the end of the last decade, foreign exchange turnover into 2011 has returned to and exceeded pre-crisis levels, a phenomenon that bodes well for all markets into the future.

European stresses and the euro

As a result of the global financial crisis of late 2008 the euro zone entered into its first recession since the inception of the continental currency. The aftermath of that recession and the slow recovery of developed market economies (principally the Atlantic economies of the US and the European Union) saw regional stresses come to the fore because previously tolerated fiscal imbalances and high sovereign debt loads in a new world of credit rationing are no longer being tolerated.

In early 2010 fears of sovereign debt crisis developed around concerns about the peripheral euro zone countries of Portugal, Ireland, Italy, Greece and Spain (called, unflatteringly, the PIIGS countries). Greece was by far the weakest, with a 15.5 per cent budget deficit and a government debt-to-GDP ratio of about 130 per cent. This weak fiscal position in the context of a continuing global credit crunch saw private lenders desert Greece, making the cost of its national debt soar into double-digit percentage levels, forcing the 'troika' of IMF, ECB and the EU to come to its assistance several times in 2010 and 2011.

This assistance was not just aimed at helping the Greek economy and banks, but also at preventing a succession of knock-on effects against the other vulnerable PIIGS economies and their respective banking systems. At the time of writing it was not clear if the EU will be successful in its support of the Greek economy and government.

In June 2011, credit agency Standard & Poor's downgraded Greek debt three notches to CCC, a rating that leaves Greece as the country with the lowest credit rating in the world.

The question of the EU and the sustainability of the euro in its current configuration is now not just a currency market issue, but a supernational political issue that has yet to fully play out. The evolving story of the euro (like the yuan and the role of the US dollar) will dominate this new decade of currency trading and likely beyond.

Excellent sources of information on foreign exchange topics

Recognising that any explanation on foreign exchange trading and the history of currency transactions in a book of this size will necessarily be incomplete, the following list of references is provided for those looking to further their knowledge. The list is web-centric because, as a retail FX trader, it's likely that you will be web-savvy and internet confident (and if you're not then you really need to be because it makes your life and tasks so much easier!).

The gold standard

<http://library.cqpress.com/cqresearcher/document>

RBA involvement in the FX market

<www.rba.gov.au/mkt-operations/foreign-exchg-mkt.html>

The RBA FX committee

<www.rba.gov.au/AFXC>

G20

<www.g20.org/about_what_is_g20.aspx>

Chinese renminbi

<www.asialink.unimelb.edu.au/publications/trading_with_china_the_rise_of_offshore_renminbi_business_-_anz_asia_society_rmb_handbook>

Euro

<www.ecb.int/euro/html/index.en.html>

European Central Bank

<www.ecb.int/home/html/index.en.html>

Bank for international settlements (BIS)

(Specifically its Triennial Central Bank Survey of Foreign Exchange and Derivatives Market Activity in 2010)

<www.bis.org/publ/rpfxf10t.htm>

Chapter 3

Show me the money!

The three-letter codes used to identify currencies — such as USD, EUR and AUD — are set by the International Organization for Standardization under ISO 4217. You will find that most trading platforms will abide by this standard and use these codes.

The most common of the currency codes you are likely to encounter are shown in table 3.1.

Table 3.1: most common currency codes

Currency	Code
United States dollar	USD
European euro	EUR
Japanese yen	JPY
Great British pound	GBP
Swiss franc	CHF
Australian dollar	AUD
New Zealand dollar	NZD
Canadian dollar	CAD

Further to these prominent eight currencies you may also encounter the currency codes shown in table 3.2 (overleaf).

Major currencies

While there are more than 160 currencies in use around the world, the majority of FX currency trading is generally restricted to, and most often conducted between, just a handful of these.

Table 3.2: other common currency codes

Currency	Code
Mexican peso	MXN
Hong Kong dollar	HKD
Chinese renminbi	CNY
South Korean won	KRW
Singapore dollar	SGD
Thai baht	THB
Malaysian ringgit	MYR
Indonesian rupiah	IDR
Indian rupee	INR
Norwegian krone	NOK
Swedish krona	SEK
Polish zloty	PLN
South African rand	ZAR

The currency involved in more foreign exchange transactions than any other is, probably unsurprisingly, the United States dollar. In fact, so dominant are transactions in USD, a BIS survey in 2010 showed it to be involved in around 85 per cent of daily foreign exchange turnover. Other highly traded currencies in order of daily traded volume include the European euro, the Japanese yen and Great British pound, followed by the Australian dollar and then the Swiss franc.

Pairs

When you buy shares in a company you receive those shares in exchange for the money you pay for them. The foreign exchange market works the same way. When you buy one currency you must give up something (another currency) in exchange. For this reason, those in the FX market do not talk about buying or selling any particular currency in isolation. Transactions in the foreign exchange market always involve two currencies, which are known as a 'pair'. If trading the United States dollar against the Japanese yen, the pair would be written as USD/JPY. If trading the Australian dollar against the United States dollar, the pair would be written as AUD/USD, and so on.

Although it is interesting to look at which individual currencies are traded the most, it is perhaps more relevant to consider which of the currency *pairs* are the most active. Again referring to the BIS 2010 survey, the results show that by far the most active currency pair is the EUR/USD, which accounts for 28 per cent of all foreign exchange turnover.

Let's put this into perspective. The BIS survey indicates that daily turnover for the EUR/USD pair is in the region of US$1.114 trillion. By comparison, the average daily market capitalisation turnover of all of the world's equity markets combined as measured by the World Federation of Exchanges (in April 2011) comes in at just US$241 billion, and includes some 45 800 individual securities.

The EUR/USD on its own is more than four times as large (in terms of daily turnover) as all of the world's equity markets combined. This is shown in figure 3.1.

Figure 3.1: comparative average daily turnover (USD billions) of global equities versus EUR/USD

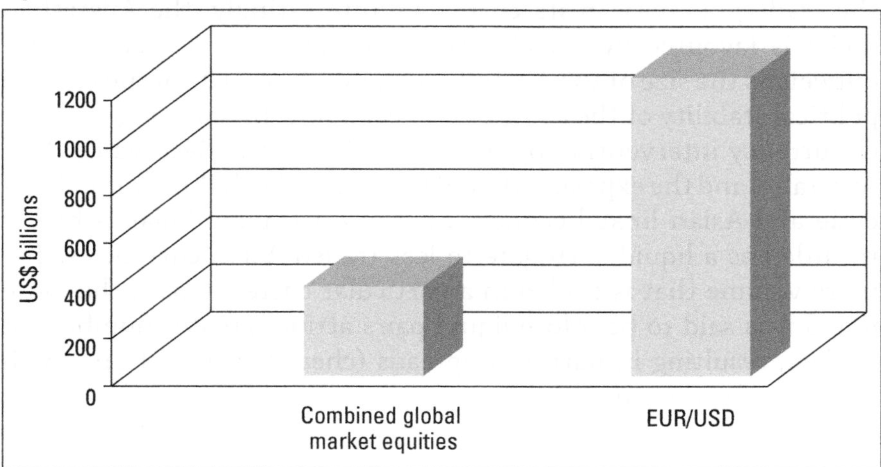

Figure 3.2 (overleaf) shows the relative size of the market share enjoyed by the most traded currency pairs. The top three pairs account for more than 51 per cent of all turnover in the foreign exchange market. The USD is involved in approximately 85 per cent of all foreign exchange turnover so it is no surprise that the USD forms one side of each of

the major pairs shown on this chart. What may perhaps come as a surprise to many is that AUD/USD is shown as the fifth most traded currency pair in the world. This is probably even more significant when you consider that Australia is not even close to getting a seat at the G8.

Figure 3.2: market share of the most traded currency pairs

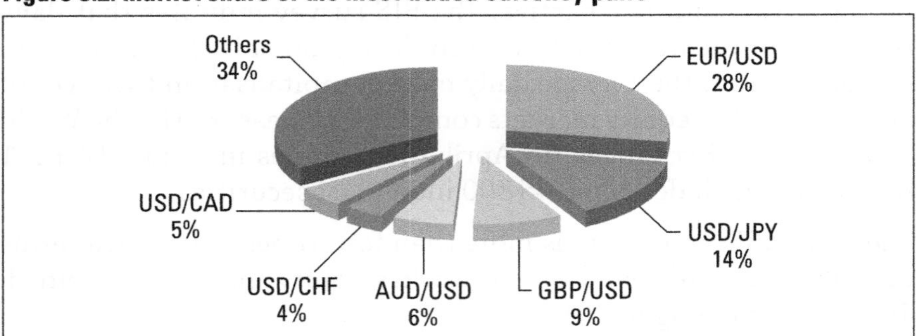

Why then the disparity between Australia's economic weight and the trading activity in its currency? Interestingly, the Australian dollar is favoured by global currency traders to a degree that far outweighs the size of the Australian economy because of the relative political stability of the country and economy, the minimal amount of currency intervention by the central bank (the Reserve Bank of Australia) and the exposure that AUD offers to both the commodities cycle and Asian linked economies. The Australian dollar is highly regarded as a liquid surrogate to less traded Asian currencies. The more volume that is traded in a particular currency pair, the more liquid it is said to be. More liquid pairs attract greater numbers of traders, resulting in narrower spreads (cheaper transactions) with less risk of price gaps.

Majors

The most actively traded currency pairs are known as the 'majors'. Usually, this group is taken to include EUR/USD, USD/JPY, GBP/USD and USD/CHF. Despite ranking highly in the 'most traded' list, it is unusual for AUD/USD to be listed as one of the key 'majors'. That said, the latest BIS survey noted that daily turnover of the

AUD/USD had surpassed that of the USD/CHF to claim fifth place as the most traded currency pair globally. The AUD, CAD and the CHF have tended to interchange positions over the years since the BIS began its survey of foreign exchange markets.

Crosses

In addition to 'majors', another term you will almost certainly come across when trading the foreign exchange market is 'crosses'. Traditionally, 'crosses' were made up of any currency pair that did not include your domestic currency. These days, and with the proliferation of North American texts on this topic, many regard a 'cross' as any pair that does not include the USD, such as EUR/JPY or AUD/NZD.

Thirds

A term that is less often used in FX markets but still crops up now and again is 'thirds'. This term is generally used in relation to regional currencies that, in comparative terms, are traded in significantly smaller amounts than the majors. In Asia, currencies such as the South Korean won (KRW) or Philippine peso (PHP) may be regarded as thirds. In Europe the Hungarian forint (HUF) may be regarded as thirds, while examples in the Americas may include the Colombian peso (COP) or the Brazilian real (BRL).

Now for the big question you're probably hoping we will provide a definitive answer to ...

Which currencies should you trade?

As with most things financial, the decision about which currencies you should trade will depend on your personal circumstances, objectives and risk profile. Just as we wouldn't tell you the groceries you should buy on a weekly basis, we will not tell you which currencies are right for you to trade. Indeed, any such decision will also depend on the opportunities available in the market at any given time.

This aside, unless you have some particular reason for doing otherwise, you are probably better off sticking to the majors plus a few of the larger crosses. Trading in these extremely liquid currency pairs offers several advantages, the main one being that they will typically show the narrowest bid/ask spread. Don't worry just at this point—we will explain what is meant by spreads in further detail later in the book—but for now suffice to say the benefit of a narrow bid/ask spread is that it makes it very cheap to trade these pairs. Also, if you are looking for research materials to support your trading decisions, it will be significantly easier to find information on the major pairs and crosses than it will be to find information on more obscure currencies.

The time zone that you are in may also influence your decision. While the Canadian dollar (CAD) and Mexican peso (MXN) both attract a lot of attention during North American market hours, interest in CAD is relatively thin during Asian hours, with even less interest usually expressed in the MXN. Similarly, the New Zealand dollar (NZD) may trade quite well during Asian hours but interest will wane during European and North American trading hours. During the European trading time, there is also considerable interest in the Scandinavian currencies, the Norwegian krone (NOK) and Swedish krona (SEK), but they are often relatively quiet corners of the market during the Asian trading time.

So for those looking to trade FX from Australia (that is, during the Asian trading time), the currency pairs that would be considered among the most liquid are:

- EUR/USD
- USD/JPY
- GBP/USD
- USD/CHF
- AUD/USD
- NZD/USD
- EUR/JPY
- GBP/JPY.

A final word on liquidity and volatility—they are not the same. It is quite possible for an FX currency pair to be quite liquid and well traded, but it may be 'quiet' in terms of its minute-to-minute or even day-to-day movement. Conversely, it is possible to have 'thinly' traded FX rates with not many participants and have quite volatile jumps in price in short to medium time frames, not to mention combinations of the above. So you need to be prepared for either eventuality, especially when you consider that in a 24-hour market like the FX market, 'shock' news that may affect the rate you're interested in may occur out of hours, in otherwise quiet or thinly traded times and certainly will not take your sleeping habits into consideration.

Just remember many of you will be starting out as part-timers or just hobby traders (and there is nothing wrong or insulting in this, we have to start somewhere). You will need to train as well as pace yourself, so this may involve initial baby-steps practice in trading certain sessions and times of the day. In practical terms, this will involve you setting aside time in the day for both research, planning and managing trades. Realistically if you have a day job this may mean you will only have the early to late evenings (or early mornings) to trade to start with. Don't worry, your momentum will come with time and the development of confidence.

If you are measured in your learning, you not only preserve your financial capital, but also your own, far more finite human capital and your sanity!

Chapter 4

Talking the talk

You have probably added significantly to your trading vocabulary. A lot more is to come, but this is nothing to fear. Even traders with prior experience in the equities or futures markets will come across certain terms that may at first be unfamiliar to them in the foreign exchange market. We have mentioned the unique three-letter ISO 4217 codes that are used to identify each currency, and the concept of majors, crosses and thirds. In this chapter we explain terms such as pips, spreads and handles, and other terms that form part of the day-to-day language of the FX trader.

It is important to realise that none of these terms or the associated language is particularly difficult to understand. However, it is only by knowing the correct terminology that you will be able to become more confident in dealing with the foreign exchange market.

Price maker and price taker

In any foreign exchange transaction there are two counterparties. The party asked to quote a two-way price (that is, a bid and an ask price) is known as the price maker, while the party that asks for the price or that deals on the price offered by a price maker is known as a price taker. In the inter-bank market, banks will switch back and forth from the role of price maker to price taker, depending on their precise circumstances at any particular point in time. However, in the retail online margin FX environment, the retail trader is almost always a price taker, having no option other than to trade at either the bid price or ask price made available by the price maker (their online margin FX provider).

A limited number of platforms allow retail traders to contribute their own bid and ask prices, thus taking on the role of price maker, albeit for a limited transaction size. However, there is usually a 'ticket fee' associated with this type of transaction. Where this is charged as a flat rate per trade, it adds to the cost of each transaction and creates a potential disadvantage for those trading smaller sized positions.

Long and short

When the buying activities of a trader outweigh his or her selling activities, he or she is said to have taken a 'long' position in the market. This is fairly simple in the case of equities or futures. If a trader buys 2000 shares in XYZ Co. then sells 500 shares, he or she is left with a long position of 1500 shares. A trader holding such a position does so in the expectation that the share price of XYZ Co. will rise and he or she will thereby profit.

The situation is reversed for a 'short' position. If the selling activities of a trader exceed his or her buying, the trader is left with a short position. For example, if a trader buys 500 shares of ABC Co. then sells 3000 shares, he or she is left with a net short position of 2500 shares in total.

With foreign exchange it is common for traders to talk about being long or short in either individual currencies or specific pairs. Determining whether you hold a long or short position for any specific currency is no different than is the case with equities and futures. If you have bought more than you have sold of a particular currency, you will have a long position; if you have sold more than you have bought of a particular currency, you will then have a short position.

When we talk about currency pairs, the terms long and short apply to the currency on the left of the quotation, which is known as the base or commodity currency (see p. 41). So, to be long the Australian dollar against the US dollar (AUD/USD) means that you have bought AUD and sold USD. Likewise, to be short the euro against the Japanese yen (EUR/JPY) means that you have sold EUR and bought JPY. The same applies when we talk about buying or selling a given currency pair. The action applies to the currency on the left of the pair. For example, if you buy USD/SGD, you are buying USD and selling SGD. If you sell GBP/JPY, then you are selling GBP and buying JPY.

Pips

For many years, the majority of currency pairs have been quoted to four decimal places in the spot market (upon which retail pricing is based). An exception has been pairs involving the Japanese yen, which have traditionally been quoted to two decimal places. Under this system, a 'pip' is simply the smallest unit of price by which a currency pair can move. It is the last decimal place of the quoted price. For example:

EUR/USD 1.4252 to 1.4253 = 1 pip

If a currency pair is quoted to just two decimal places, one pip equals 0.01. For example:

USD/JPY 77.33 to 77.34 = 1 pip

In recent years, nearly all retail FX providers have expanded the number of decimal places used in their pricing. For example, the EUR/USD may be quoted to five decimal places rather than the historic market convention of quoting to four decimal places. By doing this, they are breaking down each pip into 10 smaller units and quotes may resemble something like this:

EUR /USD = 1.38952/1.38971, resulting in a spread of 1.9 pips

Whether prices are quoted to four decimal places or five decimal places, the value of a single pip remains the same — it is a move of 0.0001. Where the price quote includes a fifth decimal, it is regarded as a fraction of a pip.

Of course, the same holds true for quotes involving the Japanese yen. A move of one pip remains 0.01. If the third decimal place is quoted, it is regarded as a fraction of a pip.

More examples are shown in table 4.1.

Table 4.1: movement of one pip

Currency pair	Price quote	One pip	One pip move higher
EUR/USD	1.38952/1.38981	0.0001 USD	1.38962/1.38991
USD/JPY	77.673/77.704	0.01 JPY	77.683/77.714
GBP/USD	1.67946/1.67981	0.0001 USD	1.67956/1.67991
USD/CHF	0.95418/0.95458	0.0001 CHF	0.95428/0.95468
AUD/USD	1.07071/1.07100	0.0001 USD	1.07081/1.07110
AUD/JPY	82.979/83.014	0.01 JPY	82.989/83.024

While it is true that narrower spreads result in lower costs, the difference between 1.9 pips and 2.0 pips is very, very small. Even if you were trading $1 million, the difference would equate roughly to the cost of a cup of coffee and a sushi roll. For an average sized retail trade, the value of a price move of one-tenth of a pip won't even buy you a postage stamp in most countries.

Because many novice retail traders focus squarely on spreads when selecting a forex provider, there is significant interest in comparing spreads from one provider to another. However, as demonstrated above, a few tenths of a pip will make very little difference to the majority of retail traders. Using the spread as your sole selection criteria would be a mistake.

Interestingly, the fifth decimal place gives retail traders access to finer price control than is available to many institutional traders. In the inter-bank FX market there are two main electronic brokers — Electronic Broker Services (EBS) and Reuters. It was only in March 2011 that EBS first started to quote spot FX prices for the major currency pairs to an extra decimal place (after starting with a roll-out to 22 pairs in the second half of 2010). This is several years after it became available to retail traders. The feedback from institutional traders was less than enthusiastic. Many of them were distracted by the appearance of a fifth decimal in the quotes and felt it caused confusion and slowed the process of trading. For these traders, the extra decimal provided diminishing marginal utility. In other words, it wasn't worth the bother! They prefer instead to trade with just four decimals where the smallest increment in price is worth $100 per $1 000 000.

Not long after EBS added the fifth decimal to spot prices, Reuters indicated that they had no plan to follow the same path. However, pressure is likely to make the fifth decimal standard in the inter-bank market before too long due to competition from forex aggregators and the demands of algorithmic traders.

It is important to note that the value of a single pip as measured in units of the base currency (the one on the left of the pair) will vary as the exchange rate varies. Consider a long position of 1 000 000 AUD/USD and a one-pip move in the rate from 1.07515 to 1.07525.

At 1.07515, AUD 1 000 000 = USD 1 075 150.

At 1.07525, AUD 1 000 000 = USD 1 075 250.

The one-pip move represents US$100, which at 1.07525 equals A$93.00.

Now, let's look at a one-pip move if the exchange rate had been considerably lower, moving from 0.86220 up one pip to 0.86230.

At 0.86220, AUD 1 000 000 = USD 862 200.

At 0.86230, AUD 1 000 000 = USD 862 300.

Once again, the one-pip move represents US$100, but this time the rate for conversion is 0.86230, which makes the equivalent amount in Australian dollars A$115.97.

Big figure

A movement in the price of a currency pair of 100 pips is referred to as a movement of one 'big figure'. Some examples are shown in table 4.2 (overleaf).

Table 4.2: movement of one big figure

Currency pair	Price quote	One big figure up	One big figure down
EUR/USD	1.38950	1.39950	1.37950
USD/JPY	77.670	78.670	76.670
GBP/USD	1.67940	1.68940	1.66940
USD/CHF	0.95410	0.96410	0.94410
AUD/USD	1.07070	1.08070	1.06070
AUD/JPY	82.970	83.970	81.970

Handle

The 'handle' is simply a truncated portion of the price, excluding the last two decimal places of the quote, or the last three decimal places if prices are quoted to the fifth decimal. For example, if you were considering the euro against the US dollar (EUR/USD) at the quoted exchange rate of 1.32613, the handle would be 1.32. Similarly, in the case of the US dollar against the Japanese yen (USD/JPY) at the quoted exchange of 77.451, the handle is 77.

This can be important, particularly in the fast-paced inter-bank market, where the handle is often not quoted as part of an initial quote because it is assumed that traders active in a particular market will know what the current handle is. For example, a EUR/USD bid/ask spread (see following page) of 1.32610/640 may simply be quoted as '610/640', with confirmation of the handle left until a deal has been executed.

On the surface it may appear that this level of knowledge is only for inter-bank traders with a high degree of experience, knowledge and confidence. However, as many of the online margin forex trading platforms become more complex and start to more closely resemble the inter-bank trading platforms, it is increasingly common to find systems that can be tailored to maximise the efficient use of available screen space by hiding the handle and/or enlarging the remaining portion of the quote—'610/640' in our example. With the fifth decimal now in wide usage, some differentiation is usually made between the full pips and the fractional pips. You will frequently find that the fifth decimal (the fraction of a pip) is shown in a smaller font than the full pips (see figure 4.1).

Figure 4.1: price quote showing full pips in larger font

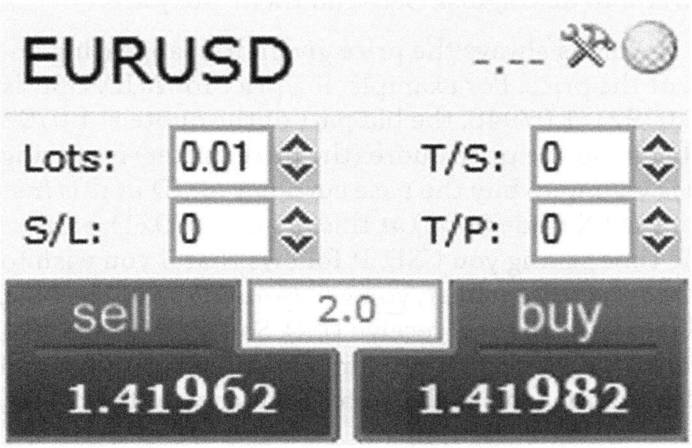

Source: © IBFX.

Bid and ask

When trading online margin foreign exchange you will notice that two prices are always quoted on your trading platform. This is because in the market usually used for transactions by retail FX traders — not the inter-bank market — your margin FX provider is effectively acting as a price maker and quoting you what is known as a two-way price. This price simply represents the price at which it is willing to buy a certain currency pair and another price at which it is willing to sell. You then have the choice of either buying or selling at the appropriate price.

In this context, the term 'price maker' applies to all non-ECN (electronic communications network; see p. 72 in chapter 6) retail FX providers, regardless of whether they are a market maker or provide straight through pricing (STP).

As noted earlier, it is common for online trading platforms to truncate price quotes in order to save space on the screen. You will often find that the 'handle' is either cut off or is shown in a smaller font than other figures.

There are two crucial components to a price quotation and you need to be careful to distinguish between them. They are:

- *Bid*: the bid is always the price given first, appearing on the left side of the price. For example, if a price for AUD/USD is given as 1.07921/1.07948, the bid part of the quote is 1.07921. The party giving the price quote (the price maker) is making the bid and is willing to buy the base currency (AUD in this instance) from the FX trader (you) at this price (1.07921), while at the same time selling you USD. It follows that if you wish to sell AUD to the price maker, you will be doing so at the bid price and in return you will receive USD. Some platforms attempt to make this clearer by labelling the bid price with a 'sell' tag, indicating that this is the price at which you (the trader) are able to sell the currency pair.
- *Ask*: the ask is the second part of the price quote, the portion on the right. Keeping with our AUD/USD sample price quote of 1.07921/1.07948, the ask price is 1.07948. The price maker is willing to sell AUD to you at the asking price of 1.07948, and in exchange you will have to pay out the equivalent amount in USD. Again, in an attempt to simplify things, some platforms label the ask price with a 'buy' tag, indicating that this is the price at which you (the trader) are able to buy the currency pair.

In a nutshell:

- If you want to buy the base currency from a price maker, you will trade at the ask price that is quoted to you. This is sometimes referred to as 'taking the offer'.
- If you want to sell the base currency to a price maker, you will trade at the bid price that is quoted to you. This is sometimes referred to as 'hitting the bid'.

Remember that your online margin FX provider is the price maker and you (the retail trader) are the price taker. Table 4.3 provides a few more examples.

These days, it is extremely rare that a retail trader will execute foreign exchange trades verbally. However, if you ever do find yourself doing this, additional terminology is frequently heard among institutional FX traders.

Table 4.3: price makers and price takers

	Price maker	Price maker	Price maker	Price taker	Price taker
Currency pair	**Quote**	**Bid**	**Ask (offer)**	**Buys at**	**Sells at**
EUR/USD	1.38930/960	1.38930	1.38960	1.38960	1.38930
USD/JPY	77.660/690	77.660	77.690	77.690	77.660
GBP/USD	1.67930/970	1.67930	1.67970	1.67970	1.67930
USD/CHF	0.95410/440	0.95410	0.95440	0.95440	0.95410
AUD/USD	1.07050/080	1.07050	1.07080	1.07080	1.07050
AUD/JPY	82.960/010	82.960	83.010	83.010	82.960

After a price taker is quoted a price in a certain currency pair, she or he will say either 'yours' if wishing to sell at the bid price, or 'mine' if wishing to buy at the ask price. For the most part, such colloquialisms will be heard only between inter-bank traders, who use such language to expedite transactions and confirm details quickly. For example, a typical conversation of an inter-bank foreign exchange transaction might go something like this:

Sam: 'Hi Fred. Price for three million AUD/USD please.'
Fred: '80/83.'
Sam: 'Yours — at 80 I sell you three million AUD.'
Fred: 'Done — I buy three million AUD from you at 1.0780, value date 20 March. Thanks.'
Sam: 'Thanks. Bye for now.'

With the fifth decimal now in wider usage, you will need to take additional care if you do ever need to place a trade verbally.

Spread

The spread is simply the number of points difference between the bid and ask in any given price quote. For example, a quote for the euro against the US dollar (EUR/USD) of 1.38758/783 has a spread of 2.5 pips.

The spread determines how far prices will need to move before a given trade will show a profit. Let's assume you are quoted a price for EUR/USD with a two-pip spread — 1.38760/780. If you choose to buy, you will pay 1.38780.

Assuming that the spread remains at two pips (and prices move in whole pips only) while the market rallies, the market will rise through a range of prices:

1.38760/780	Buy at 1.38780.
1.38760/780	If you sell before prices move, you lose two pips.
1.38770/790	If you sell here you lose one pip.
1.38780/800	Break even—you could sell here to 'scratch' your trade.
1.38790/810	From here on your long trade is in profit.

However, if the spread was four pips, you would need to see a more significant move in the market before you would be able to break even and then move into profit:

1.38740/780	Buy at 1.38780—if you sell at this level you lose four pips.
1.38750/790	If you sell here you lose three pips.
1.38760/800	If you sell here you lose two pips.
1.38770/810	If you sell here you lose one pip.
1.38780/820	Break even—you could sell here to 'scratch' your trade.
1.38790/830	From here on your long trade is in profit.

In general, the most liquid currency pairs (the majors) will have the narrowest spreads. Less liquid pairs will have wider spreads. This can have a significant impact on trading success, especially for those seeking short-term moves in prices.

Many foreign exchange traders regard the spread as one of the major costs associated with trading foreign exchange. Accordingly, they seek to minimise this cost by seeking out brokers with tight spreads. As a result, many brokers advertise that they have extremely tight spreads with headlines such as, 'Spreads from just one pip' for major pairs such as EUR/USD. Some even use the benefit of the fifth decimal to quote a minimum spread of less than one whole pip. It is important to look beyond the headlines and find out what the average spread is for the pairs you are interested in trading.

You should also bear in mind that FX providers are in business to make a profit. Some do this by charging a ticket fee on each trade in exchange for passing through tight spreads. Others add a small mark-up to the spreads they receive from the inter-bank market. Although each method has vehement supporters and detractors, the bottom line is that the broker is providing a service and one way or another it is only fair that traders pay to access that service.

While spread is one factor to consider, selecting an FX provider should be based on a much broader set of factors. We will cover this in more detail in chapter 6.

Quoting conventions—which currency comes first?

Every currency available for trading is represented by a three-letter ISO 4217 code and currencies are always traded in pairs. For each pair we obviously have two of these three-letter codes, such as AUD/USD if trading the Australian dollar against the United States dollar.

To the casual observer, it may not seem to make too much difference in which order these codes are written. In the example of Australian dollars and United States dollars, it is possible to use either AUD/USD or USD/AUD. However, there is a very important difference between these two variations. The fixed unit of currency on the left of any currency pair is known as the 'base' or 'commodity' currency, while the variable unit of currency on the right is known as the 'terms' or 'quoted' currency. The terms are:

Fixed/Variable
Base/Quoted
or
Commodity/Terms
or
Base/Terms

A given exchange rate, then, reflects the number of units of the 'terms' currency that can be exchanged per unit of the 'base' currency. In any currency pair, one unit of the base currency is worth 'x' units of the terms currency. For example, if we are given an

AUD/USD exchange rate of 1.07120, it means that one Australian dollar can be exchanged for 1.0712 United States dollars; that is, 107.12 US cents. In other words, AUD 1 = USD 1.0712. A USD/JPY exchange rate of 77.660 indicates that each United States dollar will buy 77.66 Japanese yen, or USD 1 = JPY 77.66.

Reversing the order of the quotation results in a completely different outcome. The exchange rate of 1.07120 for AUD/USD is no longer correct if we change the quotation around to become USD/AUD. Instead, the correct rate for USD/AUD is the reciprocal of the AUD/USD rate. So, the rate for USD/AUD is one divided by 1.07120, which equals 0.93353 when rounded to the fifth decimal place.

Therefore, if the AUD/USD rate is 1.07120, we can also say that one United States dollar is equal to 0.9335 Australian dollars (A$0.93), or USD/AUD equals 0.93353. This highlights the need to ensure that you have your quotations around the right way.

As a general rule of thumb, the USD is usually on the left side of any given pair, except in the case of several of the Commonwealth currencies. If one of these Commonwealth currencies (for example, GBP, AUD or NZD) is involved in the pair, it will usually be the base currency—the one on the left. However, in the case of CAD, it is most often quoted against the USD as USD/CAD. Another exception to the rule is the European euro (EUR), which is also most commonly quoted as the base currency (for example, EUR/USD).

Direct and indirect quotes

Two terms are used to describe which way a particular currency pair is being quoted. These are 'direct' and 'indirect'. Many texts you read on this topic will inform you that a pair is regarded as being quoted in 'direct' (or American) terms if the base currency (the one on the left) is not USD. The same texts will tell you that if the USD is the base currency the pair is regarded as being quoted in 'indirect' (or European) terms.

In fact, the application of the terms 'direct' and 'indirect' is dependent upon the specific geographic location in which you trade. Because the majority of texts on this topic have been written from an American perspective, the terms are often used as described above. However, if we substitute 'local currency' for 'USD', we end up with the following: where the local currency is the variable (or terms) currency and appears on the right-hand side, the quotation is a direct quotation. Where the local currency appears as the base currency (the one on the left), the quotation is an indirect quotation.

This means that for a typical FX trader in Australia, a quote for AUD/USD is an indirect quotation. However, the same quotation would be regarded by a person in the United States as a direct quotation.

What about AUD/NZD? To a person in Australia this is an indirect quotation, but the same quote in New Zealand would be regarded as a direct quotation. However, in another twist, when AUD and NZD are quoted as a pair in New Zealand, a person in New Zealand usually quotes the pair as NZD/AUD, which is an indirect quotation from their point of view.

While there are some broadly observed conventions in relation to which way currency pairs are quoted, it is always worth making sure you know how it is done in the market in which you plan to participate. As you can see, local market anomalies can crop up and it is important to be fully aware of the specifics of the market in which you hope to successfully trade.

There are two more important reasons for ensuring the currency pair you wish to trade is quoted in the correct order. When you trade a particular currency pair, you will generally trade one pair in large round numbers, while the amount of the other currency to be traded is determined by the current exchange rate and can end up being almost any number. For example, if buying a standard retail size contract of a pair such as USD/CHF, it is likely that you would be looking to buy something in the order of a multiple of US$100 000 and selling a proportionate amount of Swiss francs (CHF 95 680 if the rate is 0.95680). This is quite different from trading CHF/USD. To calculate the rate for CHF/USD we simply determine the reciprocal of the USD/CHF rate. So, if USD/CHF = 0.95680, then CHF/USD = 1 ÷ 0.95680 = 1.04515. Therefore, a trade in 100 000 Swiss francs at CHF/USD 1.04515 would equate to US$104 515.

This brings us to the next important point: calculating how much money you've earned (or lost) on a particular trade.

Calculating profit or loss for an FX trade

Continuing the example from above, if you initially buy 100 000 USD/CHF and later in the day sell 100 000 USD/CHF, your profit or loss will be in the form of CHF. The purchase and sale of 100 000 USD nets out perfectly, and you are left with a difference in CHF, as determined by the change in the USD/CHF exchange rate between the time of your purchase and the time of your sale. In simple terms, the profit or loss on any trade will always be achieved in the 'terms' currency. Some retail FX providers will automatically convert any profit or loss on closed out trades back into the currency in which your trading account is denominated. Others will leave the profit or loss in the currency in which it was achieved and will only convert this back to your 'home' currency upon request. Policies on this vary from company to company, so it is worth reading the fine print. For example, if your account is held in Australian dollars and you make large profits on a EUR/USD trade, these profits may be whittled away if there is a large rise in AUD/USD before you convert the USD profit back into AUD.

Let's look at four practical examples to better explicate this situation.

Example 4.1

Consider a situation in which USD/CHF is bought at 0.91330, then sold at 0.91780.

1	Buy 100 000 USD at 0.91330	=	Sell 91 330 CHF
2	Sell 100 000 USD at 0.91780	=	Buy 91 780 CHF
	Net result	=	Profit 450 CHF

This profit can be converted back into USD:

$$450 \div 0.91780 = 490.30 \text{ USD}$$

Or it can be converted to AUD:

$$450 \div 0.98240 = 458.06 \text{ AUD}$$

(assuming an AUD/CHF rate of 0.98240)

Example 4.2

AUD/USD is trading at 1.07040 and your analysis leads you to expect a fall towards 1.06000 as the AUD weakens in relation to the USD. For this trade you would sell AUD/USD at the current price with a view to buying it back at a lower rate.

1	Sell 100 000 AUD at 1.07040	=	Buy 107 040 USD
2	Buy 100 000 AUD at 1.06000	=	Sell 106 000 USD
	Net result	=	Profit 1040 USD

This profit can be converted back into AUD:

$$1040 \div 1.06000 = 981.13 \text{ AUD}$$

Example 4.3

Assume GBP/AUD is trading at 1.53050 and you anticipate a climb towards 1.54800 as GBP outperforms AUD in the near term. To take advantage of this move you buy GBP/AUD at the current rate, looking to sell once the exchange rate has risen.

1	Buy 100 000 GBP at 1.53050	=	Sell 153 050 AUD
2	Sell 100 000 GBP at 1.54800	=	Buy 154 800 AUD
	Net result	=	Profit 1750 AUD

Example 4.4

If your analysis suggests USD/JPY should fall from the 77.450 level towards 76.250, you may decide to sell 100 000 USD/JPY with the intention of buying it back once the market has fallen. However, in this example, say you were incorrect, and the market actually rallied away from your sell price of 77.450, hitting 78.100 before you bought your position back and squared up.

1	Sell 100 000 USD at 77.450	=	Buy 7 745 000 JPY
2	Buy 100 000 USD at 78.100	=	Sell 7 810 000 JPY
	Net result	=	Loss 65 000 JPY

Other influences on profitability

We have already mentioned that some retail FX providers will charge a ticket fee per transaction. This may also be referred to as brokerage or commission. Where this applies, it will need to be included in the calculations shown above.

Another consideration that applies to all FX traders is rollover, or swap. This relates to the net interest that either accrues or is charged to your account for any trades that are held 'overnight', or from one trading day to the next. Remember, in the FX world one day finishes and the next begins at 5.00 pm New York time. Although the majority of FX providers follow this convention, some do not. It is best to check when your provider rolls from one day into the next.

In simple terms, at rollover you will earn interest on whichever currency you have bought and you will be paying interest for the currency that you have sold. So, it all comes down to interest rate differentials. If rates are higher in the country of the currency you have bought than in the country of the currency you have sold, you should end up earning a small sum at rollover. On the other hand, if rates are lower in the country of the currency you have bought than in the country of the currency you have sold, you are likely to incur an interest charge. This is often calculated with reference to the relevant swap rate between the countries concerned. Some providers refer to this benefit (or charge) as the daily swap.

We take a closer look at rollover (swap) in chapter 11 when we examine a strategy that has evolved to take advantage of these interest rate differentials.

Note for Muslim traders

Earning and paying interest is not acceptable to many Muslim traders. For this reason, a number of retail FX providers now offer 'no swap' (interest free) accounts specifically tailored to meet the needs of Muslim clients. For more, visit <www.alexdouglas.com>.

Bulls and bears

In your trading career you will hear a lot about bulls and bears. Why bulls and why bears? Explanations vary. Suffice to say, a bullish market is one that is rising, as though thrown higher on the horns of a bull. By contrast, a bearish market is one that is heading lower, as if it were being clawed at by a bear. When discussing a security from the equities or futures market, it is a simple matter to determine whether a particular move has been bullish or bearish. If the market rises, it is a bullish move. If the market falls, it is a bearish move. Simple as that.

But, as always, things are not quite so simple in the FX market. For example, you may find yourself reading research reports or articles that claim the Japanese yen has been firmly bullish (stronger) against all currencies (see figure 4.2), but the accompanying 'yen chart' of USD /JPY shows a distinct move lower during the time in question. Why is this?

Figure 4.2: a 'bullish' move for Japanese yen—from 100.57 to 76.097

Source: MetaTrader 5, © 2001–2011 MetaQuotes Software Corp.

In the specific example of USD/JPY, a move lower on the chart (lower exchange rate) indicates that each USD can be exchanged for fewer JPY than was the case when the market was trading at a higher level. We can therefore say that the USD is comparatively weaker than JPY when the USD/JPY rate falls. This is the same as saying the JPY is stronger against the USD — in comparative terms — as the USD/JPY exchange rate falls. If JPY is comparatively stronger against many currencies, it may be said to be 'broadly firmer' or 'firmer across the board'.

Let's consider another example. If the EUR/USD rallies strongly, it means that each EUR will now buy you more USD than it would previously. If the relationships with all other currencies have remained steady, we could say that in general terms EUR was bullish while USD was bearish. If the USD posted similar losses against a number of currencies while the EUR remained relatively steady against those same currencies, it would be more accurate to say that the sharp jump higher in EUR/USD was due to USD bearishness.

Inverted charts

Although it is rare, you may occasionally encounter a chart that has been inverted so that the direction of the currency at the heart of the commentary is reflected more intuitively in the chart. For example, a EUR/USD chart may be turned upside down so that a discussion of 'firmer USD' is accompanied by a chart that appears to be rising. This is usually only done by news services catering to their domestic audience, and is not likely to be encountered in broader global media outlets — but it is worth being aware of.

The warning then is clear: always check charts against the rates and your understanding of the market's movement to confirm the direction and general sentiment surrounding the FX pair you are following at that time.

Local media reporting

Another peculiarity of local media outlets is their reporting of currency rates in terms of the local currency unit. This means, for example, that reports on Australian radio or television news services regarding the price of JPY or EUR are likely to be in terms of AUD/JPY and AUD/EUR respectively. These prices will be significantly different from the USD/JPY and EUR/USD levels that you will become familiar with as your FX trading career blossoms.

For example, the local media might claim that the Australian dollar is trading at 80.28 Japanese yen or 0.7294 euro. However, when you check the majors on your FX margin provider's trading platform you will find the Japanese yen and the euro most likely quoted against the US dollar; for example, USD/JPY = 76.957 and EUR/USD = 1.43045. This is shown in table 4.4.

Table 4.4: comparison of local media and FX markets

Local media (A$1 =)		FX markets	
JPY	80.28	USD/JPY	76.957
EUR	0.7294	EUR/USD	1.43045

It's not inconceivable to imagine traders who are relatively new to FX markets getting quite a shock as they drive along listening to the business news on the car radio and hear that the euro is now quoted at 0.7294 — especially when they were long at 1.43045 about 10 minutes earlier!

This concludes the formal section on FX jargon and terminology, although it is obviously very likely that you will continue to encounter new phrases, expressions and particular nuances relevant to FX markets as you read the book. We'd encourage you to always check their appropriateness in the market that you intend to trade. Next, we turn attention to the main players in the FX game.

Chapter 5

Who's who at the FX marketplace

Okay, by now you're probably thinking that you understand the basic language, have a fair idea of the concept of free-floating currencies and you're ready to take the plunge. But before this can happen, you need some idea of the playing field and just who the main players are.

Why does foreign exchange trading exist?

At the root of it all, international trade is the most obvious reason for the existence of the foreign exchange market. Importers buying goods in a foreign country need to sell their local currency and buy foreign currency to pay for the goods they have bought in the currency of the country in which they have bought them. On the other side of the trade equation, exporters will often receive payment for the goods they sell overseas in the currency of the country to which their goods have been sent. In the majority of cases, these exporters will then need to convert the foreign currency they have earned back to their local currency.

As mentioned in chapter 2, the exchange of currencies from different countries and regions for the purpose of international trade can be traced back thousands of years to merchants travelling the Silk Road through Asia and trading in the bazaars of Mesopotamia. These days, with the advent of globalisation and the ever-growing cross-border trade in goods and services, international mergers and acquisitions, and 24-hour financial markets, FX transactions are even more prevalent.

Three broad groups of participants

Before looking too closely at exactly who is doing all the trading in the foreign exchange markets, it is helpful to have a broad view of the three major groups of participants. In very general terms, these are the inter-bank (or wholesale) entities, the clients of the wholesale entities (both retail and corporate), and the intermediaries that help bring these parties together and facilitate trade (the brokers). Although each participant in the foreign exchange market will fit within one of these groups, it is worth bearing in mind that there is also frequent interaction between these groups.

Inter-bank (professional/wholesale)

As the name suggests, this is the market in which banks of all types (investment, merchant, commercial, central) trade with one another. Trades are executed by dedicated dealers on the treasury department dealing desks, either directly with another bank or via specialist inter-bank brokers. Because of the size of the transactions taking place on this market, it is the activity of the participants in the inter-bank market that sets the approximate prices on which everybody else involved in the foreign exchange markets will trade.

Within the inter-bank market there is a further division between the various participants, determined by the specific foreign exchange products that they trade. We cover these specific products in more detail in chapter 11, but briefly there is a division between products known as 'spot', 'forwards' and 'options'.

Spot market (or today plus two)

The spot market is where the plain, basic 'vanilla-flavoured' trading takes place. Basically, two traders agree to opposite positions and trade straight away at a specific price, with settlement to take place in two business days' time (hence 'today plus two').

For the retail trader it is important to understand that in most instances, unless otherwise specified, the prices made available on the online margin FX trading platforms are based on the inter-bank spot market prices. As you get further into this game, the old-time professionals will tell you when you see the price on the screen that 'screen prices don't deal'. In other words, when you see the price on the computer screen it is only an indication of where the market will likely trade at the next price offering, but not necessarily the price that will be available to you.

Forward market (trading for anything but spot value)

The key point that differentiates a spot transaction from a forward transaction is the settlement date of the deal. As noted above, settlement for a spot transaction takes place two business days after the execution of the deal. A forward transaction is a deal with a settlement date on any day other than two days after the execution of the deal. The settlement date may fall either three or more days after the deal is executed or, in the case of 'short-date' transactions, the settlement date may fall earlier than the second business day after the execution of the deal. It may be one day after (value tomorrow) or even on the day of the deal itself (value today).

When discussing forward prices it is important to remember that it fundamentally is a function of not just the spot price mentioned earlier, but also the relative difference between the interest rates of the two currencies for a given maturing forward contract, called 'FX swap' points. In other words, a forward foreign exchange contract is equal to the spot price plus (or minus) the net difference in interest rates between the currencies for a given maturity expressed in FX price points.

On this basis, the volatility of forward FX values are a combination of spot FX price moves, domestic or base currency interest rate moves and foreign currency money market moves. Each constituent market of course is likely to have a traded life of its own all at the same time. As you can gather, already trading forward FX is an even more complex art than just spot trading, because in effect you are trading three different markets at the same time.

Options and other derivatives markets

Traders in the options and other allied FX derivatives markets such as futures and non-deliverable forward markets (called NDFs) seek to profit from change, or a lack thereof, in the volatility of the currencies they are following. As a part of their trading strategies, they are likely to also participate in both the spot and forward markets from time to time.

While many of you would be familiar with futures markets, which are in effect exchange-traded standardised forward FX contracts, non-deliverable FX forwards are not traded on an exchange but between banks and between banks and their clients. It is a cash-settled, short-term forward contract on usually non-convertible currency (such as the Chinese yuan), where the profit or loss at the time of the settlement date is calculated by taking the difference between the agreed upon exchange rate and the spot rate at the time of settlement for a previously agreed upon notional amount of funds. They are especially popular for corporations seeking to hedge exposure to foreign currencies that are not traded, or where the laws of the country inhibit direct domestic to foreign currency transactions.

Regardless of which subset of the professional FX markets banks trade in, one of the key reasons that banks participate in the global foreign exchange market is to meet the needs of their customers, in particular their corporate customers with specific exposure to foreign currencies seeking to convert export receipts, convert funds to pay for goods to be imported, or hedge the risks associated with holding assets in other countries. Traders in the banks use their specialist knowledge of the market to skew the prices they quote to their clients very slightly, depending upon factors such as market trends, order flow and the intentions of the client to either buy or sell—if known. By skewing prices slightly, the bank opens up the potential for it to profit from price differentials in its FX transactions. Saying this, increased competition in recent years has left banks with far less room to profit by quoting a price to a client that is too far removed from the current inter-bank price. A difference of more than a few pips is now likely to see the client call another bank, but as recently as the early to mid 1990s it was not uncommon for a bank to pad out a price quoted to a corporate client by 10 to 20 pips or more. Ten years before that it would have been possible for a bank to quote a price that was 50 to 100 pips away from the inter-bank market.

By meeting the needs of their corporate customers, the banks themselves end up with exposure to foreign currency that they must then also manage. Traders in the banks use their skill and knowledge of the market to decide whether they are better off to immediately offset the positions they are left holding after conducting transactions with a client, known as 'squaring up' or 'jobbing', or whether they stand to gain by holding the position and waiting for a better price before exiting the position. The majority of exposure generated by client dealings will be squared up by the end of each day.

Banks that have investments or assets in foreign countries will be similarly affected by fluctuations in exchange rates. For them, if no action is taken to address these fluctuations, an otherwise profitable investment may easily turn into a loss-making investment, with unfavourable moves in the exchange rate wiping out the profits. To avoid this problem, it is common for banks with foreign investments to take measures in the foreign exchange market to protect themselves against currency fluctuations. This is known as 'hedging' and may involve a simple currency transaction or more advanced techniques such as the use of options or FX forwards.

Separate to both client-related transactions and in-house related hedging transactions, banks also participate in the inter-bank foreign exchange market with the specific goal of profiting through speculation on anticipated market movements. Trades will be initiated specifically to profit from expected changes in exchange rates, with multi-million-dollar transactions adding further to the liquidity of the market. The treasury departments of some banks add significantly to the bottom line of the bank's performance when these speculative traders are successful. Of course, on the flip-side, there is also the risk of substantial loss if trading is not conducted responsibly—just ask the National Australia Bank about its foreign currency option trading problems of 2003.

Central banks

A major government body involved in the wholesale sector of the foreign exchange market in many countries is the local central bank. In Australia this is the Reserve Bank of Australia (RBA) and it is good practice to get to know the central bank in your country (see the end of this chapter for a quick tour of central banks that count in our region). While the RBA states that it does not specifically target any preferred level for the AUD exchange rate, it can and does take action in the open market (the inter-bank market) to 'smooth' moves that are deemed to be uncharacteristically large in one direction or the other. When there is such a move in the market or when volatility becomes excessively high, traders will be on the lookout for any signs of activity by the RBA. Other central banks can and do play far more active roles with consequent regulation in their respective currency markets for various public policy and historical reasons.

Unlike other participants in the foreign exchange market, central banks do have the monetary muscle to move exchange rates (albeit temporarily) through their trading activities, either buying or selling hundreds of millions of dollars over a relatively short time. They, unlike anyone else in the market, have the ability and authority to literally print money (called 'quantitative easing'), something the US Federal Reserve, for instance, has done twice in recent years in the aftermath of the GFC.

In fact, the ability of a central bank to move rates is such that a simple rumour of the presence of a central bank in the market will often be enough to cause a ripple in prices. Some central banks use this to their advantage, openly calling around to different banks—price makers—and asking for quotes in the particular currencies they are interested in. Even if they do not trade on the prices they are quoted, the news that the central bank was checking prices will quickly spread through the market, sometimes resulting in trade moving in the direction sought by the central bank without them needing to trade at all. When a central bank openly expresses its desire for the currency to move in a particular direction, or even to a particular level, it is known as 'jaw-boning'.

While the RBA does not target a specific level for the AUD, other central banks are more vocal about their desires. The Bank of Japan (BoJ) is notable for making repeated statements that the Japanese yen (JPY) is too strong and for taking steps to sell JPY against other currencies, particularly the USD. Although the initial strengthening of JPY (as a part of broader USD devaluation) was planned and agreed to under the Plaza Accord of September 1985, once the USD/JPY retreat from the 250 region neared 140 in mid 1987, the BoJ started attempting to slow the ascent of the JPY (reflected by a falling USD/JPY). Despite significant bouts of intervention in the years since, attempts to artificially cap the JPY have had only brief success. Market forces defeated the central bank at 140, at 120, and again at 100, with trade probing below this level in 1994–95.

Throughout Asia, central banks in the region have a variety of policy styles, objectives and regulations that affect and institutionally frame the market you would deal in. For instance in (mainland) China the trade in yuan is heavily regulated with controls on the amount and purpose of currency exchange, whereas Hong Kong currency markets are relatively unregulated. It is therefore good practice to know the currency laws of your and the currency counterparties' lands as well as doing the research to know what your local central bank does and is thinking. It helps you to be a better trader and investor and not to be blindsided by events and trends that are otherwise public knowledge.

Price maker/price taker

Recapping this topic (mentioned at the start of chapter 4), a bank that is willing and able to quote both a bid and an offer (a two-way price) on a certain currency pair when requested to do so by a counterparty is known as a 'price maker'. As the name suggests, price makers set the prices other participants must trade on. Price makers must be prepared to deal on either side of the transaction, becoming either the buyer or seller of the pair quoted based simply on taking the opposite side to that selected by the counterparty.

Although a bank may be a price maker in some currencies—for the most part those that it specialises in—it may at the same time be a price taker in other currencies. Clients of the wholesale group (including retail participants) also fall under the heading of price takers. Again, as indicated by the name, price takers do not make prices; rather, they transact at the prices quoted to them by a price maker. Other than choosing not to trade at a given price, price takers have very little power on an individual basis to affect the prices on offer from the price makers.

Clients (of the wholesale participants)

This client group includes participants as diverse as governments, fund managers, hedgers and companies with foreign currency expenses or receipts, such as importers and exporters. This is also the group to which you (the retail trader) belong.

In years gone by there was a definite pecking order within this group. Clients that brought the most business to the banks with the most regularity also generated the most profits for the banks. It is understandable therefore that these customers were frequently given access to better prices (narrower spreads) than other customers, and that they were the first ones to receive a call from the dealing desk if there was a significant event taking place that may influence the foreign exchange market. Personal relationships between clients and banks also helped to lift clients in the pecking order—back in the days of the long business lunch. However, in these days of electronic trading platforms, equal access to data and fierce competition, the prices (spreads) available to all types of clients are more or less the same, with size and personal relationships now counting for little.

Retail

As recently as the mid 1990s, very few avenues were open to the average retail investor wishing to participate in the foreign exchange market. Those who did venture in found a far less transparent, more expensive and less competitive marketplace than we enjoy today.

Travellers making many small transactions with travellers' cheques and credit cards have traditionally dominated the retail involvement in the FX market, but recent advances in technology have opened the door to much wider involvement from the retail segment.

The surge in online trading platforms (including contracts for difference, or CFD, providers) and their wide acceptance as a method of executing trades began with equities trading, but the arrival of numerous online margin FX companies now means that retail traders from just about anywhere can participate in the foreign exchange market on an almost level playing field with the biggest investment houses and banking institutions in the world. The majority of this retail activity has now transformed from the practical task of exchanging money while travelling, and purchasing goods and services in foreign currencies while on holidays, to one that is largely speculative in nature, with traders seeking to directly profit as a consequence of changes in exchange rates. Although retail traders may still be faced with spreads that are one or two pips wider than those available to inter-bank traders, this is a vast improvement over the spreads available for travellers' cheques. In comparison to other markets, such as equities or futures, the cost of executing transactions in the foreign exchange market (the spread) is very small.

Governments

Governments have numerous reasons to be involved in the foreign exchange markets. These involve everything from simply running the affairs of government and maintaining foreign embassies to spending on infrastructure and defence projects. Delivering foreign aid will also often involve significant foreign exchange flows; after all, there isn't much use for Australian dollars once you step too far beyond the borders of Australia. Under normal circumstances, governments will conduct all of their foreign exchange business as customers of their respective central banks.

Sovereign wealth funds and debt offices

Sovereign wealth funds are in effect investment managers for a country's foreign exchange surpluses. In days gone by the task of managing a country's foreign exchange reserves were the exclusive preserve of either the central bank or treasury of a national government, but over time, the build-up of significant foreign reserves between a few far-sighted countries has seen the need for a more specialised investment management agency tasked to preserve and enhance the public's investable assets over very long time frames, if not in perpetuity. This is particularly the case for non-renewable commodity exporting countries, such as oil-exporting Arab Gulf states, and coal- and iron ore-selling Australia, which are not necessarily guaranteed either volumes or prices for their product in the future.

Sovereign wealth funds are not insignificant players in the foreign exchange marketplace. In July 2011, according to the Sovereign Wealth Fund Institute, there was something like $US4.7 trillion in funds under management by just the top 40 agencies alone. Examples of such funds include Australia's Future Fund with about $US75 billion under management, Singapore's Government of Singapore Investment Corporation (GIC) and China's SAFE Investment Company. The world's largest fund is currently the United Arab Emirate's Abu Dhabi Investment Authority with $US657 billion under management. Each of them has different mandates and objectives, but all have the job of ensuring their country's surplus wealth is deployed to maximise the return to those reserves within their defined risk parameters.

On the other side of the balance sheet spectrum is the role played by national debt management offices. These government agencies handle the liabilities and debts of government, ensuring a continuance of their access to funding as well as managing within defined parameters the interest rate risk implications of their borrowing programs, which sometimes involves the borrowing of foreign exchange.

Both types of government agencies tend to be very shy about their investing and, to a lesser extent, their borrowing activities. It is no surprise that debt management office bankers and investors tend to demand a higher level of scrutiny as opposed to sovereign wealth funds that tend to be more commercially discreet about their intentions and portfolios. What can't be ignored is their significance in the FX marketplace.

Supernationals

This category of currency market beast(s) is one that periodically grabs the headlines, but most of the time tends to be ignored by the markets. The most prominent ones include the International Monetary Fund (IMF), the World Bank and the Bank for International Settlements (BIS). These supernationals are nominally funded by developed and, to a lesser extent, developing economies.

The IMF was established to smooth world commerce by reducing foreign exchange restrictions and using its reserve of funds to lend to countries experiencing temporary balance of payments problems so they could continue trading without interruption. The World Bank focuses on making loans to governments to rebuild railroads, highways, bridges, ports and other public infrastructure. The BIS was founded in 1930 to administer the war reparations of Germany to the victorious Allies after World War I.

The supernationals are usually mentioned when a country or region is having financial difficulties and needs some sort of financial assistance or debt restructuring (read 'bail out'). Not that they're universally loved. When Asia went through its financial crisis in 1997–98, the IMF was heavily criticised for its harsh, uncompromising stance on economic and financial restructuring of Asia's (then) damaged economies, an experience that both the IMF and Asia's political elite have since learned from. The IMF (along with the EU and European Central Bank) has shown relative generosity with respect to the problems of Europe's southern periphery economies. Asia's governments, in their turn, wishing to never yield temporary financial sovereignty again, have built up vast and to an extent, unwieldy and wasteful foreign reserves.

We should not ignore these institutions though, as often they are the last financial lifeline for nations in financial distress and indeed are significant currency managers in their own right. For instance, the BIS manages about 10 per cent of the value of foreign exchange reserves of the world's governments.

Corporations (including transnationals)

Companies involved in importing or exporting of goods need to engage in foreign exchange transactions as a part of their normal everyday business dealings. Importers need to sell the local currency in exchange for a foreign currency to pay for the goods they intend to import. Exporters have the opposite requirement, needing to convert the foreign currency they have received for the sale of their goods back into their local currency for repatriation. Discussion of exporters applies not only to companies but also to many primary producers whose output (such as wool, cotton and wheat) is sold into the global markets.

Importers are not only companies that import finished goods ready for sale. This group also includes companies that use foreign-sourced materials in the production of their goods. For these companies, a fall in the value of the local currency will mean that they need to fork out more of their local currency in order to buy the same amount of materials from the foreign source. On the other hand, an increase in the relative strength of the local currency will mean that less of the local currency is required to acquire the foreign imports, leaving more money in the hands of the local company.

If companies are able to forecast their foreign exchange requirements in advance, they are able to use various instruments and tools within the foreign exchange market to 'hedge' their exposure to future movements, effectively locking in a price today for a transaction that will occur in the future. If there is an unfavourable move in rates between the date the rate is locked in and the date of the eventual physical transaction, the company (or individual) is protected. If there is a favourable move, the company may miss out on the benefit, but the trade-off is the comfort that comes with certainty and the removal of foreign exchange risk. (In chapter 11, we will take a closer look at 'forwards', whereby participants lock in a future rate, and at 'options', which may be used to protect the user from losses while still leaving room to gain from favourable moves in the market.)

Transnational corporations are like the ordinary corporations mentioned and have the same requirements to buy, sell and manage their currency flows. This is, however, with the added complexity of importing and exporting across multiple national and currency boundaries with costs and revenues accrued in many currencies. This presents a challenge in the risk management of FX cash flows and balance sheet assets and liabilities, not to mention the problem of reporting in multiple currency terms and jurisdictions.

The turnover of some transnational corporations is larger than the gross domestic products of some emerging nations, so their potential clout in the market is huge. Transnationals had a substantial impact on currency flows, but with the deregulation of financial markets and the integration of previously disparate national markets into regional and even continental blocs, the influence of transnationals over currency markets has shifted to the next category of player we will look at: fund managers.

Fund managers and hedge funds

Investment houses charged with achieving the best returns available on their clients' funds will rarely be content to invest purely in their domestic market (unless restricted to that market by their charter). As the managers of these funds identify superior opportunities in other countries, they will shift the funds from one country to another, with each move involving an exchange in the FX market.

According to the BIS, for every dollar of trade-based currency transactions, something like nine dollars of FX transactions is involved in the investment (capital) flows of fund managers and the like. It is for this reason the individual and collective investment decisions of fund managers tend to influence currency rates far more than that of transactional trade-based flows.

Once an investment has been made in a foreign country, the investment manager is likely to employ a strategy to hedge the risk presented by future currency fluctuations. Such strategies are often referred to as 'currency overlay', and they may be passive, simply reacting to current exchange rates, or active, with the degree of hedging in part determined by the currency overlay manager's anticipation of future currency movements.

Hedge funds form a more aggressive subset of the general category of fund manager. While the history of hedge funds and their many styles and shades is a separate book in itself, here we should use their correct title of 'absolute returns' funds. It is a bit of a misnomer nowadays to call them hedge funds. In fact they don't usually hedge, but unlike traditional fund managers they tend to focus on making an active and absolute commercial return rather than just passively investing in an asset. Absolute returns funds tend not to tolerate losses and are quick (and more ruthless) in cutting a loss and exiting a currency or national market.

The impact on currencies of absolute returns funds is far more pervasive and in keeping with the multiplicity of trading styles. They also have a broader influence on currencies and more accurately price them, having an impact on currencies from very short time frames to very long time frames.

In the very short time frame we have also seen in the past decade the rise of high-frequency traders (HFTs). They are (usually) dedicated funds that use sophisticated technology to trade by analysing market data to capture trading opportunities that may open up for only a fraction of a second to several hours. Aiming to capture just a fraction of a currency unit on every trade, HFTs move in and out of short-term positions several times each day. While they do provide more liquidity to the market, the jury is still out on whether they add to market efficiency or are a dangerous destabilising factor in a market in times of stress.

Speculators and investors

Speculators have no underlying fundamental reason to participate in the FX markets. They simply seek to profit from fluctuations in exchange rates. Speculators may be found in banks on proprietary trading desks, in investment funds (some of which are specifically set up to speculate in currencies) and among the ranks of retail traders. Although speculators have sometimes been given a bad name in the markets, the liquidity they add to the market helps significantly to contribute to the overall efficiency of the FX market.

One of the best known currency speculators is George Soros. He shot to fame, or notoriety, in 1992 when he and his Quantum Fund, which took large bets on international market trends, took on a very large speculative short position in pounds (GBP), reportedly in excess of $10 billion. His expectation for GBP to weaken was directly opposed to the view of the Bank of England, which was reluctant to either let GBP weaken or raise official interest rates. Ultimately, market forces dominated, and GBP did indeed fall heavily, forcing the Bank of England to withdraw GBP from the European Exchange Rate Mechanism and earning Soros a reported US$1.1 billion, along with the title of 'the man who broke the Bank of England'. As with many 'trading legends', what you tend to hear less about are the losses. It is rarely mentioned that just a couple of years later (in 1995), Soros lost hundreds of millions of dollars in a similar speculative attack on the Japanese yen. In 1997, he was accused of being behind the fall of the Malaysian ringgit (MYR) and Thai baht during the Asian currency crisis of 1997–98. Not many speculators are so influential (or profiled), but as a group they make up a large part of the activity within the foreign exchange market.

The term 'speculators' carries negative connotations of a person who seeks greedily to profit from the misfortune of others, but in foreign exchange markets this is not necessarily so. Speculators are investors who buy and sell a commodity, share or currency, based on their expectations. Speculators have a lot of confidence in a price or exchange rate. Lose that confidence and people begin to sell.

This is not an act of greed, but of fear. The first sellers of Thai and Malaysian assets during the Asian currency crisis of 1997 were in fact local Thais and Malaysians themselves.

It is not the role of investors (or speculators) to support government policy; rather, it is the role of governments to give confidence to investors to invest and have faith in a country's prospects and currencies. Speculating and investing are essentially the same. When you buy or sell a currency you are both investing and speculating.

Brokers

Brokers are simply the facilitators of the activities of other participants in the foreign exchange market. Their role is to bring together buyers and sellers, resulting in price discovery and increased liquidity for all participants. There are a variety of brokers, depending on the type of clients they are trying to 'mediate' or 'broker' for.

For the inter-bank market, the traditional voice brokers have largely given way to electronic brokers, which first started to emerge in the early 1990s. Previously, teams of FX brokers would sit in rooms quoting prices down dedicated open phone lines directly into bank trading rooms, but these systems are now largely a thing of the past, although a handful do still exist, mostly in London. The emergence of electronic broking through systems such as Reuters and EBS provides traders with a more transparent system, with faster matching of buyers and sellers and less room for costly human error.

From a retail perspective, the 'broker' is in effect the platform provider or company with which you trade, which is also your sole counterparty. Every trade you open with your 'broker' (your online margin FX platform in the retail FX trading scene) must be closed out with the same company. The same applies to CFD providers who provide a margin deposit service whereby their clients can participate in the FX market and trade largish amounts with only a deposit put down as collateral to begin with.

Who else is in the FX 300?

Some of the traditional lines of distinction between the three broad groups outlined above are becoming blurred as online margin FX providers begin to act as price makers to their clients. These clients are often retail, but some of the larger online platforms also cater to large corporations and even to some of the smaller banks. These online margin FX companies frequently turn over as much volume as many of the banks, and are significant players in the global foreign exchange market as they seek to offset the positions created by the activities of their clients.

The foreign exchange market is dominated by the global inter-bank (wholesale) sector, which is where the majority of money is exchanged and is the source of the general price levels that all other participants in the market trade on. These other participants make up the second group we looked at, the clients of the wholesale sector. In this group we include corporations, fund managers, investors, even governments and sovereign wealth funds. It is also the group to which retail traders belong. Bringing all of these parties together are the members of the third group, the brokers and facilitators.

Key central banks

- European Central Bank <www.ecb.int>
- Bank of England <www.bankofengland.co.uk>
- US Federal Reserve <www.federalreserve.gov>
- People's Bank of China (English version) <www.pbc.gov.cn/publish/english/963/index.html>
- Bank of Japan (in English) <www.boj.or.jp/en>
- Bank of Canada <www.bankofcanada.ca>
- Swiss National Bank <www.snb.ch>
- Reserve Bank of Australia <www.rba.gov.au>

- Reserve Bank of New Zealand <www.rbnz.govt.nz>
- Reserve Bank of India <www.rbi.org.in/home.aspx>
- Bank of Korea <www.bok.or.kr/eng/index.jsp>
- Monetary Authority of Singapore <www.mas.gov.sg>
- Hong Kong Monetary Authority <www.info.gov.hk/hkma>
- Bank Indonesia <www.bi.go.id/web/en>
- Bank Negara Malaysia <www.bnm.gov.my>
- South African Reserve Bank <www.resbank.co.za/Pages/default.aspx>
- Bank for International Settlements <www.bis.org>
- International Monetary Fund <www.imf.org/external/index.htm>
- World Bank <www.worldbank.org>.

In the next chapter we will take a more detailed look at the companies that facilitate trading on the foreign exchange market for retail traders — the online margin FX providers.

Chapter 6

Trading platforms for retail traders

The growing popularity of foreign exchange trading among private investors is reflected in the continuing explosion of companies now catering specifically to the needs of this segment of the market. These new online margin FX trading platforms are supported by continual technological advances and are making dramatic inroads into the world of private trading through a broad acceptance, user familiarity and genuine enthusiasm for online trading platforms. In this chapter we examine some of the key differences between traditional inter-bank brokers and these online 'brokers', more accurately described as margin FX providers.

As we discuss further in chapter 10, the role of inter-bank foreign exchange brokers is to assist in the price discovery process, bringing together the highest bid and lowest ask prices, then seeking to match two separate counterparties (banks) willing to take the opposite sides of a trade at the quoted price. In effect, the inter-bank broker is simply the intermediary between two independent counterparties. Once a deal has been executed between these two counterparties, there is no need for them to trade with each other again to close out the initial trade. Each is free to trade with any counterparty of their choosing, subject to their respective in-house counterparty risk guidelines.

In contrast, an online 'broker', or margin FX provider, takes the place of the counterparty to all trades executed by its clients. It in effect makes the market by agreeing to take the counter position to the retail FX trader. So, when you trade with one of these 'brokers', your counterparty is always the broker itself. As a result, any positions you open with a given broker must be closed out by executing an opposite trade with the same broker. If you buy $100 000 AUD/USD through the trading platform provided by XYZ Forex Broker, for example, you would need to sell $100 000 AUD/USD through the same company in order to close out the position. Because the market in which you initially deal is made by the particular margin FX platform provider, in this case XYZ Forex Broker, you could not close the position by selling on another platform or selling through another company.

In summary, an inter-bank broker seeks to extract the highest bid and lowest ask prices from its clients in order to come up with a price with the narrowest possible spread for each currency pair, while an online margin FX provider plays the role of price maker and quotes a two-way price (bid and ask) to clients. And, fortunately for the retail FX trader, the fierce competition between online FX platforms means that the prices they quote to their clients are always very close to the underlying inter-bank market rates, with spreads often within a single pip or two of being as narrow as those on offer to the world's biggest banks and financial institutions. Any broker that is seen quoting prices that differ notably from the broader market will rapidly lose customers. Thus this self-interest and its necessary contribution to the bottom line of margin FX providers largely removes the risk of retail clients being quoted consistently 'bad' prices — although there is still the risk of an occasional wayward price spike.

Importantly, although the online margin FX provider is the counterparty to all trades executed on its trading platform, different types of providers will have different ways of handling client positions. Some will lay off their risk by passing the trades straight through their liquidity providers to the inter-bank market. Others will match off client trades against one another and hedge the balance, while another group may decide to take the risk of holding the opposite side of client trades. So long as both the price being quoted to clients and the execution of trades are fair and free of manipulation, it should not make any difference to the client which method the FX provider is using to manage its risk exposure.

Choosing an online margin FX provider

All online margin FX providers offer broadly the same services; that is, the ability for retail investors to participate in the foreign exchange market with the opportunity to significantly leverage their funds and enjoy competitive pricing, comparable to the prices available to the world's biggest traders in the inter-bank market. However, due to the 'over-the-counter' nature of the foreign exchange market, there are some significant differences between these companies that you should consider when deciding which one to open an account with. Key differences to consider include the following:

- pricing model
- size and backing of the margin FX provider
- margin and leverage
- trade sizes available — 100 000/10 000/any amount
- spread width — is it fixed or variable?
- trading platform — ease of use and need to download software
- charting service — ability to create your own indicators and/or back-test trading systems
- number of currency pairs available to trade
- access to other markets
- regulatory environment.

We will now examine each of these considerations separately to give you some idea of the issues that you will need to consider when choosing your online margin FX provider.

Pricing model

The three main pricing models you are likely to encounter as a retail FX trader are:

- straight through pricing model
- market maker model
- electronic communications network (ECN) model.

If you read information posted on internet trading forums you will quickly discover that many traders have firm views regarding each of these models. Online discussions regarding their relative merits frequently dissolve into heated arguments as the supporters and detractors of each model attack each other with passion. These forums rarely do more than perpetuate widely believed misconceptions and inaccuracies.

Although we can make some broad general comments about each of these models, the reality is that each FX provider does things slightly differently. As technology advances and regulatory changes continue to alter the trading environment, pricing models are also evolving. At times, the boundaries between the different models can appear somewhat blurred.

In very broad terms, here are some of the features that define each of these models.

- *Straight through pricing:* As the name suggests, FX providers that employ this model pass prices directly from their liquidity provider/s through to their retail clients. Although they may add a small mark-up to the wholesale spreads they receive from the inter-bank market (in lieu of charging commission), they generally do not have a traditional trading desk and do not get involved in manual execution of clients' trades. Prices and spreads fluctuate in line with the underlying inter-bank market and the automatic execution results in all clients being treated equally.
- *Market maker:* A traditional definition of a market maker is a provider (broker) that is willing and able to continually quote a two-way price (bid/ask) in a given security. Although a market maker derives its prices from those of the underlying market, it does not necessarily offset all client trades in the underlying market. This way, it can provide additional liquidity to the marketplace. Market makers usually have a trading desk that manages the risk created by the open positions of clients.
- *Electronic communications network (ECN):* As a general rule, an FX provider using the ECN model is providing a marketplace where multiple liquidity providers, banks, market makers and traders provide competing bids and offers. Instead of earning revenue by adding a margin to the spread, ECN

providers usually charge a fee for their services. There are as many different methods of charging this fee as there are ECN providers. Although their tight spreads appear attractive, traders generally need to trade higher volumes before the tighter spreads offset the cost of the commissions paid.

Although this gives a broad overview of the different types of FX providers you are likely to encounter, it must be stressed again that each provider is different. Each will offer its own unique combination of pricing and execution methodology. It is up to you, the trader, to research which model is used by any given provider and to decide whether or not it suits you.

There is one other important point to reiterate here. Many traders are concerned by the idea of their provider being the counterparty to their trade and effectively trading against them. If you are trading with a provider that is obliged to meet strict regulatory requirements, this should not be an issue (see the section later in this chapter on regulatory environment). Despite this, people still don't like the idea of losing money to an FX provider that takes the opposite side of their trade. However, so long as the prices you receive fairly reflect the underlying inter-bank FX market and are not manipulated by your FX provider, it should not make any difference whether it is your provider or the market that benefits from your losses, or pays for your wins.

Size and backing

Although many jurisdictions around the world have increased the capital requirements for FX providers in recent years, it remains a fact that some have considerably more financial backing than others. When selecting which company you will entrust your FX trading funds to, it is worth considering how secure your funds will be.

In doing this, it is also useful to determine exactly which entity will be holding your funds, as many of the smaller companies in the market act as 'introducing brokers' or provide 'white label' versions of trading platforms run by other companies. Companies that develop online trading platforms for their clients sometimes seek to expand the number of people trading on their platforms by making the trading platform available to other online 'brokers' either as 'introducing brokers' or as a 'white label' version, which the second 'broker' may emblazon with its own name and logo. The second broker can offer its clients a first-rate trading platform without spending a fortune to reinvent the wheel, and the originator of the platform enjoys increased trading volumes.

While your broker may be small, this is not necessarily a problem as the entity responsible for holding your funds may well be very much larger, perhaps even being a significant player in the broader global foreign exchange markets.

Margin and leverage

The terms 'margin' and 'leverage' are often used interchangeably, although there is a slight difference in their meaning. Margin is the amount of money required to hold a certain open position. Leverage refers to the amount by which your trading power is magnified by your FX provider.

In October 2010, the Commodity Futures Trading Commission (CFTC) in the United States placed a cap on leverage of 50:1 for the major currency pairs and 20:1 for other pairs. In August 2011, the Financial Services Agency (FSA) of Japan placed a cap on leverage for retail FX traders of 25:1 after having reduced it to 50:1 a year earlier.

In other jurisdictions, such as Australia, it is still common (in late 2011) for FX providers to offer leverage of 400:1 or even 500:1. This means that with just $1000 in a trading account, a trader could place a trade for as much as $500 000.

Let's assume you trade with a provider that offers leverage of 50:1. If you have US$20 000 in your account, you will be able to place trades with a face value of up to $1 000 000.

If you trade one standard lot of USD/JPY at 76.680, you will be taking a position of US$100 000 against JPY 7 668 000. With leverage of 50:1, the margin required to hold this position open will be one-fiftieth (or 2 per cent) of US$100 000, which equals US$2000.

Taking the same trade with an account using leverage of 400:1 would require considably less margin. In this instance, the margin required for the same trade would be just US$250, or one four-hundredth (0.25 per cent) of US$100 000.

Whether the available rate of leverage is 50:1 or 400:1, it could be said in this instance that the trader has effectively employed leverage of just 5:1 by taking a position with an initial value that was only five times larger than the funds on deposit. It would be rare (and foolish) for a trader to leverage trades to the maximum extent allowed. Doing so would leave no room for any adverse price fluctuation. In fact, because of the bid/ask spread, the margin requirements would be likely to exceed the available funds almost straight away.

In the example above, the base currency is the same as the currency in which the account is denominated, USD. When this is not the case, the margin is frequently quoted in the same currency as that in which the account is denominated.

For example, let's assume you hold US$20 000 in your account and wish to trade one lot of EUR/USD at 1.45390. You will be taking a position of EUR 100 000 against US$145 390. When trading on leverage of 50:1, the margin requirement will be EUR 2000; however, many FX providers will instead show that the margin requirement is the USD equivalent, which in this instance is US$2907.80.

It is *extremely important* that traders understand that leverage is a double-edged sword. Although it can help you to grow your account with dramatic speed when you trade with the market, it can also cause you to lose your funds just as quickly in the event that the market turns against you.

Although it might at first seem attractive to have as much leverage as possible on your account, it is highly likely that anybody utilising the full leverage available to them is taking excessive risks and not employing sound money management techniques. In reality, you will probably find that an effective leverage rate in the region of 10:1 through to about 50:1 is sufficient in most situations. By all means, sign up for the account that offers leverage of 500:1, but don't feel as though you are compelled to use all of the margined funds that are available to you.

Trade size

In years gone by, the standard default size for a trade in the inter-bank spot FX market was 5 000 000 units of the base currency. For example, a standard-sized EUR/USD trade would be for 5 000 000 EUR, with the USD amount fluctuating as dictated by the prevailing exchange rate. Although the usefulness of average figures is questionable in a market with such a large variation in trade sizes, research shows that average trade sizes have fallen. In May 2011 the research and consulting firm Celent produced a report entitled *Technology Systems in the Global FX Market*. Celent estimates that the average ticket size in the inter-bank spot FX market has fallen from $4.3 million in 2004 to just $1.8 million in 2011 despite the overall growth of FX volumes. This reduction in average ticket size is attributed to the growth of algorithmic trading and the rapid growth of the retail FX market.

Within the retail FX market, many online trading platforms have adopted a quasi-standard size 'contract' equal to 100 000 units of the base currency. They borrow a term from the futures markets and call this amount 'one lot'. Many providers also offer an account that is based on a 'mini-contract' where 'one lot' is equal to 10 000 units of the base currency.

Some platforms, including the popular MT4 platform, allow traders to trade less than one whole lot. This allows traders to fine tune their position size. For an account set up to trade standard lots, the ability to trade just 0.01 lots reduces the trade size from 100 000 units of the base currency to just 1000 units of the base currency (or any multiple thereof). In the same manner, trading 0.01 lots of a 'mini-contract' reduces trade size to just 100 units of the base currency. At this level, a one pip move in price represents a change in value of just 0.01 units of the terms currency. For example, if trading 0.01 lots of a mini-contract in EUR/USD at 1.45250, you would be trading EUR 100 against US$145.25. An increase in price of one pip to 1.45260 would increase the USD amount by just one cent, to US$145.26. Where the terms currency of a trade of this size is Japanese yen, a one pip change in price would result in a change in value of JPY 1.

Other margin FX providers do not require you to trade in multiples of 100 000 or 10 000, or fractions thereof. Some will allow you to trade any amount from $1 upwards, while others may impose some limit on the minimum trade size. For example, some platforms will require each trade to be for at least US$10 000 or equivalent, while others will allow any size trade but will charge a commission fee if the trade is smaller than US$50 000 or equivalent.

The key point is that each online margin FX provider has its own rules, and you need to make sure you are aware of these rules before you start to trade. You cannot assume that the rules you have learned for one platform will be applicable to another.

Spread width — fixed or variable?

Unfortunately, there is an excessive focus on spread width when novice retail FX traders are selecting a provider to trade with. In a market that has become so heavily commoditised, where key differences are mostly behind the scenes, it is a fairly simple marketing strategy to equate tighter spreads with lower costs. After all, who doesn't want to save money where possible?

However, the actual amount of money that an average retail trader will save by executing trades on a tighter than average spread is relatively small. Any such saving needs to be weighed up as a part of the overall package offered by a given FX provider.

Beyond the headline-grabbing average width of the spread, traders should also consider whether their trading is best suited to a provider with variable (floating) or fixed spreads.

In the inter-bank FX market, spreads vary from second to second as multiple banks around the world add, remove and alter their bid and ask prices. Retail FX providers that quote their clients raw inter-bank prices (like an ECN) or add a small mark-up to inter-bank prices will have spreads that may vary from time to time as conditions in the underlying market change. This is most obvious when spreads widen due to relatively low liquidity, as is common first thing on Monday morning in Asia or around the time of major data releases.

Other retail margin FX providers quote their clients fixed spreads. While this does offer a degree of certainty for traders, the trade-off is that the fixed spread is usually slightly wider than the average spreads of those providers that offer a variable spread. Because of the nature of offering fixed spreads, this model is synonymous with market makers as distinct from brokers that provide straight through pricing (with or without a mark-up).

The narrowest spreads are quoted on the most liquid currency pairs — EUR/USD, USD/JPY and GBP/USD — with most platforms offering a spread of between two and four pips on these pairs. Once you move into more 'exotic' currencies, it is not uncommon to see spreads widen out to 20 pips or more, making them much more expensive to trade in comparison to the major currencies.

Data releases

Major data releases can cause relatively big moves in currency prices, so many retail traders regard these events as good trading opportunities. While it is indeed possible to trade these events successfully, it is worth understanding what is going on behind the scenes. In the moments prior to the release of a major piece of economic or statistical data, many institutional FX traders will withdraw their orders from the market. This has the effect of reducing overall liquidity, which can result in a widening of spreads. While internet chat rooms and bulletin boards will light up with accusations that retail FX providers are responsible for widening the spreads at such times and taking advantage of their clients, in most instances it is actually just a reflection of what is taking place in the underlying inter-bank FX market.

Trading platform

There are a great number of different FX trading platforms, and they all have a different look and 'feel' in the way they present market information, trading screens and account information. Many FX providers have their own proprietary trading platforms, while others provide access to a platform provided by a third party, such as MT4 from MetaQuotes. Most companies will allow you to trade on a 'demo' version of their platform before you open a live account and deposit real money. It is a good idea to take advantage of these demonstration accounts so that you ensure you select a platform that you find easy to understand and navigate. Trading is complicated enough without having to struggle to understand your trading platform.

Mobility is one question to consider when choosing a trading platform. How and where are you most likely to be trading? Will you always be trading from your computer at home or from your personal laptop? Or will you also require access to your trading platform from other locations, computers and devices? Will you want to trade from numerous branch offices of your company or while on the road in an internet café or hotel? Your answer will determine whether you should consider a trading platform that requires software to be installed on your computer, a platform that simply requires you to visit a web page and log in, or perhaps even a platform that can be accessed on your smart phone, tablet computer or some other device. In general, a platform that requires software to be downloaded will provide greater functionality and security, while a platform that you simply log into via the internet offers mobility but may offer reduced functionality. Continuing improvements in technology are already bringing the two types of platform closer together.

Ease of use is another major factor to consider. Trading the foreign exchange markets often requires a quick response to events in the marketplace. You need to be able to move around the order entry screens quickly and have a clear indication of the current level of the market. Most platforms make this information very clear and easy to access, with some even allowing you to trade with a single click on the bid or offer price showing on the screen.

A simple display of open positions, current orders and stop-loss orders is also important. Ideally, this will include an indication of the current value of your open positions and overall account balance, updated in real-time. Your trading platform should also provide you with access to a complete listing of your trade history and all activity on your account.

Building a new trading platform from scratch costs millions of dollars. Considerable cost is also associated with maintaining a trading platform and tweaking it to keep it up to date with changes in the market and customer requirements. This is a huge financial commitment for any FX provider. It is also potentially a significant risk. What if traders simply don't like the platform, or what if it has stability issues?

Although many companies have built very good trading platforms that are available exclusively to their clients, there are alternatives. One of the most popular is the MT4 platform from MetaQuotes.

In recent years, more and more retail FX providers have made MT4 available to their clients. As users have churned from one broker to another, many have chosen to switch to another MT4 provider due to familiarity with the platform. As a result, even some of the large FX providers with their own high-profile platforms have been compelled to include MT4 as an additional trading option due to customer demand.

One highly attractive feature of the MT4 platform for many traders and money managers is the expert advisor (EA) tool. Users can program their own EA to execute trades automatically, based on their own specific criteria. This is particularly useful for traders who are unable to sit and monitor the markets themselves. It also means that traders can take advantage of opportunities that arise 24 hours a day, throughout the trading week.

A newer trading platform, called MT5, is available from MetaQuotes. Although it looks and feels much like MT4, the architecture behind it is quite different. One of the intended benefits for users is an integrated tool to help with the creation of expert advisors, removing the need for specific code-writing skills. At the time of publication, a handful of FX providers are offering MT5 as a demo or in beta. However, MT4 has a loyal user base that appreciates its stability and vast library of add-ons. So far, there has not been a rush by either traders or the brokers to switch to the newer platform.

We cover this topic more in chapter 14, on new technology.

Trading on your phone

Since it has become possible to access some trading platforms via smart-phones, there has been strong customer demand for all providers to offer this service. Although volumes may pick up in the future, it appears at this stage that little actual trading is conducted via these mobile devices. When selecting a broker, you should consider the features that will actually help you to trade, rather than being seduced by features that you are unlikely to use.

Charting service

Technological advances have seen a significant increase in the sophistication of charting packages that are automatically provided with online trading platforms. As well as offering intraday charts, right down to five-minute, one-minute and possibly even tick charts, you want to ensure that the charting package available to you allows you to draw trend lines and other indicators onto the chart. The better charting packages allow you to create and apply your own indicators, with some even allowing you to back-test your trading ideas and trade directly from the chart.

Number of currency pairs available to trade

While some trading platforms make a big fuss over the number of trading pairs they have available on their platforms, unless you have a specific requirement there is little reason for retail FX traders to stray beyond the largest four or five currency pairs. The EUR/USD alone accounts for some 28 per cent of all daily FX market turnover, with USD/JPY and GBP/USD accounting for a further 14 per cent and 11 per cent respectively. Just these three pairs account for more than 50 per cent of all FX market activity.

Access to other markets

Traders who don't wish to be confined purely to the FX markets may consider choosing a company that offers online trading in other markets as well. Some companies offer integrated trading platforms that allow users to trade numerous different markets, often from the same single trading account. However, be sure that in its attempts to provide a 'one size fits all' solution, your online platform does not force you to endure too many compromises.

Regulatory environment

The degree to which retail foreign exchange trading is regulated depends greatly on geographic location. In the past, foreign exchange trading was largely restricted to over-the-counter operations between banks. As a result, there was little need for rules to protect retail traders, who did not have access to the market. However, in recent years, a number of jurisdictions have introduced extensive regulations aimed primarily at providing protection for retail traders against fraudulent, misleading, unfair and deceptive conduct by those involved in the industry.

The section following gives a brief outline of the regulatory bodies of Australia, the United Kingdom and the United States, where many of the larger margin FX providers are based.

Australia

Margin FX providers operating in Australia must be registered with the Australian Securities and Investments Commission (ASIC) <www.asic.gov.au> as the holder of an Australian financial services licence (AFSL), as set out in the *Corporations Act 2001*.

Unless a company or individual is the holder of an Australian financial services licence or is an authorised representative of an AFSL holder, it or he or she is not permitted to provide financial product advice or arrange for people to deal in financial products.

The following is taken directly from the ASIC website.

> **What we do**
>
> ASIC is Australia's corporate, markets and financial services regulator. We contribute to Australia's economic reputation and wellbeing by ensuring that Australia's financial markets are fair and transparent, supported by confident and informed investors and consumers.
>
> Source: ASIC <www.asic.gov.au>.

United Kingdom

In mid 2010 it was announced that the existing regulator of retail foreign exchange trading in the UK, the Financial Services Authority (FSA) <www.fsa.gov.uk> would be disbanded. This move is part of an effort to resolve inefficiencies within the tripartite regulatory system involving the FSA, the Bank of England and the UK Treasury.

Under the new regime, the responsibilities previously held by the FSA will be divided between the Bank of England (which will establish a new financial policy committee) and two new agencies: The Prudential Regulatory Authority (PRA) and the Financial Conduct Authority (FCA).

The changeover is due to take place in 2012. Once the new agencies are in place the FCA will oversee regulation and conduct of financial services firms, including those that provide retail FX services, while the PRA will be responsible for ensuring firms adhere to the relevant financial requirements.

The United States

In the US two bodies oversee the activities of margin FX providers: the National Futures Association (NFA) <www.nfa.futures.org> and the Commodity Futures Trading Commission (CFTC) <www.cftc.gov>, which is responsible for registering entities as futures commission merchants (FCM).

An FCM must maintain stringent financial standards and comply with certain investor protection regulations. These requirements are enforced by the NFA and investors with a complaint can contact either the NFA or the CFTC.

Questions to ask when choosing a broker

ASIC has created a list of questions that it recommends you ask when choosing which contracts for difference (CFD) provider to trade with. Because ASIC treats CFDs and margin FX as similar products, this list may also be useful for those choosing an FX provider. Here is the list, adapted for FX:

- What is the financial position of the FX provider?
- What is the FX provider's policy on the use of client money?
- How does the FX provider determine prices?
- Can the FX provider change or re-quote the price after you have already placed your order?
- When processing FX trades, does the FX provider enter into a corresponding position in the market for the underlying asset?

- If there is little or no trading going on in the underlying market for an asset, can you still trade margin FX contracts over that asset?
- Does the FX provider let you trade margin FX contracts even if the underlying market is closed?

There are not any intrinsically 'wrong' or necessarily 'bad' answers to the questions above. The intent behind these questions is to make sure that brokers provide proper disclosure and that clients are adequately informed regarding the characteristics of the market in which they are participating.

How do margin FX brokers make money?

It should not come as any surprise that margin FX providers are in business to make a profit. They provide traders with a service and, quite rightly, expect to be rewarded for doing so. Once again, each broker does things slightly differently. Some of the more common sources of broker revenue are outlined below.

The most obvious way for a broker to make money is to charge a commission. This method is most commonly used by ECNs, which represent a relatively small portion of the overall retail FX market. Among those that do charge a commission, this charge may be in the form of a fee per trading ticket, a fee for trades below a certain amount (say $50 000), or a fee calculated on total monthly volumes.

Other direct fees and charges may be levied in relation to deposits, withdrawals and other account administration activities. In general, these charges represent little more than cost recovery for the brokers and are not a key driver of profits.

Many FX providers do not pay interest on client deposits, yet they are likely to be earning interest on that portion of client funds that have not been allocated to open positions. For larger brokers with millions of dollars on deposit, this can be a good source of risk-free revenue.

The daily rollover provides another revenue opportunity. Some brokers have the ability to add a small mark-up to the swap rate (interest rate) applied to open positions at the end of the FX day (usually 5.00 pm New York time), when they are rolled from one day to the next.

For FX providers that do not pass all of their trades directly through to an inter-bank counterparty (liquidity provider), there is an opportunity to match client trades against each other. If they have their back-end systems configured correctly, every buy from a client that offsets a sell from another potentially allows the broker to pick up the value of the spread as profit.

For example, in table 6.1 let's assume an online margin FX provider is quoting EUR/USD at 1.45150/170. If one client buys EUR 1 000 000 at the ask price of 1.45170 and another sells EUR 1 000 000 at the bid price of 1.45150, the broker has effectively bought at 1.45150 and sold at 1.45170 for a profit of two pips, or US$200.

Table 6.1: example of a quote from an online margin FX provider

Broker quote: EUR/USD 1.45150/170			
Client 1:	Buy	1 000 000 EUR at 1.45170	Broker: sells at 1.45170
Client 2:	Sell	1 000 000 EUR at 1.45150	Broker: buys at 1.45150

Continuing from our example above, if Client 2 had not sold EUR 1 000 000 at 1.45150, the broker would have been left with a short EUR/USD position as a result of Client 1 having taken the offer at 1.45170. So, the broker is short EUR 1 000 000 at 1.45170 and needs to buy EUR to square up. Through their liquidity providers, online margin FX providers have solid relationships with one or more of the major players in the inter-bank FX market, and have access to price quotes that are often the same as those in the inter-bank market. While the online margin FX provider is quoting EUR/USD at 1.45150/170, it may be trading in the inter-bank market at 1.45158/163. If the short EUR 1 000 000 at 1.45170 position can be squared up by buying at 1.45163, the online broker automatically makes a profit of seven-tenths (0.7) of a pip.

Built into the previous example is one of the other key ways in which many margin FX providers make their money. The example shows that the broker is quoting a price for EUR/USD of 1.45150/170, while the underlying inter-bank market is showing a price of 1.45158/163. In this example, the margin FX provider has added a small margin to the inter-bank price, resulting in the spread widening from 0.5 pips to 2 pips. This is the major source of income for many FX providers that pass trades directly through to their liquidity providers and don't charge commissions. However, this margin of 1.5 pips is not all profit. From this relatively small mark-up in prices, FX providers need to pay their liquidity providers as well as covering the costs of staff, technology, marketing and even rebates to partners and introducing brokers. You can see why these providers rely on high trading volumes.

There is another source of revenue for market makers that stirs up quite a bit of controversy among retail traders. Market makers have a trading desk and do not usually pass all their clients' trades through to the inter-bank market. Instead, the traders employed by these brokers are tasked with managing the exposure that is created by the trading activity of their clients. Usually, these traders will be guided by procedures that allow their exposure to build only to a certain level. If client trades result in this exposure exceeding a certain level, some of the risk will be 'taken off' by the traders taking a counterposition in the market. However, while exposure remains within predetermined risk parameters, the traders have the choice of either covering the client positions (by taking a countering position in the market) or leaving the position unhedged. In effect, this is the same as taking the other side of the clients' trade. If the client loses and their trade was unhedged, the losses go straight to the market maker. On the other hand, if a client wins on a trade that has not been hedged, the profit made by the client is paid for by the market maker.

As outlined towards the start of this chapter, if clients are receiving price quotes that are a true reflection of the underlying market and trade execution that is fair and free of manipulation, the method of risk exposure used by the broker should not make any difference to the client. Whether you lose to your broker or lose to the market (as you do with equities) makes no difference. The same applies if your trades are winners.

To ensure that a market maker is treating you fairly and providing trade execution that is free of manipulation, it is wise to use a provider that is registered in one of the more tightly regulated jurisdictions. Fines for brokers caught doing the wrong thing in these countries can run into millions of dollars.

One key point is worth mentioning at this juncture. Perhaps the biggest benefit of all that retail traders gain from the existence of online margin FX companies is access to a market that would otherwise be inaccessible to them. Online margin FX trading gives retail traders the ability to participate in price moves that emanate from the inter-bank foreign exchange market, the biggest market in the world. Despite suggestions to the contrary that you might read on the internet in chat rooms and forums, the inter-bank market is a closed shop unless you happen to be a bank with a decent credit rating. Given that online margin FX providers make it possible for retail traders to participate in this market, we can hardly begrudge them earning a pip or two above the inter-bank rate (which the retail trader cannot access anyway).

The next step

When selecting a trading platform and the associated online margin FX provider, it is worth doing some basic checks, even if the company boasts a well-known name. Is that company, for example, registered in a known tax haven, or perhaps in a country famous for corruption and financial scams? Or is it registered in a tightly regulated country such as Australia, the UK or the US? Is the demo version of the software intuitive and easy to use? Do the margin, spread and standard trade size meet with your satisfaction?

There are many online margin FX trading platforms for you to choose from and they all have slight differences. Your best bet is to select a short list, then try out the demonstration versions to see which one suits you best.

One thing is certain: as technology evolves, trading platforms will continue to improve, offering more features and greater ease of use. For updates on the latest developments, please visit <www.alexdouglas.com>.

Chapter 7

Factors influencing FX markets

Over the longer term, it is undeniable that underlying economic fundamentals will drive the currency markets in one direction or the other. In the shorter term, however, elements of fear, greed and herd behaviour drive the foreign exchange markets. This herd mentality can be reflected in short-term movements that are often a reaction to market rumours, or might evolve as a longer term phenomenon because traders are paying undue attention to one area of market influence while virtually ignoring another. We saw this in the late 1990s, when the United States and the USD became the 'flavour of the month' among global investors, despite the everpresent trade deficit.

Many factors in each country can and do affect the economy of that country and the value of its currency. To make matters worse, it is the interrelationship between these factors that drives the markets. This is complex enough when just looking at one country, but in the currency markets we are looking at how all of these factors interrelate, not just within the borders of each country, but how they interrelate across borders around the world. This makes it extremely difficult to accurately pinpoint exactly which factor is responsible for any particular movement in a market. This is the challenge for the FX trader.

Nonetheless, it is worth having a broad understanding of the theoretical way in which various fundamental and economic factors are generally seen to affect the foreign exchange market, and this is what we examine in this chapter.

Supply and demand

Prices (or exchange rates) are ultimately determined by the relative influence of the forces of supply and demand. If there is very high demand for a particular currency, its value would be expected to increase in relation to currencies that there is less demand for. On the other hand, if there is a desire among holders of a particular currency to dispose of that currency in exchange for another, its value is likely to decline in relation to other currencies.

The sources of supply and demand in the foreign exchange market were outlined in chapter 5; namely, banks, governments, money/investment managers, corporations, retail traders and speculators. We now come to the motivations behind the actions of these participants, although we've partly examined some of the more practical of these, such as those governing the commercial business of importers and exporters.

Before you form a 'view' on a currency it is critical to remember that a foreign exchange rate is a 'ratio' of one currency for another. It is not an absolute in, say, a strong or weak currency. The bet you make on a currency will not be about whether it is good or bad, but *how* good or bad it is relative to that particular counter-currency. It is important to get this right. For instance, if you have two strong currencies, the trade you would make would be to buy the 'better' of these two good currencies and sell the other. The logic works conversely, where one buys the less weak of two weak currencies and sells the other. This is a game that all of the participants in the FX market try to anticipate and trade accordingly, looking for the best future currency to buy or the weakest currency to sell.

When these groups detect an opportunity in a particular currency, either for direct appreciation or for higher investment returns, demand increases for that currency and buyers will outbid one another, resulting in currency appreciation. When the opportunity moves to another country/currency, holders of the first currency may then seek to sell that currency in exchange for the currency linked to the new opportunity. A term that is often heard in relation to funds that constantly flow around the world in search of the greatest returns is 'hot money'.

So what moves hot money?

The balance of payments

Traditionally FX dealers first focus on a country's balance of payments (BoP), or trade balance as it is known in the US. The BoP is simply the net result of all importation to a particular country against all the exportation from that country. As shown in table 7.1, a country that exports more than it imports is said to have a trade surplus, while a country that exports less than it imports is said to have a trade deficit.

Table 7.1: outline of a country's balance of payments (BoP)

Trade activity	Trade result	Currency result
Country exports more than it imports	Trade surplus	Firmer currency
Country imports more than it exports	Trade deficit	Weaker currency

All other things being equal, we would expect to see a country that exports more than it imports to have a firmer currency than a country that did more importing:

In highly simplistic terms, all other things being equal, a country that has a trade surplus is thought to be generating more foreign receipts than foreign debts. In order to convert these foreign receipts back into the local currency, there is a need to sell foreign currencies and buy the local currency. This buying of the local currency exceeds the selling that is undertaken by importers converting their funds into foreign currencies to pay for their purchases. The excess demand for the local currency would then, in turn, help to lift its value relative to other currencies. This can be represented as shown in table 7.2.

Table 7.2: lifting the value of currency relative to other currencies

Exporters	Importers
Buyers of local currency to convert foreign-denominated revenue from the sale of the export.	Sellers of local currency in exchange for foreign currency to pay for the import in the country of origin.
Want to see a weak local currency so that their foreign currency can be converted into the highest possible amount of local currency.	Want to see a firm local currency so that their sale of the local currency will provide the maximum possible amount of foreign currency.

In Australia, specific figures for BoP data are released on a quarterly basis by the Australian Bureau of Statistics (ABS). A monthly report on goods and services also provides a rough guide in between releases of the BoP data. The US trade balance data is released on a monthly basis and can be accessed through <www.census.gov>, as well as other current US economic indicators. In China, crucially important data for our region and international trade data are reported (in English) on <www.stats.gov.cn/English>. As the second largest economy in the world and in many cases the largest trading partner of all Asian countries, it is doubly important to keep track of trends in China, our largest customer.

Since late last century the US has been in a chronic state of trade deficit with Japan, a source of much trans-Pacific anguish and irritation. The US now has an even larger deficit with China. Persistent trade imbalances (where one country has large surpluses against another country's trade deficits) usually point to the need for their currency cross to appreciate in favour of the surplus country and for the deficit country's currency to decrease in relative terms. This has been demanded by US trade negotiators with the Chinese as the Chinese yuan continues to appreciate against the US dollar.

Interest rates and money supply policy

There are numerous theories and models on the source of currency exchange rates, some of which are examined in chapter 9. Central to many of them is the impact of interest rates.

Interest rates are traditionally set by the official 'monetary policy' in each country and have a major influence on exchange rates. In general terms, the short-term interest rate differential between two countries has a significant impact on the exchange rate of the countries' two currencies, although the longer term impact of the absolute and real interest rates also plays a part.

The interest rates of most importance to traders in the currency markets are those rates set by the central banks in each country. Working on this premise, the major central banks to watch are the:

- US Federal Reserve Bank (known as 'the Fed')
- European Central Bank (ECB)

- Bank of Japan (BoJ)
- Bank of England (BoE)
- Reserve Bank of Australia (RBA), for those trading the AUD
- People's Bank of China (PBC).

All of these central banks utilise the fact that by varying the rate of 'official' interest rates it is possible to influence the level of economic activity and the behaviour of borrowers and lenders in their currency, be they residents or non-residents. At the same time, a change in interest rates will alter the relative returns available to investors in the country concerned compared with other currencies, which will in turn influence currency exchange rates.

If an economy is seen to be expanding too quickly (and perhaps heading towards problems with inflation), official monetary policy may be 'tightened', which basically means interest rates are raised. This is generally achieved through the increased sale of government securities, which has the effect of taking money out of the financial system, increasing the 'cost' (or interest rate) for the funds that remain in the system. The higher cost of funds eventually flows through to all borrowers, including those who are traditionally most reported on in the news — the mortgage holders and users of credit cards. Businesses also find it more expensive to borrow funds for the expansion of their activities. The net result is that the pace of growth in the economy overall will slow.

However, higher interest rates also have the effect of generating higher potential returns for investors and investment funds scouring the world for the best possible returns. A lift in interest rates in a particular country will therefore help to strengthen the currency as more investment funds are attracted to that country.

On the other hand, an economy that is sluggish and is viewed by its central bank as needing a boost may see an 'easing' of official monetary policy; that is, a lowering of interest rates. To achieve this, the central bank buys back government securities, thus injecting more funds into the financial system. A simple matter of supply and demand will then lead to a fall in the cost of funds as they become more plentiful.

Lower interest rates provide investors in that country with lower returns on their investments. This encourages investors to seek higher returns elsewhere, resulting in selling and a weakening of the currency of a country that lowers its interest rates.

In the developed economies of the world interest rates are the fastest and quickest mechanism to affect borrower and investor behaviours. In lesser developed economies it is not the only mechanism by which their spending patterns can be affected. In China, which is a vast economy, interest rate settings are not the only channel by which the central bank and government influences spending. China has an evolving financial market status and still uses direct credit controls where it effectively takes money out of the banking system (and thus the available pool of funds) when it demands that banks increase reserves held with the central bank, or conversely puts money back into the system by decreasing reserve deposit requirements, which has a similar effect to raising and cutting interest rates.

A country with persistently high interest rates relative to other countries may see its currency weaken if the high interest rates are a symptom of high inflation or expectations of high inflation. High inflation would result in an erosion of value for holders of the high inflation currency.

Speaking of inflation...

Inflation and deflation

Inflation has both long-term and shorter term implications for the foreign exchange market and must be analysed within the context of the broader economic outlook.

In very simple terms, the traditional, or longer term, view of inflation is concerned with the way in which inflation eventually results in higher costs of production. Such costs then flow through to higher prices for goods, which in turn make exports less competitive, eventually leading to falling exports and a weakening of the domestic currency.

In the financial markets there is also a shorter term view of inflation. Provided inflation is not increasing too rapidly or erratically, modest signs of inflation may actually aid in lifting the domestic currency as traders anticipate the possibility of the local central bank attempting to slow inflation by raising interest rates, thus increasing the relative attractiveness of the domestic currency.

Inflation in the medium to long term has the effect of making a country's exports less competitive (by being higher cost) and conversely opens the local market to competition from imports. Inflation or inflation that is higher than that of international competitors exerts a downward pressure on the currency as it loses market share of trade.

Deflation (the opposite of inflation) has a more insidious effect on currencies. An uncontrolled fall in prices is usually a sign of economic depression (not good for a country) and is accompanied by low interest rates because of the lack of economic activity. The fear of the effects of deflation among global investors in the aftermath of the 2008 global financial crisis has led to a demand away from the popular major currencies to a more stable store of value, such as gold and commodities.

Asset prices

In this context, assets include items such as bonds, equities and even real estate (commercial, industrial and residential). When assets such as these are enjoying a buoyant market in a particular country, they are likely to draw the attention of international investment managers seeking to maximise their returns. The relatively high returns will attract buying of the domestic currency as foreign funds flow into these strongly performing assets.

Commodity prices and terms of trade

Traditionally currency traders around the world refer to Australia, New Zealand, Canada and South Africa as being members of the 'commodity bloc', the implication being that the currencies of these large commodity-exporting nations are significantly influenced by broad trends in commodity prices. In recent times this list has been expanded to include Chile (especially in relation to the price of copper), Norway (oil), Brazil (agriculture) and Russia (oil).

If trading one of these countries' currencies, it is worth staying in touch with commodity price movements and news of shortages or excesses in supply. For example, those watching the Australian dollar will want to be aware of issues affecting Chinese demand for steel (China is the world's largest producer of steel) because this will be reflected in the prices of coal and iron ore.

Copper is of particular interest, because it is often seen as a leading indicator of the broader commodities market due to its wide range of industrial and building applications. Chile is the world's largest copper exporter and demand for copper is a key driver of its relative currency value.

Of course other currencies have other specific commodity drivers; for instance, the price of export dairy and lamb meat prices can affect the relative value of the New Zealand dollar.

In recent years there has been a significant re-rating of the value of commodities relative to other investor assets, ostensibly on the back of a booming, mineral hungry and industrialising China, as well as a degree of safe-haven investment away from problematic major currencies like the USD and the euro in favour of emerging markets and commodity producing countries. For example, there has been a rise of 30–100 per cent in the currencies of countries like Brazil, Australia and Chile in less than 10 years.

This improvement in commodity prices in turn pushes up the relative terms of trade of a country, improving its balance of payments situation on a structural basis and pushing their currency higher, all things being equal. For example, the Australian dollar traded near the 47 US cents level in 2001, but 10 years later is exceeding 1.10 to the USD, largely on the back of the twin positives of a generally weaker USD (the counter-currency against all currencies) and once-in-a-century boom in commodity prices.

One of the best sources of information on the level of commodity prices in general is the CRB Index, published by the Commodity Research Bureau, which can be found at <www.crbtrader.com>. The index to look for is the CRB Spot Index, which often has a fairly high correlation to the Australian dollar. This broad correlation can be seen in the chart in figure 7.1, which displays both AUD/USD and the CRB Index over a period of slightly more than 24 years.

Figure 7.1: CRB versus AUD/USD

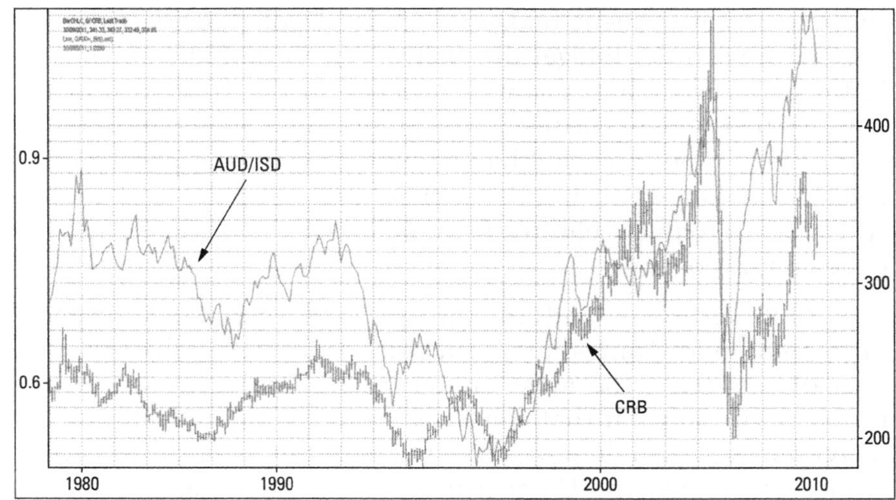

Note: left-hand scale = AUD/USD, right-hand scale = CRB Index.

Source: © Reuters.

Government budget and fiscal policy

The government budget and fiscal policy refers to the mix of taxes and government spending undertaken by the controlling regime of the day. Some distinctions that FX traders need to comprehend are:

- *Tighter* fiscal policy refers to a situation in which the government favours higher taxes and less government spending. The net result of tighter policy is less money is flowing through the economy as people have less in their pockets after tax and less money is being spent by the government. Eventually this results in a slowdown in economic activity, resulting in a similar outcome to higher interest rates, although without the need to actually raise interest rates.
- *Easier* fiscal policy refers to a situation in which the government favours lower taxes, leaving people with greater disposable income, and there is more government spending. The net result of easier policy is that more money is flowing through the economy, stimulating economic growth.

Until recently, traders did not take into too much consideration the role of government budgets and fiscal policy, aside from the days leading to the budget day delivery or in periodic updates by National Treasury bureaucrats. However, in the aftermath of the 2008 financial crisis, the need for a number of advanced economies to fix their balance sheets has become urgent. The problem is a collision of long-term trends in their demographics and welfare spending or, to put it bluntly, fiscal policy that is too loose and has gone on for too long.

The 2008 recession and the prospect of their slow recovery prompted more immediate concerns about the solvency of a host of countries, the most famous being Greece. However, the problems are so great that concerns about the US budget position increased in the middle of 2011 to the point that the erstwhile riskless borrower, the US government, felt the need to raise its self-imposed borrowing limit beyond the US$14 trillion mark and above 100 per cent of gross domestic product, a source of great medium-term uncertainty and anxiety to investors around the world, not just because of the unlikely risk of the US defaulting on its debts, but because of a more likely credit rating downgrade, which we will discuss next.

Credit ratings

Just as companies have credit ratings, so too do countries. The major credit ratings agencies, such as Standard & Poor's Ratings, Moody's Investor Services and Fitch Ratings, all rank countries via a generally similar ratings system that assesses a country's ability to service its domestic (and foreign) debt obligations when they fall due, both in the short term and the long term.

The eventual rating is an assessment of how safe it is to lend to a country. The rating is awarded on the basis of a combination of key financial and qualitative criteria, such as:

- political risk (of a country not caring to honour its debts)
- economic structure
- growth prospects (can a country service its future interest bill against future income growth?)

- fiscal policy and whether a government needs to borrow in the case of a deficit
- debt burden, usually expressed as a ratio of net liabilities against a country's gross domestic product (or in other words, national income)
- balance of payments/trade balance; effectively the difference between imports (foreign currency outflows) and exports (inflows)
- external debts
- inflation outlook.

A downgrade in the credit rating of a country implies that it has become relatively riskier to invest in that country and/or hold its currency and/or its debts. Investors and certainly institutional investors would then reassess the value of remaining invested in that country, and there would be significant risk of funds being withdrawn to be invested elsewhere.

Australia's Foreign Currency Credit Rating was lifted to the top level, AAA, in the early 2000s, largely on the back of a significant reduction in government debt. A high credit rating implies lower risk of default, which in turn results in a lower cost of borrowing for both the government and for companies based in that country. In comparison, Greece was rated CCC in 2011 by Standard & Poor's, meaning it was assessed as being currently vulnerable and dependent on favourable business, financial and economic conditions to meet financial commitments.

It is important to note that ratings agencies are not perfect judges of countries and have come in for their share of criticism for being either too late to correctly assess a (usually poor credit) country's decline, as in the case of Asian economies during the 1997–98 financial crisis, or too hard with a country's rating, a sentiment that is, not surprisingly, usually voiced by the country receiving the rating.

Regardless of one's view of the worth or effectiveness of credit rating agencies, market participants do take a lot of notice of them and try to anticipate any changes in a country's credit ranking because it directly affects the pricing of currencies and local assets.

Currency controls

Currency markets as a rule are not and hardly ever are free and unregulated. Governments and central banks around the world are far too cautious and risk aware to allow the value of their currency to be left to the often fickle devices of free-market valuation. (Remember that central banks and local governments are more focused on controlling local inflation and interest rate levels than keeping foreign exchange dealers happy!) For that reason quite often prescriptive and quantitative controls are imposed on national currency transactions and holdings, be it by local citizens or foreigners.

Hardly any country has a free-floating currency. In the Asian region for instance, the Hong Kong dollar continues to operate under a linked exchange rate system in which the Hong Kong Monetary Authority (HKMA) guarantees that it will exchange HKD for USD, and vice versa, at a rate of 7.80 HKD for each USD. In practice, the HKMA allows the value of USD/HKD to drift within a band of 7.75 to 7.85. Market forces therefore keep prices close to the 7.80 target, as any rise above will see local banks handing in their HKD in exchange for USD, leading to a reduced supply of HKD and a fall in the USD/HKD rate (as the HKD firms). By contrast, a slip below 7.80 will encourage local banks to exchange USD for HKD, resulting in a greater supply of HKD and a rise in the USD/HKD rate back to 7.80, as the HKD becomes comparatively weaker and each USD will buy more HKD.

There can be no discussion of currency markets and controls in Asia without mentioning China's currency, the yuan (CNY). In July 2005, the fixed peg against the USD (in place since 1994), was broken and revalued by the Chinese authorities, with USD/CNY falling from 8.28 to 8.11 as the CNY was officially strengthened. The exchange rate is now tied to a basket of currencies made up of the currencies of China's major trading partners. While the pattern of a strengthening yuan was temporarily halted in 2008–10 in the aftermath of the global financial crisis of 2008, the float remains managed, with daily movements widened marginally to no more than +/– 0.5 per cent of the previous day's closing price.

Most analysts believe these continuing changes to the degree of currency controls of the CNY are part of the evolution towards allowing market forces to play a greater role in setting the value of CNY in the years ahead, and part of an eventual move towards making the CNY a fully convertible currency, able to be traded freely in the inter-bank market.

Other Asian central banks have analogous currency policies and controls of their currency. For instance, Singapore has a like basket basis for its currency and is quite strict, with its rules around the forward FX market attempting to discourage 'hot' investment flows destabilising its local money market. However, Asian central banks generally do tend not to regulate — or cannot effectively do so — third currency dealings, where the two currencies traded are both non-local.

Malaysia also deserves a mention in this section. In response to the Asian currency crisis of 1997, the then prime minister, Mahathir bin Mohamad, introduced currency controls to restrict the flow of money out of the country and oversaw the instigation of a currency peg, with the Malaysian ringgit (MYR) fixed against the USD at a rate of USD/MYR 3.8. These measures helped Malaysia stage a strong recovery from the crisis of 1997 (much to the chagrin of the International Monetary Fund), but the peg was dropped on 21 July 2005, the same day that China dropped its peg to the USD. As with China, the Malaysians have elected to follow a managed float system based on a basket of currencies, with initial moves seeing the USD/MYR rate slip as the MYR strengthened along with CNY. This fact alone is a reminder to market participants to be aware that central banks do talk to each other and often coordinate currency policy with each other to ensure that their own policy actions are not at cross-purposes and to make doubly certain it will be effective for their purpose.

Politics and wars

Political considerations at local, regional and geopolitical levels can and do have a significant impact on currency markets. As with many other markets, participants in the currency markets do not like uncertainty and risk, especially political uncertainty because of its capacity to cause unintended consequences not initially priced in by traders and investors. Countries facing general elections or political turmoil will often find that this is accompanied by uncertainty about future government directions and policies on both domestic and international issues, leading to risk aversion and a tendency of markets to avoid currencies in the lead up to these 'risk events'. When faced with uncertainty of this type, investors will often delay making major decisions or committing to major projects until the outcome is known and the future is clearer.

In modern, open democracies such as Australia and the US, a change in government from the incumbent party to the major opposition party is likely to result only in relatively small changes to the broad policies of the prior government. However, in other countries, a change in government can bring about tremendous political, social and financial change that will significantly affect the direction of that country. Previously open markets may suddenly become closed or heavily taxed to foreigners, or there may be alterations to existing or planned trade agreements, which would have trade balance and flows implications.

When trading the major currencies, election results are likely to have only a relatively small impact over the broader time frame. However, it is always worth asking yourself, 'What would it mean to the currency markets if the opposition were to win the election?' Having a preconceived notion of the potential fallout will have you well placed to take action ahead of the crowd once the result is declared.

Finally we should never lose sight of the fact that markets do not exist in isolation, but are nested in the societies around them. While political turmoil is one consideration, the possibility of armed conflict is sadly an all-too-frequent risk faced by investors. Recurring regional conflicts, for instance in the Persian Gulf since the 1980s that perennially affect the price of oil and the USD (as a safe-haven currency) with knock-on effects on Gulf currencies, would be familiar to many. While major wars in our region have been rare since the end of the Vietnam War in 1975, border squabbles persist between countries. There is a risk of the Korean Peninsula conflict escalating in the future, with lethal exchanges of artillery fire still being seen in 2010, almost 60 years after the Korean War ended.

If countries go to war a host of disruptive events and behaviours kicks into play. Trade flows and economic activity are disrupted, banned or attacked. Inflation rises as government spending and borrowing goes into overdrive to fund wars and private investment flees currencies where human, physical and financial capital is being destroyed. There is a bitter dictum in wartime investing — sell battlefield currencies and buy arsenal currencies; or, in other words, invest in those making the guns and don't lend money to those using them.

Investors must be prepared for such events, even if they are unlikely, and to act very quickly when they do occur.

Industrial relations, social unrest and nature

Elections and wars have certain predictable cycles — they are either won or lost, or drag on as a form of institutional regional uncertainty.

Industrial disputes that involve widespread and extended strikes or disruption to the production and transport of goods can, if they escalate far enough, have a significant impact on the broader economy, and in extreme cases may result in political instability or even a change in government. Examples from the not-too-distant past include the social unrest that pervaded South-East Asia (in varying degrees) at the height of the Asian financial crisis of 1998 as many firms failed and people lost their jobs and took to the streets in protest at their own government's and the IMF's measures to reform their respective economies. Some governments fell as a direct consequence (most notably the regime of Suharto in Indonesia). Images of protesters burning banks and government buildings in Jakarta and other Asian capitals does not encourage investors, regardless of where they are, and it is no accident that, as the currencies of Asia collapsed, both local and foreign investors exited these markets.

The Australian and New Zealand dollars also fell in sympathy with their Asian neighbour currencies at this time, even though they did not have anywhere near the degree of social dislocation. This emphasises that we are all related or, in other words, that no man or market is an island.

In 1998 in Australia the major dispute between the Maritime Union of Australia (MUA) and Patrick Corporation occurred. This involved a series of rolling strikes around the ports of Australia and bans on performing overtime work. At one point there was a threat by the Australian Workers' Union (AWU) to shut down oil refineries in support of their MUA colleagues. The dispute was eventually resolved, and the financial impact was restricted to specific companies and individuals rather than the broader Australian economy and currency; however, if it had been allowed to continue, there would potentially have been a significant negative impact on the Australian dollar.

Where there is significant instability or uncertainty, investment funds are likely to seek out other opportunities in countries that provide more stability and 'safer' investment opportunities.

As a final point, do not forget the power of nature. While there is much global anxiety about the warming of the planet and its effect on human civilisation, more immediate natural catastrophes have had the power to overwhelm the deeds and works of humans, such as earthquakes, tsunamis, nuclear accidents, floods and other catastrophes. In 2011 Christchurch in New Zealand was rocked by a lethal earthquake with consequent effects on its (and Australia's) currency. In the northern hemisphere, Japan was hit by an earthquake and tsunami, resulting in damage to the Fukushima nuclear reactor and leakage that has disrupted global supply chains and affected the immediate prospects for a sustained Japanese recovery, if not the region and world.

We must be prepared to respond as quickly as possible to whatever nature throws at us and our markets.

Market sentiment

In general, markets are affected by the psychology of large crowds, often resulting in market sentiment oscillating between extremes that are unsupported by the underlying fundamentals. The currency markets are no different. A notable case involved the state of the US markets since the late 1990s, when there was strong and consistent demand from around the world for investment in the US markets. In fact, in 1999 some 72 per cent of all global fresh investment capital went to the US. The 'new economy' was booming. Bricks and mortar were dead. In these glory days of riches for everyone, people managed to turn a blind eye to the massive trade deficits of the US.

Then it all fell apart; the dotcom bubble burst, the US economy slowed, there was a broader equity market downturn, corporate scandals were unmasked by the receding tide, there were the terrorist attacks of September 11, and, in the background, regions that had been struggling now looked good again — regions such as South-East Asia, China and Eastern Europe. Investor sentiment and optimism has shifted significantly to Asia and emerging markets, and the USD began a notable decline, as can be seen on the chart of the USD index in figure 7.2.

Figure 7.2: the USD index

Source: © Reuters.

It is fascinating to speculate about the fate of the USD, given it has just experienced more than ten years of decline and is still floundering.

Big trades

Foreign exchange trades usually involve significantly more money than the average equity trade. In the inter-bank market, trades are commonly executed for $5 million or more. Any amount less would be considered small. Exactly what constitutes a 'big trade' in the foreign exchange market depends on the amount of activity in the market at the time a particular trade takes place.

Volumes in the foreign exchange market tend to be heaviest during the European session that overlaps with the US morning session in particular, with a little overlap at the end of the Asian session. In the early morning Asian session, a deal of $100 million may have a notable short-term impact on market prices, but if the same deal were executed during the European session it may pass by virtually unnoticed by most participants.

One area of business closely watched for big currency flows is cross-border merger and acquisition activity. If a large company in one country buys another large company in a different country, a significant currency transaction is likely to be involved, sometimes involving hundreds of millions, or even billions, of dollars. However, often firms have already bought the currency or arranged their borrowing facilities, so the announcement of a corporate action may not necessarily coincide with the currency transaction. It may have been done beforehand or been deferred.

Data releases, speeches and minutes

The release of economic and statistical data can also have a significant impact on the value of a country's currency.

In Australia, the most significant data releases come from the Reserve Bank of Australia <www.rba.gov.au> and the Australian Bureau of Statistics <www.abs.gov.au>. In New Zealand the comparable organisations are the Reserve Bank of New Zealand <www.rbnz.govt.nz> and Statistics New Zealand <www.stats.govt.nz>.

For links to these and other central banks from around the world, refer to the chart at the end of chapter 5 (p. 66).

It is not just data releases that affect currency rates. Speeches by key central bankers (and, to a lesser extent, politicians) can have immediate impacts on exchanges, particularly if the speech or minutes of a key policy meeting are in relation to interest rates. It is good practice when planning your trades to be aware of and plan for the schedule of speeches and announcements by central bank bosses, particularly those that relate to your currencies, as well as the top five major traded currencies. Sometimes comments by these figures periodically disrupt FX price relationships. Don't forget some of these announcements or speeches may in fact be 'surprise' events so be on your guard.

One of the most important things to understand in relation to the release of economic and statistical data and speeches is that the market does not react simply to the actual figure released—often known as the 'headline figure'. Instead, the market will make an instantaneous comparison between the actual result and the result that the market had been anticipating, as reflected in the market consensus forecasts. The reaction then seen in trading is a response to the difference between the actual result and the anticipated result.

Prior to the release of important economic figures, statistics or a speech, participants in the market will take action on the anticipated outcome, buying if they expect bullish results or selling if they expect bearish results. Although such pre-release activity does not necessarily result in the anticipated outcome being fully priced into the market, there is often a move that reflects the broad market consensus of expectations.

Where the data release is broadly in line with the figures that had been expected, the actual release of the data will often result in little significant impact in the market. However, if the actual data release does not closely match the expectations of the market, there can be significant volatility and opportunities as the market seeks to realign itself with the facts as indicated by the data release.

This can lead to situations that at first appear 'wrong' to the uneducated observer. Consider a data release that appears on the surface to be a positive piece of news for a particular currency; say, firm retail sales data. On the back of the data release, on its own it would be fair to say we would expect to see the currency strengthen on the release of this data.

However, if analysts and the broader market consensus had indicated that results would be three times stronger than they were, the actual data release would come as a disappointment to the market. Traders who had already positioned themselves on the basis of a firmer result would look to wind back their positions and you may well see a situation where the market falls on the release of apparently bullish headline data.

Many of the major data releases and speeches for most countries are pre-scheduled, and with the evolution of the internet all market participants have equal and instantaneous access to this data, whether they be sitting in the dealing room of a global investment bank in Sydney, New York or London, or sitting in an internet cafe in Alice Springs. Most trading platforms will provide you with a list of pre-scheduled data releases for the week ahead, and many will also include a guide to the current market consensus expectations for the major releases. If your platform does not have such a guide, you will find one fairly easily by performing an internet search. Be aware that some calendars have a clear bias towards focusing on data releases for the country in which the website is based. This is true for many, though not all, US-based sites.

Exactly what a certain data release will mean for the markets on any given day will depend largely upon the broader context of the markets at that time. It will also depend on which of the various data releases is viewed by the market as being the most important. This may sound obvious, but the focus of the market shifts over time. In the past, there was a major focus on money supply data, but these days clearly much greater emphasis is placed on employment data, especially employment data for the US, which is released on the first Friday of the month, with the key figure being that for non-farm payrolls. But of course that is not the only release we should be alert to.

In the following section, we give a broad indication of the type of statistics that influence FX rates and that are likely to be seen on the release of some of the more significant figures. Remember, though, that stating specifically that move 'y' is due entirely to event 'x' is virtually impossible. Pinpointing specific causes for moves in the market is a little like trying to unscramble an egg—but, assuming all other elements remain steady, we can make some generalisations.

The consumer price index (CPI)

The CPI is a statistic that provides a measure of inflation by tracking changes in the prices of a specific basket of goods and services. Modest gains in the CPI may help to support the local currency if there is potential for higher interest rates to be used to dampen the economy. However, if CPI (and therefore inflation) is rising notably faster than had been anticipated, local assets will become less attractive due to the premium required by investors for holding assets that are being eroded by inflation.

Don't forget that an almost universal mandate of central banks is to regulate inflation via the use of monetary and interest rate policy. Reported and expected CPI is a key driver of a central bank's interest rate settings. Traders accordingly keep an eye on a country's inflation rate for clues about where interest rates (and the currency) will go in the short and long term.

Retail sales

Interpretation of retail sales data is based on the premise that when consumers feel financially secure and confident about their future they will be more inclined to spend freely, and even to take on additional financial commitments and debt. By contrast, when consumers start to feel less financially secure or less optimistic about their financial future, they will tend to rein in their spending activities and will be less inclined to take on new debt.

It follows therefore that strong retail sales imply that the economy is performing well and expanding. An economy that is performing well is likely to be attracting foreign investment, which will help to support the currency. Additionally, if the economy continues to grow firmly there may be a situation in the future in which the government seeks to dampen the economy by raising interest rates. This will also help to support the local currency.

The next five data releases we examine were originally specific to the United States, but have been increasingly adopted around the world as important and useful data for market participants and regulators to get a better take on their economies. The USD is involved in some 85 per cent of all FX transactions, so it is useful for us to be aware of the issues driving it.

The producer price index (PPI)

Just as the CPI measures the cost of a specific basket of goods and services used by consumers, the PPI in the US is an index that tracks changes in the cost of a specific basket of goods and services used by producers. In Australia and China this is further broken down into raw, intermediate and final producer prices for an even finer measure of 'upstream' price pressures in the economy. Traditionally a rapid rise in the PPI means that the costs of production have risen, and this can be expected to flow through to the prices consumers have to pay for their goods and services, thus feeding inflation.

Industrial production (IP)

IP is a measure of the physical output of the manufacturing, mining and utility industries in the United States and is released monthly. One of the uses of this data is to gauge capacity utilisation, although its accuracy is questionable. In broad terms, moderate growth in IP is regarded as a positive for the USD, although sharp gains can point to potential bottlenecks in the economy and inflationary pressures.

Durable goods orders

Durable goods are those items that have an intended lifespan of three years or more. The dollar values of orders, shipments and unfilled orders are viewed as a leading indicator of manufacturing activity, with extra emphasis given to results that are reflected across a wide range of sectors rather than being confined to just one or two sectors. If the data shows a sharp enough rise to suggest that demand may be outstripping supply, there may be a flow-through threat to the pace of longer term economic growth, with this in turn weighing on the value of the USD.

The purchasing managers index (PMI)

The PMI is extracted from the monthly report of the National Association of Purchasing Managers (NAPM), and is calculated on a weighted average of data for new orders, production, employment, deliveries and inventories. A figure above 50 implies an expanding economy, which suggests the USD is attractive to foreign investors and may also lead into higher interest rates, thus supporting the USD. A comparable China PMI is tabulated by Hong Kong Shanghai Bank (HSBC) and reports measures of Chinese economic activity. It is also closely watched as a forward indicator of economic activity in the 'Middle Kingdom' (China).

Employment

Employment data has a similar impact in each country that reports this statistic, but it is the US employment data, or non-farm payrolls data, that attracts the most attention in the foreign exchange market. Again, because the USD is involved in such a large percentage of all FX trading activities, US data releases have the potential to have a significant impact across all currencies.

US non-farm payrolls data is one of several data series derived from the 'establishment survey', which is one of two surveys conducted each month by the Bureau of Labor Statistics <www.bls.gov>. Conveniently for the financial markets, this data is released at 8.30 am New York time on the first Friday of each month (with the occasional variation). This timing overlaps with the European trading session, so any shocks in the result will have a very wide impact.

In general, firm employment data reflects a buoyant and growing economy, which is attractive to investors, thus supporting the currency. Also, if there is a concern that the economy is growing too quickly, traders may see the potential for the government to raise interest rates in an attempt to slow the pace of growth a little, making the domestic currency relatively more attractive.

Other elements of the employment data — such as 'average hours worked' — are also useful to those seeking deeper insights into an economy. If people are working longer hours, it may indicate that industrial production will be strong, along with personal earnings and wages. Average hours worked needs to be viewed in the context of the broader business cycle, as high numbers early in the cycle may point to confidence in the economy and increases in employment in the months ahead, while high numbers later in the cycle may suggest that the market is being stretched to capacity and employers are having trouble finding suitable employees.

It is important to remember that the markets react not simply to the actual headline figure, but to the difference between this actual result and the markets' expectations for the data release. Let's consider an example. Figure 7.3 (overleaf) shows market activity for the USD/JPY at the time of the release of non-farm payrolls data. Each bar in this chart represents one minute of trading.

Figure 7.3: USD/JPY

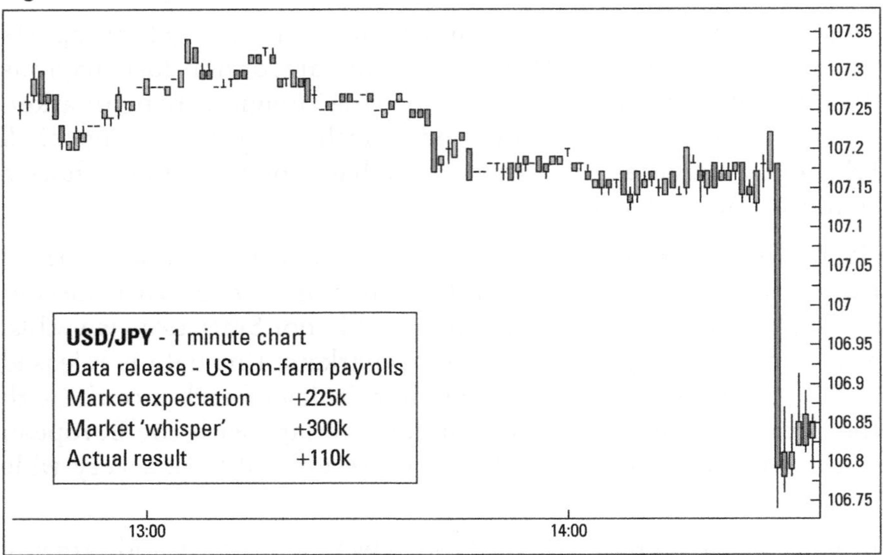

Source: © Reuters.

Remember, we suggested above that a firm rise in employment should be supportive of the currency, as it suggests a growing economy, which provides an attractive investment environment and may eventually see an increase in official interest rates in an attempt to cool the market. However, despite the fact that the data indicated growth in the number of people employed, with 110 000 jobs added during the reporting period (month), the knee-jerk reaction of USD/JPY was to fall on the release of the data, as the USD weakened in relation to the JPY.

The market fell despite reasonably firm growth in employment, because the market consensus expectation prior to the release of the data had been for an increase in employment in the region of 225 000 jobs. On top of this, in the final few minutes before the release of the data, a rumour went around the markets suggesting that those with inside knowledge were looking for a figure closer to 300 000 new jobs. This so-called market whisper may well have been responsible for the last blip higher seen in the final minute before the collapse that accompanied the release of the result.

Seen through the eyes of market participants, a result of 110 000 was significantly weaker than the 225 000 that traders had been looking for, and even weaker than the 300 000 that some had expected. When the reality and the expectations of the market are so far out of line, there is a sharp move as traders seek to unwind previously entered positions that had been established on the back of the expected results (that is, expectations that had been 'priced in' to the market).

It should also be pointed out that major data releases, especially the monthly non-farm payrolls data, are often periods when liquidity in the inter-bank market evaporates considerably. Many professional inter-bank traders prefer not to hold positions over the release of such volatile data, and will refrain from placing bids and offers in the market until the data is released or a clear direction is established. In these times of relatively low liquidity, moves in the market are often exaggerated significantly, with relatively small trades causing large moves in price until the regular flow of trade is re-established. Because of the ability of relatively small trades to notably move the market in these circumstances, the knee-jerk reactions you see on the release of major data such as non-farm payrolls may stem from the activities of just a handful of market participants. These participants may have specific reasons for taking a particular stand in the market that may initially seem at odds with the data. These factors all add up to make major data releases very tricky to trade.

A whole slew of economic data is released in most countries on an almost daily basis. Most of it does not have a direct or material bearing on your FX trade, so be careful of information overload. Here and above all we have concentrated on those statistics and driving factors that you need to know for your trading plan.

Fundamentally, its only a beginning

This chapter has given you a broad view of a number of the factors that influence foreign exchange prices. We will investigate a few of these areas in greater detail in chapter 9, but as 'fundamentals' can be a rather dry topic, let's change tack for a little while and discuss the other major school of market analysis, technical analysis.

Chapter 8

Technical analysis for traders

Many dozens of books cater specifically to the needs of those people wishing to learn more about the art of technical analysis. Attempting to give a comprehensive explanation of this vast topic in just a few pages would be unrealistic, but we will cover some of the analytical methods, broad concepts and indicators, and some of the issues that relate specifically to foreign exchange.

If you want to learn more about technical analysis, we suggest the following books:

- Robert D Edwards and John Magee, *Technical Analysis of Stock Trends*
- John J Murphy, *Technical Analysis of the Financial Markets*
- Martin J Pring, *Technical Analysis Explained*
- J Welles Wilder, Jr, *New Concepts in Technical Trading Systems*.

What is technical analysis?

The three authors of this book were all members of the Board of Directors of the International Federation of Technical Analysts (IFTA) <www.ifta.org>. This global umbrella organisation ties together many of the individual country-based technical analyst societies and associations of the world. The Market Technicians Association (MTA) <www.mta.org> is another global technical analysis organisation. It provides excellent resources for its members including chapter meetings, regional seminars, regular educational online live and archived webinars, and an extensive online knowledge base. Within the ranks of both organisations are the best, brightest and most senior members of the field of technical analysis. The following is an extract from the IFTA Constitution as at October 2010:

Principles and Policies

...The Federation asserts that the technical analysis of stocks, commodities, bonds, currencies, etc. price movement and the supply-demand relationships underlying them can make a vital contribution to the process of decision making involved in efforts to preserve and enhance the investor's capital.

The Federation makes this assertion on a number of grounds, including the following considerations:

Technical analysis deals with the generally undisputed fact that the market price of a stock, commodity, currency, etc. does not necessarily, nor indeed usually, at any given time coincide with its intrinsic value, which itself is often a matter of controversy. In dealing with the frequently very elastic differential between market price and underlying value, technical analysis and fundamental analysis, insofar as they relate to specific common stocks, commodities, currencies, etc. and to all financial markets the world over, can properly be regarded as complementary, and, in fact, interdependent.

In a broader perspective, technical analysis concerns itself also with supply-demand relationships affecting the equity, commodities, currency, etc. markets as a whole and with potential future shifts in these relationships that may be instrumental in shaping future price movements. In pursuit of this concern, it extends to examination of flow of funds. Moreover, the tendency of price trends to persist and of investors' behavioral patterns to recur enables the technical analyst to recognize and anticipate potentially favorable or unfavorable investment environments.

Indeed, the recognition of extremes in investor psychology is one of the technical analysts' unique contributions to the field of investment techniques.

> The Federation asserts, in sum, that the technical analysis of stocks, commodities, currencies, etc. price movements, and the supply-demand relationships underlying them, is a valid, indeed an indispensable, element in the formulation of a 'reasonable basis' for investment decisions.
>
> Source: © IFTA.

Broadly speaking, technical analysis involves the analysis of market-generated data (price, volume and open interest). Using this data, the supply of and demand for a security (or currency) is analysed to identify the current mood of market participants (bullish or bearish) and to determine the probability of that mood either continuing or changing. Because of the loose definition of technical analysis, it is not uncommon to find all sorts of unrelated fields of analysis thrown in under this heading — many of which clearly do not belong. Thus, according to our definition, if a study involves anything other than price, volume, open interest (where available) or time, then it is not technical analysis.

There is also an almost indefinable element of 'art' involved in technical analysis. It is not, as some would assume, a simple science with black and white rules that suit all occasions. Knowing when to use each of the various technical tools available to traders is a part of the skill that comes with experience. Recognising the imperfections and limitations in each of these tools and using your ability to interpret them is an important step towards the successful use of technical analysis. Hopefully this knowledge will also help to protect you from accepting the signals of 'black box' systems without knowing how or why the signals are generated. ('Black box' is the term given to computerised trading signal generators that produce buy and sell recommendations without the user necessarily having any understanding of how or why these signals have been generated.)

Technological advances and the falling cost of personal computers in recent years mean that virtually everybody is now able to display charts of dozens of markets from around the world on their PC with just a few clicks of the mouse, regardless of where they happen to be. It would be a very rare trader indeed (especially in the inter-bank market) who did not at least glance at the chart of a security he or she intended to buy or sell prior to executing the transaction.

On the surface, this massive explosion in access to the tools of technical analysis seems like a positive event for the field of technical analysis. However, because it has become so easy for people to call up charts and apply numerous indicators to them, many traders are not making the effort to learn how to correctly use the tools of technical analysis. Unfortunately, these uneducated traders often wind up losing money and many of them nominate 'technical analysis' as their scapegoat when they search about for a reason for their losses. We've all heard the saying, 'A good tradesperson doesn't blame the tools'. The same holds true for technical analysis. Putting in the time and effort to learn how to use the tools of technical analysis will pay off in the long run.

One important thing to realise is that you do not need to master all of the technical indicators (also known as 'technical tools', or simply 'tools') that are supplied with your charting package. You are better off selecting a small number of them (around four to six) and learning them inside out. Learn how they are calculated. Understand what the resulting plot is telling you about the bullishness or bearishness of the market. Learn in which market conditions the indicator works best and in which conditions it is not so good. Once you have a thorough understanding of an indicator, you should start to be able to anticipate what that indicator will look like even before you apply it to a particular chart. The simplicity of the techniques that are used by many of the analysts and traders in major international financial institutions would probably come as quite a surprise to many private traders. Sure, there are some that use neural networks and organic algorithms, but far more of them use the tried and trusted basic tools that are found on nearly all commercially available technical analysis computer software.

When selecting your indicators, be aware of what is known as the 'collinearity trap'. This occurs when you select two indicators that basically give you the same information. An example is the simultaneous use of the directional movement index (DMI) and moving averages, both of which are basically giving you an indication of the trend, even though they use quite different methods of calculation. Although you may have similar indicators within your group, be aware of the risks of using the similar ones at the same time. One way to overcome this is to group indicators into different types, such as trend indicators, momentum indicators and hybrid indicators. Table 8.1 provides an example of six indicators you might select to learn thoroughly.

Table 8.1: six indicators you may wish to learn thoroughly

Trend indicators	Momentum indicators	Hybrid indicators
Moving averages	Relative strength index (RSI)	MACD
Parabolic SAR	Slow stochastics	
Directional movement index (DMI)		

When using technical analysis for instruments with accompanying volume data, it is a good idea to use an indicator that includes volume in its calculations, such as the money flow indicator (MFI). However, for foreign exchange we are restricted to indicators that use price data only.

Technical analysis is widely used in the foreign exchange markets, both for determining the overall trend and for shorter term timing of trades, with fundamental analysis used to paint a broader background view. While it is certainly possible to base all of your trading decisions purely on technical analysis of the relevant price charts, ignoring potential fundamental analysis inputs is effectively denying yourself the opportunity to benefit from a very useful source of market intelligence. It is advisable, therefore, to at least have a basic grasp of the major fundamental issues that may influence the specific currencies that you are intending to trade. Basing your decisions on a broader set of inputs (including the fundamentals) is likely to lead to more profitable outcomes and fewer unexplained shocks to your trading account. At the very least, being aware of fundamental issues should help to prevent you taking a greater risk than necessary, such as taking a large position immediately prior to the release of important economic data or remaining oblivious to a significant policy change announced by a foreign government that has a direct bearing on your foreign currency trades.

In support of technicals, it must be said that while you could base all of your trading decisions on signals generated by technical analysis, it would be significantly more difficult to trade successfully using only fundamental data, especially for a short-term trader.

The following methods, indicators and concepts may help you in your efforts to apply the methods and techniques of technical analysis to the foreign exchange markets. However, they are not in any way to be regarded as a substitute for making a more detailed study of the art of technical analysis. Many books and courses are available on the topic of technical analysis and these will help you to build a solid knowledge base. Joining a technical analysis association such as the Market Technicians Association (MTA) <www.mta.org>, which has many chapters throughout the world, or joining a member association of the International Federation of Technical Analysts (IFTA) <www.ifta.org> will provide you with excellent networking opportunities with technical analysts at all levels of knowledge. In addition, if you can find an experienced mentor with suitable credentials, this will often help lift your technical analysis skills considerably.

Assumptions made in technical analysis

Technical analysis is based on several assumptions about the way markets work.

The market discounts everything

A major assumption of technical analysis is that everything that is known about a stock—past, present and potential future influences—is reflected in the price that market participants are prepared to pay for it. Changes in price reflect changes in opinions of these influences, which affects supply and/or demand for a security.

Prices move in trends

Another major assumption is that prices tend to move in trends. This is contrary to an academic theory that price action is random and that market information is disseminated immediately and efficiently and is acted upon in a rational manner. In the real world, market information is taken up at different times by various market participants, leading to perhaps increased or decreased demand for, or increased or decreased supply of, a security over a period of time as participants form an opinion based on that information. This inefficient uptake of information leads to trending action. Market information is also not always acted upon in a rational manner by participants. Irrational emotional factors, such as fear, greed and 'group mentality' may have a profound effect on securities prices from time to time, perpetuating strong trending action in a particular direction.

History tends to repeat itself

Technical analysts also assume that past history will tend to be repeated in a general sense. As human beings we are driven by emotions such as fear, greed, ego and desire. Under certain circumstances market participants will repeatedly tend to react with these raw human emotions. At certain times market participants also tend to act as a group rather than as individuals. A skilled technical analyst can generally recognise warning signs of these emotions at play and use it as a tool to take appropriate action in the marketplace.

Short-term chart analysis

Short-term analysis is the study of the components that make up a single time unit on a chart; for example, a bar on a bar chart or a candlestick on a candlestick chart. The components are the open, the close, the high and the low. The distance between the high and the low determines another component, called the range. Analysis of these components enables technical analysts to understand the relative strength of the bulls or the bears at that point in time. This understanding may be very important for timing entry into and exit out of the market.

Short-term trend determination

Determination of the trend in the short term—that is, on a bar to bar basis—is crucial to determining the trend on a larger time scale basis.

Trends in the short term, bar to bar basis, are defined as follows:

> An up trend is a series of higher highs and higher lows.
>
> A down trend is a series of lower highs and lower lows.

Interpretation is not too complex. Simply, the bar prior to the bar which is being analysed is the 'reference bar' and the high and low of the current bar is only compared with the high and the low of that reference bar.

Figure 8.1 shows a first time frame up trend and down trend.

Figure 8.1: first time frame up trend and down trend

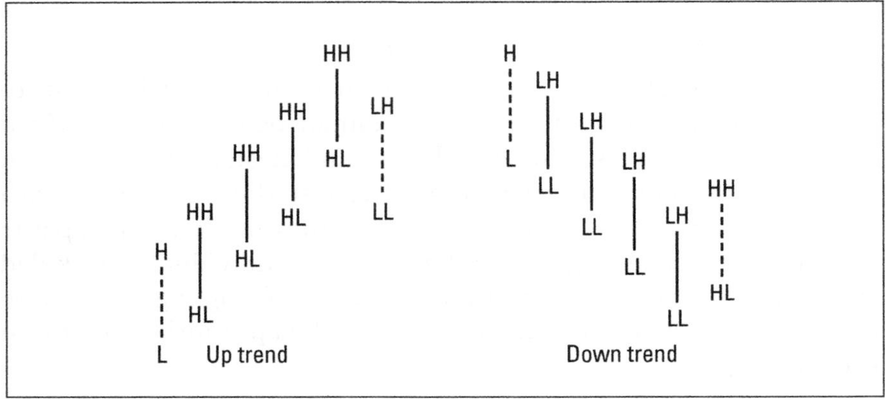

Source: © Kaplan Education Pty Ltd.

A trend changes when we have the opposite configuration of highs and lows in place and we can define a trend ending sequence:

> An up trend is ended by a bar that has a lower high and a lower low.
>
> A down trend is ended by a bar that has a higher high and higher low.

Note that the end of an up trend is also the beginning of a down trend and vice versa.

Determination of trend on a bar to bar basis enables a trader to identify when a swing in bars making a trending price action in a certain direction has finished and to enter a trade in the direction of the new trend.

There are some bars that can complicate our perfect trend-ending model. They are called 'inside bars' and 'outside bars'. Figure 8.2 shows inside and outside bars.

Figure 8.2: inside and outside bars

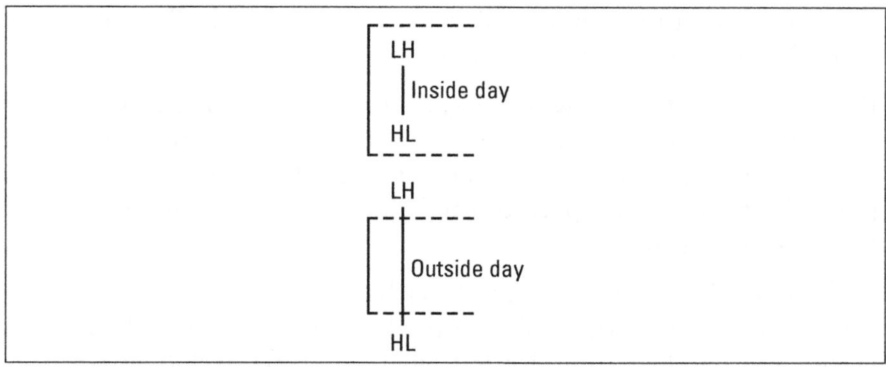

Source: © Kaplan Education Pty Ltd.

An inside bar is a bar with a lower high and a higher low when compared with the previous bar (the reference bar); that is, the range of the bar being analysed is completely within the range of the previous bar. An outside bar is a bar with a higher high and a lower low when compared with the previous bar (the reference bar); that is, the range of the bar being analysed is completely outside the range of the previous bar. These types of bar do not meet the criteria for trend determination and thus fail to end the trend that is in existence. So, for example, if a previous up trend was in existence for, say, the previous three days and the current bar has a higher high but lower low when compared with the previous bar (an outside bar), then at that point in time the trend remains up. The importance of these bars is that, even though they don't change the trend, they do raise doubt about continuation of the trend because the required configuration of highs and lows no longer exists.

There are other possibilities with the configuration of highs and lows, such as equal highs and/or equal lows. These bars are treated in a similar manner to inside and outside bars and have no effect on the determination of the prior trend.

Position of the close in the range

The position of the closing price within the range gives an indication of the relative strength of the bulls or bears in a period of time.

If the close is at the high we can say that the bulls were in control and were committed when the time period closed. It is the relative strength of the bulls that pushes price higher. If the market closes at the highest point for that trading period, then the bulls were in the ascendancy at that period of time.

If the close is at the low we can say that the bears were in control and committed when the time period closed. It is the relative strength of the bears that pushes price lower. If the market closes at the lowest point for that trading period, the bears were in the ascendancy at that period of time.

If the close is at the midpoint level between the high and low we can say that neither the bulls nor the bears were in control and both lacked and had lost commitment when the time period closed. It is the relative strength of the bulls that pushes price to the high and the relative strength of the bears that pushes price to the low during the trading period and in this situation we can say that the battle between the bulls and the bears was not resolved at the close.

Figure 8.3 shows how a technical analyst can understand the relative strength of the buyers and sellers by analysing the position of the close in the range. This figure is of a five-minute bar chart of the USD/JPY.

Figure 8.3: five-minute bar chart of the USD/JPY

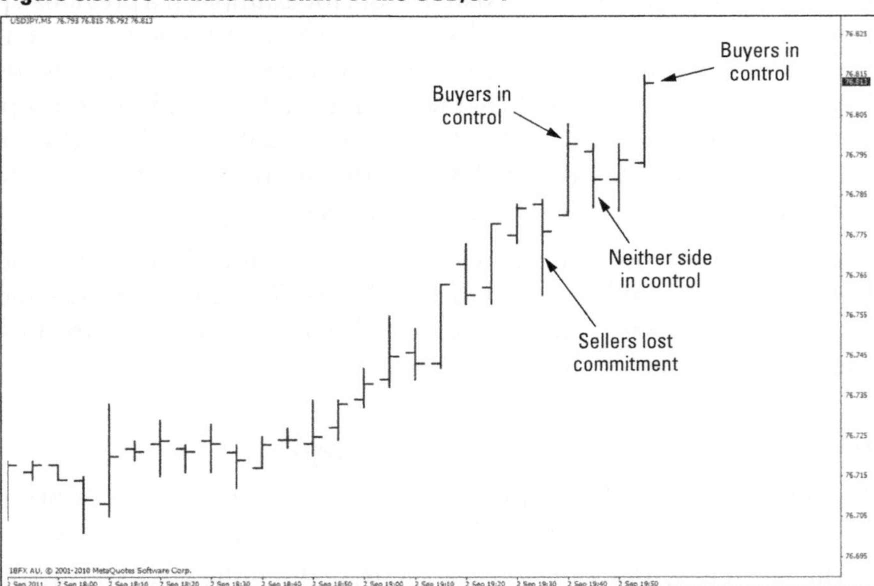

Source: MetaTrader 5, © 2001–2011 MetaQuotes Software Corp.

Long-term bar chart analysis

Earlier we examined how we determine the trend in the short-term time frame (on a bar to bar basis). In this section we will look at the bigger picture and apply a similar concept to a longer time frame.

Longer time frame trend analysis

It is very important for all traders to be aware of trends in multiple time frames. Trends in higher time frames tend to have a larger effect on the movement of price action within a certain direction. It is better for a trader to be in unison with these larger trends, which exert a greater force on the market, than to trade against them. By trading with the higher time frame trends, traders will receive a greater 'bang for their buck' because the lower time frame swings of trends in the direction of the higher time frame trend will generally be greater than the lower time frame swings of trends against the higher time frame trend. In the higher time frame, the lower time frame swings counter to the higher time frame trend will tend to be minor retracements and will tend to terminate lesser in terms of net price than lower time frame swings that move in unison with the higher time frame trend.

To determine the trend in the next higher time frame than a bar to bar basis, called the second time frame, we slightly alter our definition for a trend. In the second higher time frame, instead of examining the relationship of the highs and lows, we examine the relationship of the peaks and troughs in the swings in the first time frame trend (the bar to bar basis).

Say that we have the market in a first time frame up trend and the trend changes to the downside, we determine the highest high in that previous sequence of up trending bars as the peak. The peak is the highest level that the first time frame up trend achieved.

If we have the market in a first time frame down trend and the trend changes to the upside, we determine the lowest low in that previous sequence of down-trending bars as the trough. The trough is the lowest level that the first time frame down trend achieved.

Following on from that we can define trends in higher time frames:

> A second time frame up trend may be defined as price action making a series of higher peaks and higher troughs.

> A second time frame down trend may be defined as price action making a series of lower peaks and lower troughs.

Figure 8.4 shows a four-hourly chart of the USD/CHF. The chart shows where the down trend began based on the USD/CHF making a series of lower peaks and lower troughs.

Figure 8.4: four-hourly chart of the USD/CHF

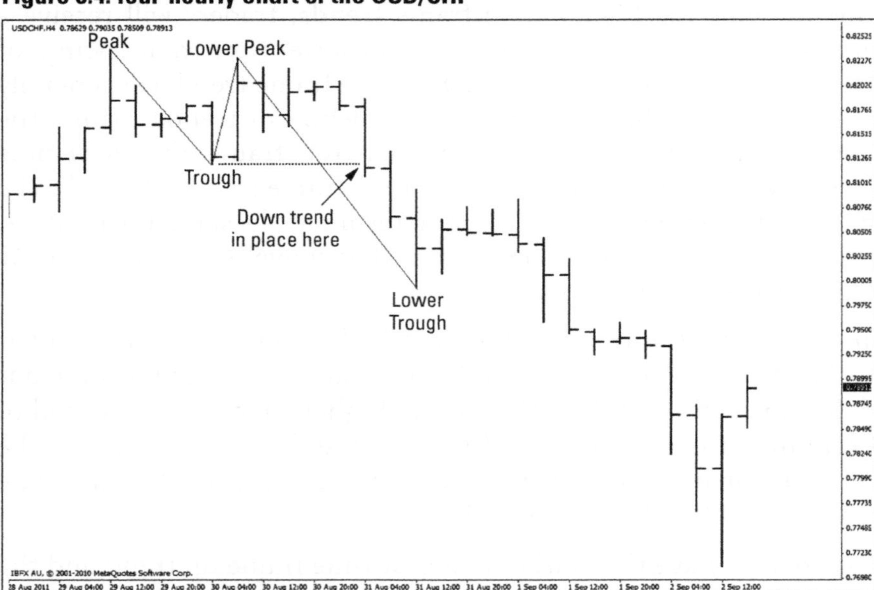

Source: MetaTrader 5, © 2001–2011 MetaQuotes Software Corp.

In a similar way to analysing the trend in the short-term time frame, a second time frame trend changes when we have the opposite configuration of peaks and troughs in place and we can define a second time frame trend-ending sequence:

> A second time frame up trend is ended by a lower peak and a lower trough, in that particular sequence.

> A second time frame down trend is ended by a higher peak and higher trough, in that particular sequence.

Note that the end of a second time frame up trend is also the beginning of a second time frame down trend and vice versa.

Having the ability to define the trend in more than one time frame allows the trader to take advantage of the more powerful forces at play in the market. Generally, the direction of a higher time frame trend determines whether a trader will look to going long or short in a market and the short-term analysis of trend and control and commitment will be used to enter or exit that trade.

Trend lines

The proper use of trend lines by traders is often misunderstood. A trend line is simply a line that represents a trend and the momentum or speed of that trend. A trend line represents momentum because the inputs into the line are price and time. Price (or distance) divided by time equals velocity or speed. Therefore, the relative angle of a trend line tells us something about the relative strength of a market.

An up trend line is drawn through the troughs of an up trend. An up trend line does not exist until a new peak is made higher than the peak which intervenes between the two troughs.

The following sequence of peaks and troughs must be in place before an up trend line can be drawn — trough, peak, higher trough, higher peak. This constitutes an up trend. It is obvious that an up trend line cannot be drawn unless an up trend exists.

A down trend line is drawn through the peaks of a down trend. A down trend line does not exist until a new trough is made lower than the trough that intervenes between the two peaks.

The following sequence of troughs and peaks must be in place before a down trend line can be drawn — peak, trough, lower peak, lower trough. This constitutes a down trend. It is obvious that a down trend line can't be drawn unless a down trend exists.

Figure 8.5 shows the model for drawing up and down trend lines.

Figure 8.5: model for drawing up and down trend lines

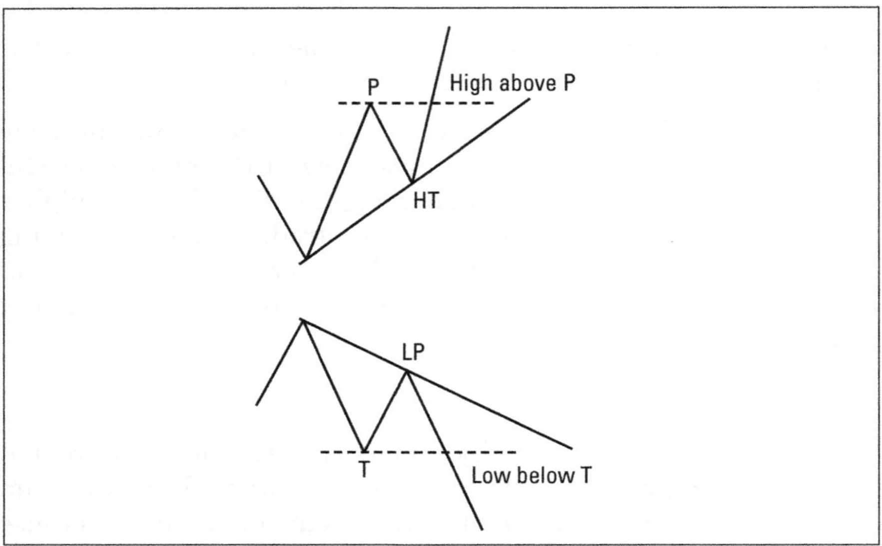

Source: © Kaplan Education Pty Ltd.

It is important to note that a break of a trend line does not mean that a trend has changed. It simply means that the momentum that the trend had prior to the break is no longer the same. This is because a trend line merely describes the speed of the trend and changes of trend are defined by peaks and troughs, not lines. A trend line break does, however, warn of the potential for a break of trend because of the loss of momentum in the trend.

Figure 8.6 shows an hourly GBP/USD chart. The chart has three trend lines drawn on it. As the trend developed to the downside, three trend lines were drawn at steeper angles highlighting the gain in downside momentum in the trend. Eventually, as the trend lost momentum, each of the trend lines was broken by price action. Also note that the down trend was still intact as the steepest trend line was broken. This warned of a potential change of trend, which occurred before the second trend line was broken.

Figure 8.6: hourly GBP/USD trend lines

Source: MetaTrader 5, © 2001–2011 MetaQuotes Software Corp.

Support and resistance

A good knowledge of support and resistance is essential to trading financial markets.

A support level is an area where the downside movement of the price action, being driven by the sellers, was stopped by buyers being strong enough to halt the movement. It is a short-term area of equilibrium in the market, where the strength of buyers and sellers becomes temporarily equally matched. Following the equilibrium the buyers take the ascendancy and move the market to the upside. This area of temporary equilibrium tends to be remembered by buyers and sellers, and the next time the area is tested the buyers are likely to come back into the market to, once again, move the market to the upside.

When a break of support occurs the buyers generally fail to reappear because their ideas of value in the market have changed. The lack of buyers means that the sellers are in the ascendancy and can push the market below the previous area of support.

A resistance level is an area where the upside movement of the price action, being driven by the buyers, was stopped by sellers being strong enough to halt the movement. It is a short-term area of equilibrium in the market, where the strength of sellers and buyers becomes temporarily equally matched. Following the equilibrium, the sellers take the ascendancy and move the market to the downside. This area of temporary equilibrium tends to be remembered by sellers and buyers, and the next time the area is tested the sellers are likely to come back into the market to move the market to the downside once again.

When a break of resistance occurs the sellers generally fail to reappear because their ideas of value in the market have changed. The lack of sellers means that the buyers are in the ascendancy and can push the market above the previous area of resistance.

Traders also need to be aware that support and resistance can reverse their roles. It is not uncommon for an area of support to become an area of resistance and vice versa.

The strength of an area of support or resistance is determined by a few factors:

- how recently the area was established
- the number of times the area has been tested
- whether the area was at a round number or an all-time high or low.

Figure 8.7 shows an hourly GBP/USD chart. This is a good example of how support and resistance can change roles. In this case previous support has become resistance and a barrier to the market trading at higher prices.

The best way for traders to approach support and resistance is to identify an area as a potential area where the market may halt and reverse, based on previous price action, and to watch the short-term price action as the area is tested once again. For example, the market may be in a first time frame down trend and trade to an area that was established as previous support. If we see the close near the high following a test of the area by the low of the trading period, we can feel confident that there may be very strong potential for the area to hold again because the buyers took control of the market. The high of the current time period should be watched for a potential higher high and higher low, a change of trend to the upside and confirmation that the area of support has held.

Figure 8.7: hourly GBP/USD support and resistance

Source: MetaTrader 5, © 2001–2011 MetaQuotes Software Corp.

Retracements

We know from our trend analysis that markets don't continue trending indefinitely. Trending markets need a rest and that rest manifests itself as either congestion or a retracement of the previous trend swing.

This retracement is short-term trending price action counter to the prior trend. Markets tend to retrace back to certain well-known percentages of the previous swing before terminating and moving back in the direction of the prior trend. The best known retracement is 50 per cent and is keenly watched for a turnaround by many traders in many markets. Other retracements that are keenly watched are the Fibonacci levels of 38.2 per cent and 61.8 per cent.

These levels should be watched by all traders as potential entry levels to trade with the underlying trend of the market. But these levels should not be followed blindly. The key to using these levels as entry and exit points is to combine short-term analysis of the relative strength of the bulls and bears and short-term trend analysis when the market is interacting with the 38.2 per cent, 50 per cent and 61.8 per cent retracements. This provides an advantage to technical analysts who put effort into thinking about price action.

Figure 8.8 shows the possible Fibonacci retracement levels in a bull and bear market.

Figure 8.8: possible Fibonacci retracement levels in a bull and bear market

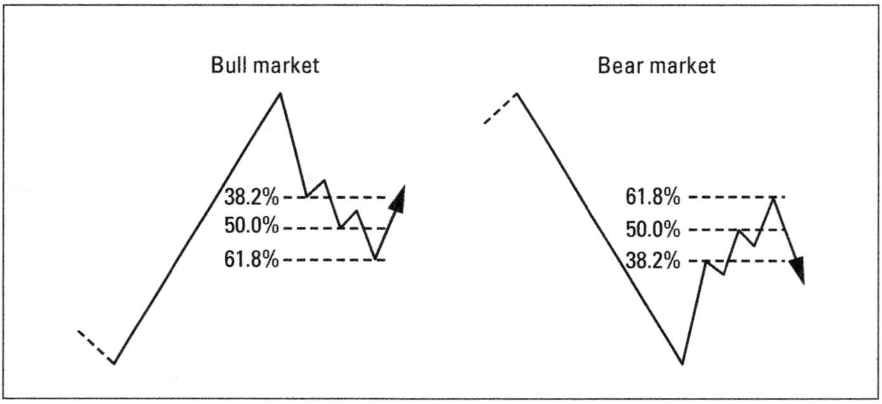

Source: © Kaplan Education Pty Ltd.

Chart patterns

In our ideal model for trending action, we tend to portray markets as trending in the direction of the dominant higher time frame trend, retracing counter to that trend and then continuing back in the direction of the higher time frame trend when the counter move has subsided. In the real world, markets don't always move that way. Quite often markets will trend in the direction of the higher time frame trend, form an area of congestion where the trending action basically moves sideways, then break out above or below the congestion area either in the direction of the higher time frame trend or against it.

Very often, these congestion areas form patterns that have distinctive price action enabling them to be recognised by technical analysts. Quite often these patterns will act in a fairly predictable manner following the breakout above or below their boundaries. The patterns tend to be classified as either reversal or continuation patterns with regard to the likelihood of whether the trend will continue in the direction of the trend prior to the pattern or in the reverse direction to the trend prior to the pattern. Generally, continuation patterns tend to be smaller in size and form faster. Reversal patterns tend to be larger and form over a longer period of time.

It is important to note that there is one common requirement for all chart patterns — that is, that there *must* be a prior trend leading into the pattern. If there is no prior trend, there is no pattern. It is also important that any pattern is not grossly larger, in terms of size, than the prior trend leading into it.

In this book we examine some of the more common patterns.

The head and shoulders reversal pattern

The head and shoulders pattern is a bearish reversal pattern that reverses an up trend only. It takes the shape of a man standing, where the prior trend is the body. A left shoulder, head and right shoulder are subsequently formed on the top of the body.

Basically, it begins with the market trending higher, making higher peaks and higher troughs. The last peak and trough in this sequence form the left shoulder. Another higher peak is made, followed by either a higher or lower trough. This forms the head. Following formation of the head a lower peak is formed, with the subsequent price action continuing to the downside. A line is drawn through the troughs that make up the shoulders and the head. This is called the neckline.

It is possible to calculate a potential target for a head and shoulders pattern. It is the distance from the peak of the head to the neckline, projected down from where the breakout occurred at the neckline.

Traders should go short on a break of the neckline, placing a stop-loss order just above the peak of the right shoulder. Quite often price action will retrace back to the neckline following the breakout.

This gives traders another opportunity to go short if the neckline holds as resistance and a stop-loss order should be placed a few pips above the neckline.

Figure 8.9 shows a four-hourly USD/JPY chart and a successful trade based on the head and shoulders pattern. A short trade would have been taken upon the breakout below the neckline with the stop loss above the right shoulder. Another short trade may have been taken following rejection from the neckline.

Figure 8.9: four-hourly USD/JPY chart and successful trade based on the head and shoulders pattern

Source: MetaTrader 5, © 2001–2011 MetaQuotes Software Corp.

The inverse head and shoulders pattern is a bullish reversal that reverses a down trend only. It takes the shape of a man standing upside down on his head and has the opposite characteristics and trading tactics of the head and shoulders pattern.

Figure 8.10 shows a one-minute EUR/USD chart with an inverse head and shoulders pattern which is testing the neckline.

Figure 8.10: one-minute EUR/USD chart with an inverse head and shoulders pattern testing the neckline

Source: MetaTrader 5, © 2001–2011 MetaQuotes Software Corp.

Double and triple tops and bottoms

The double top is a bearish reversal pattern that reverses an up trend only. First we have up trending price action leading to two peaks at approximately the same level. The pattern is complete when price action breaks out below the trough which intervenes between the two peaks.

The target for this pattern is the distance between the peaks and the intervening trough projected down from the breakout below the intervening trough.

Traders should go short on the breakout below the intervening trough and place a stop-loss order just above the peaks of the pattern.

The double bottom pattern is a bullish reversal pattern that reverses a down trend only. The characteristics are the inverse of the double top pattern and the pattern is complete when the price action breaks out above the intervening peak.

Triple tops and bottoms are similar to double tops and bottoms but, obviously, have an extra peak or trough in the pattern. For the triple top, the trading tactics involve going short on a breakout below the lowest of the intervening two troughs (which should be in roughly the same area). For the triple bottom, the trading tactics involve going long on a breakout above the highest of the intervening two peaks (which should be in roughly the same area).

Figure 8.11 shows the model double and triple tops and bottoms.

Figure 8.11: model double and triple tops and bottoms

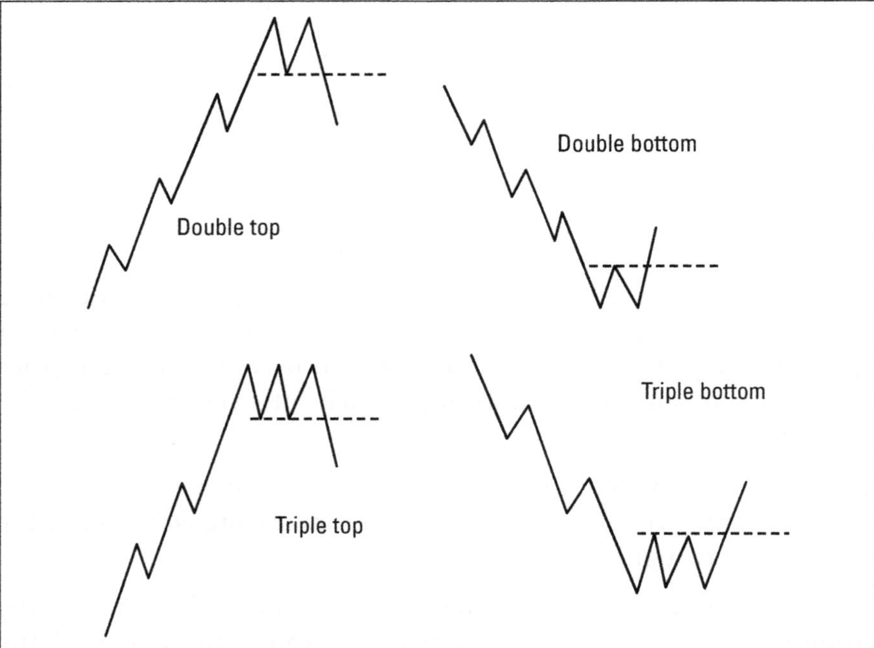

Source: © Kaplan Education Pty Ltd.

Flags

The flag is a continuation pattern where the trend continues, after breakout, in the same direction as the trend prior to formation of the pattern.

If the initial trend is an up trend, price action gives way to an area which forms a series of minor highs and lows which are generally counter to the prior up trend. Two lines drawn through the counter trend highs and lows are approximately parallel. The pattern is complete when price action breaks out above the boundary line drawn through the highs in the pattern.

The target for this pattern is the distance of the up trend leading into the pattern projected up from the area of breakout above the line representing the boundary of the highs in the pattern.

Traders should go long on the breakout and place a stop-loss order just below the lowest low in the pattern.

If the initial trend is a down trend, price action gives way to an area that forms a series of minor highs and lows which are generally counter to the prior down trend. Two lines drawn through the counter trend highs and lows are approximately parallel. The pattern is complete when price action breaks out below the boundary line drawn through the lows in the pattern.

The target for this pattern is the distance of the down trend leading into the pattern projected down from the area of breakout below the line representing the boundary of the lows in the pattern.

Traders should go short on the breakout and place a stop-loss order just above the highest high in the pattern.

Figure 8.12 (overleaf) shows a monthly chart of the USD/CAD with two flag continuation patterns which would have produced two successful short trades.

Figure 8.12: monthly chart of the USD/CAD with two flag continuation patterns that would have produced two successful short trades

Source: MetaTrader 5, © 2001–2011 MetaQuotes Software Corp.

Triangles

Triangle patterns come in three forms: symmetrical, ascending or descending. They may be either reversal or continuation patterns.

For the symmetrical triangle, trending price action gives way to a congestion area that has lower peaks and higher troughs within its boundaries. Generally they are continuation patterns, but also manifest themselves as reversal patterns.

For the ascending triangle, trending price action gives way to a congestion area that has equal peaks and higher troughs within its boundaries. In an up trend it is often a continuation pattern and in a down trend it is often a reversal pattern.

For the descending triangle, trending price action gives way to a congestion area that has lower peaks and equal troughs within its boundaries. In an up trend it is often a reversal pattern and in a down trend it is often a continuation pattern.

The target for all triangles is the maximum distance between the boundaries of the triangle at the base projected from the area of the breakout and in the direction of the breakout.

For all triangle patterns a position should be taken in the direction of the breakout with a stop-loss order placed on the opposite side of the triangle.

Figure 8.13 shows a symmetrical triangle for the EUR/USD.

Figure 8.13: symmetrical triangle for the EUR/USD

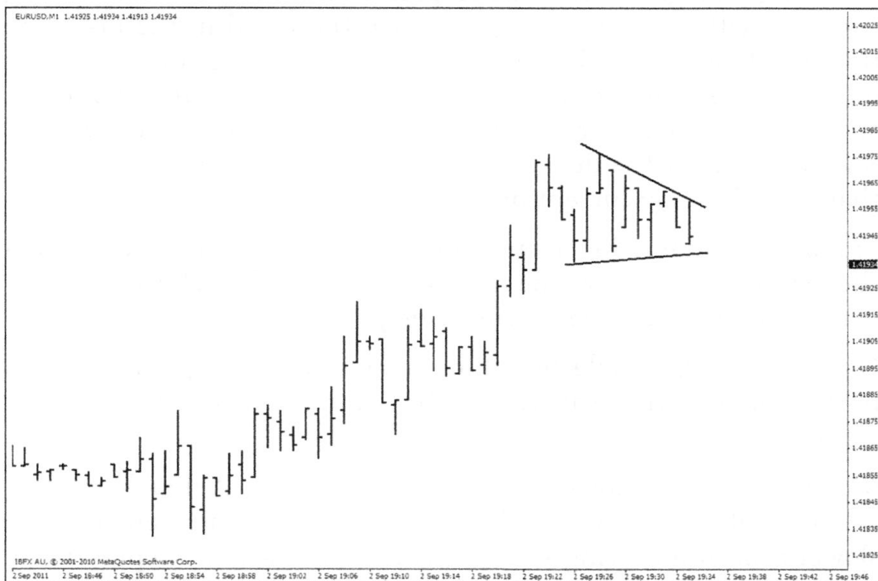

Source: MetaTrader 5, © 2001–2011 MetaQuotes Software Corp.

Trend following indicators

Trend following indicators use one or more of the components of a bar, the open, high, low or close, to mathematically calculate a chart that is drawn on either the main chart with price action or as a subchart. They are used to reveal the underlying trend in the chosen time frame and, sometimes, the strength of that trend.

Moving averages

The most commonly used trend following indicator is the moving average.

A moving average is defined as the sum of *n* period closes divided by *n*, where *n* is the number of bars in the lookback period. This is often called a simple moving average. There are many other types of moving averages with variations on the above formula: exponential, weighted, adaptive, etc.

A moving average is a smoothed representation of the trend. Moving averages with short time inputs reveal the trend in the fast time frame and they are fairly quick to respond to changes in price action but the more whipsaw trades result. The longer the time input, the smoother the indicator and the longer the time frame of the trend revealed. One of the drawbacks with the longer moving average is that it tends to lag current price action.

Trading rules for using a single moving average is to go long when the market closes above the moving average and go short when the market closes below the moving average.

Quite often the angle by which a moving average points in a particular direction can reveal the strength of the trend being represented.

Moving averages may also be used in multiples. A double moving average will usually consist of a fast time unit moving average with a slower time unit moving average, with the fast average representing the trend in the short-term time frame and the slower average representing the trend in the longer time frame.

Trading rules for using two moving averages is to go long when the fast moving average crosses above the slower moving average and go short when the fast moving average crosses below the slower moving average.

Figure 8.14 shows a monthly chart of the USD/CAD with an 11 period simple moving average. The chart shows where long and short entries would have been taken based on the moving average. You can see that the moving average generally describes the trend quite well and the short trades were quite profitable.

Figure 8.14: monthly chart of the USD/CAD with an 11 period simple moving average

Source: MetaTrader 5, © 2001–2011 MetaQuotes Software Corp.

The disadvantage of the above two trading methods is that the trader is kept constantly in the market. This is good if the market is continually trending, but we know that markets also have periods of sideways price action when these methods lead to whipsaw trading, eating up profits.

Using three moving averages together attempts to have the trader in the trend during trending periods and out of the market during sideways trading.

The three moving average method employs a fast, medium and longer term moving average. The idea is that the trader only trades when all time frames are in unison.

Trading rules for using three moving averages is to go long when the fast moving average is above the medium moving average and the medium moving average is above the longer moving average. The long trade is closed when this condition no longer exists. The trader may also go short when the fast moving average is below the medium moving average and the medium moving average is below the longer moving average. The short trade is closed when this condition no longer exists.

Figure 8.15 shows a 5, 20 and 50 period triple moving average on a five-minute EUR/USD chart. The chart shows where a trader would have entered a short position, closed that short and subsequently entered a long position based on the trading rules.

Figure 8.15: 5, 20 and 50 period triple moving average on a five-minute EUR/USD chart

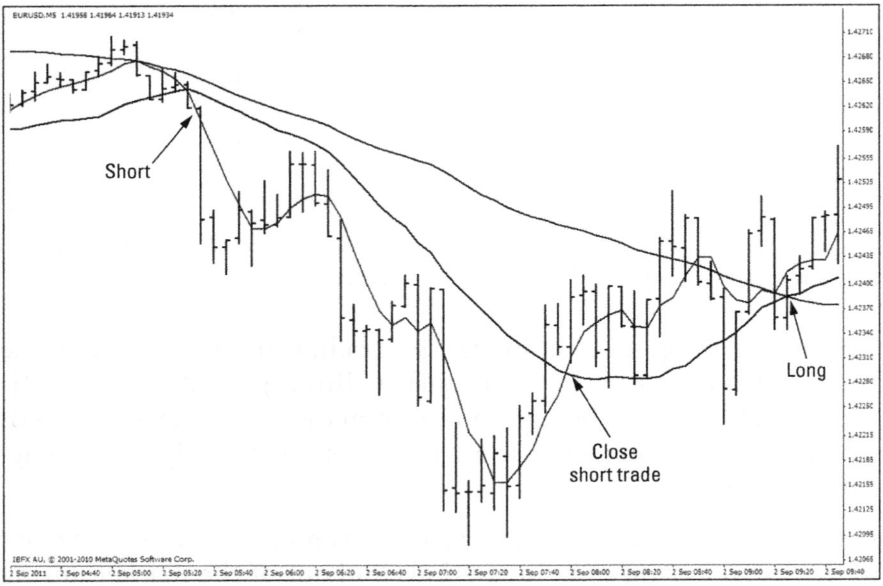

Source: MetaTrader 5, © 2001–2011 MetaQuotes Software Corp.

Momentum oscillator indicators

Momentum oscillators are used to measure the change in the speed of the market. They tend to oscillate above and below a centre line and move between overbought and oversold conditions. Momentum oscillators generally don't lag price action as various trend following indicators do and are used to enter into and exit out of the swings in a sideways or trending market.

The relative strength index (RSI)

The most popular momentum oscillator is the relative strength index or RSI. It differs from many other oscillators in that it has upper and lower limits to which it may travel. The standard time input into the RSI is 14 periods, but it is quite often used with an input of seven time periods and in some trading methods two or three.

In sideways markets, the overbought level is set at 70 and the oversold level is set at 30. This provides us with some trading rules: go long when the RSI falls below 30 and rises back over it and go short when the RSI rises above 70 and falls back under it.

In a trending market, oscillators tend not to move between extremes and will be biased towards higher levels during an up trend and lower levels during a down trend. For this reason, adjustments are made to the overbought and oversold levels in a trending market. In an up trend the levels are shifted up to 80 and 40 and in a down trend the levels are shifted down to 60 and 20. This provides us with some rules: go long in an up trend when the RSI falls below 40 and rises back over it and in a down trend go short when the RSI rises above 60 and falls back under it. Note no signal is provided to go short in an up trend nor long in a down trend, ensuring that the trader does not trade against the trend.

An interesting way to adjust RSI levels is to apply Bollinger Bands to the indicator to normalise these levels for volatility. This results in a dynamic level of overbought and oversold, which can often be more useful than the levels originally proposed.

Traders may also use trend lines and pattern analysis on the RSI when the market is trending.

Figure 8.16 (overleaf) shows a five-minute chart of the AUD/USD with a five period RSI subchart. The chart indicates where a trader may have entered long positions based on the market being in an up trend and the RSI crossing above the 40 level after falling below it.

Figure 8.16: five-minute chart of the AUD/USD with a five period RSI subchart

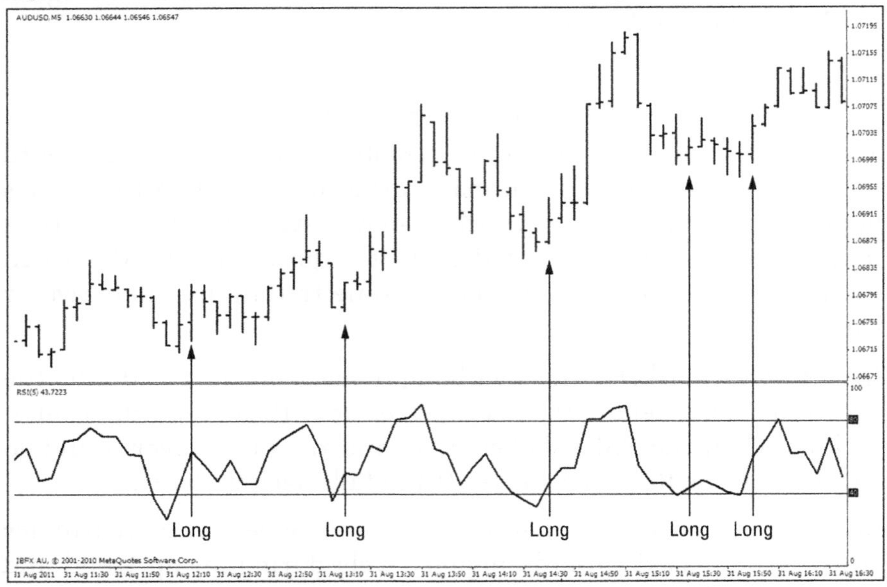

Source: MetaTrader 5, © 2001–2011 MetaQuotes Software Corp.

The moving average convergence divergence indicators (MACD)

The MACD is a popular indicator that is used for trend following, but is derived in a similar manner to an oscillator. It is calculated by subtracting a longer term exponential moving average from a shorter one. A 'signal line' is derived from this calculation which generates buy or sell signals based on the crossovers of the two lines.

The MACD histogram is a derivative of the MACD and is always drawn as a histogram chart. It is calculated by subtracting the MACD line from the signal line. A bullish signal is given when the MACD histogram turns up when it is below its zero line and a bearish signal is given when the MACD histogram turns down when it is above the zero line.

Both the MACD and the MACD histogram generate very strong signals when the peaks and troughs in the indicator diverge from peaks and troughs in price action.

Figure 8.17 is a weekly chart of the AUD/USD. It highlights how the MACD histogram can be used to generate buy signals in an up trend and shows divergence between the peaks of the indicator and the peaks of price action.

Figure 8.17: weekly chart of the AUD/USD

Source: © AmiBroker.

Bollinger Bands

Bollinger Bands are an extremely useful and adaptable indicator that reveal the status of another element of the market — volatility. The indicator consists of a moving average, which we discussed earlier, and a line above and below the moving average at, usually, two standard deviations away.

Bollinger Bands employ the standard deviation of price action as an input, so the majority of price action should be contained within the bands. For this reason, a bullish move above the upper band or bearish move below the lower band suggests that the price action is very strong and is likely to continue in that direction. This can be used as a trading signal only when confirmed by other indicators.

In their simplest form, Bollinger Bands can be used to detect periods of relatively low volatility in the market, reflected by the bands drawing together. These periods are often followed by a sharp breakout and sudden increase in volatility, presenting traders with the opportunity to enter trades that offer significant gains with minimal and well-defined risk. Visit <www.bollingerbands.com> for more information.

Figure 8.18 is a five-minute chart of the EUR/USD with 20 period Bollinger Bands. Notice how the bands squeeze together before a breakout occurs.

Figure 8.18: five-minute chart of the EUR/USD with 20 period Bollinger Bands

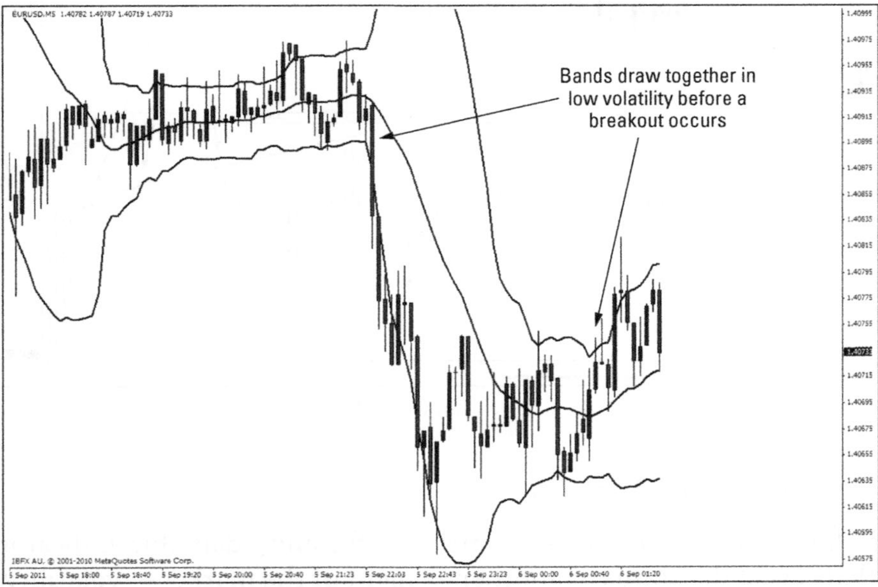

Source: MetaTrader 5, © 2001–2011 MetaQuotes Software Corp.

Candlestick charts

Candlestick charting originated in Japan centuries ago. It was used to convey information about price action in the Osaka rice markets. Candlestick techniques have developed and are the main price chart used in Asian markets, as well as being extremely popular in Western markets.

Some traders have the mistaken belief that candlesticks provide more information than bar charts. That is not correct and a good trader who understands short-term analysis and is able to assess the relative strength of the bulls and the bears sees the same information in both charts. The advantage of candlesticks, however, is their graphic nature; it is very easy to quickly see the size of the bodies of the candles and the shadows on the top or bottom.

Candlestick charts use the same components as a bar chart but are depicted differently. The area between the open and close is drawn as a box, called the real body, and is shaded with colour, generally red, if the close is below the open. The real body is not shaded or shaded green if the close is above the open. This allows traders to instantly observe whether the sellers or buyers were in the ascendancy when the market closed and also observe the strength they had during that period as evidenced by the size of the body. If the close is below the open, the sellers made net bearish progress in that time period between the open and the close. If the close is above the open, the buyers made net bullish progress in that time period between the open and the close.

Figure 8.19 shows how a candlestick chart is constructed.

Figure 8.19: how a candlestick chart is constructed

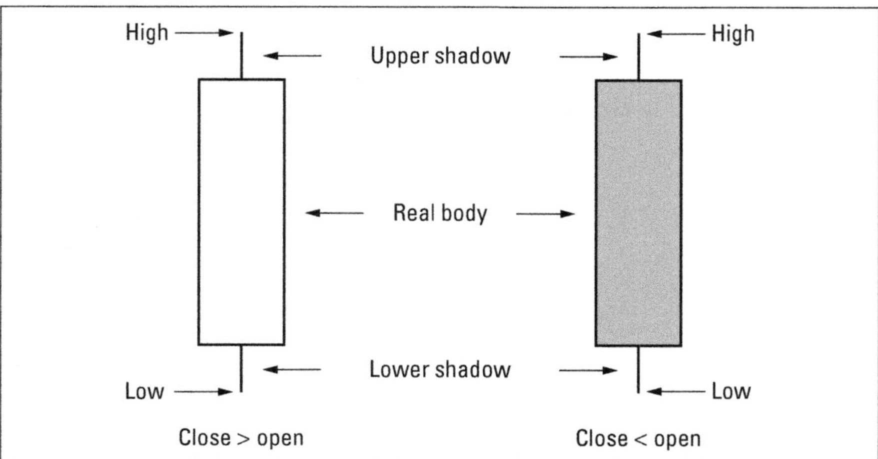

Source: © Kaplan Education Pty Ltd.

As in bar charts, the range — the distance between the high and the low — is drawn as a vertical line. The real body of the candle is drawn over the top of the line so that the only part of the line showing is that which extends beyond the open and the close. The part of the line above or below the body is called the shadow.

Shadows are very important because they represent price rejection or an area where the market traded to but was unable to end the trading session at that level. It is for this reason that candlesticks are very useful in highlighting price rejection from areas of support and/or resistance.

The interpretation of the candlestick lines makes the technique extremely useful for timing entry into and exit out of trading positions.

Figure 8.20 shows how the shadows on the candlesticks highlight an area of support and resistance.

Figure 8.20: the shadows on the candlesticks highlight an area of support and resistance

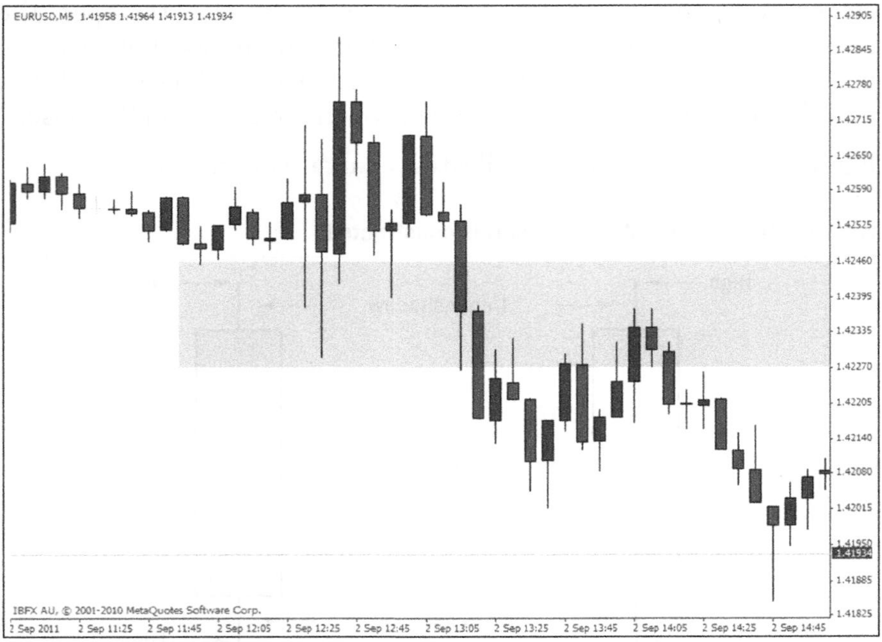

Source: MetaTrader 5, © 2001–2011 MetaQuotes Software Corp.

The method also has a series of defined candlestick patterns that are potential reversal or continuation patterns in the short-term time frame. Some of these patterns are quite robust and offer strong signals for traders. The patterns will not be covered in this book but they can be found in many books on the subject or on many websites.

Ichimoku Kinko Hyo charts

The Ichimoku Kinko Hyo or 'equilibrium at a glance' chart is a trading method that tends to highlight higher probability trades. It is relatively new to Western technical analysis, but its popularity has been increasing among financial markets traders.

Ichimoku charts apply a series of indicators on one chart, allowing traders to assess price action in three time frames — long, medium and short. This style of analysis enables the trader to see the 'whole' picture for any particular security.

Figure 8.21 shows an hourly Ichimoku chart of the EUR/USD. This chart highlights the bearishness in this market in the long, medium and short term time frames by price action trading below the Kumo, Kijun Sen and Tenkan Sen.

Figure 8.21: hourly Ichimoku chart of the EUR/USD

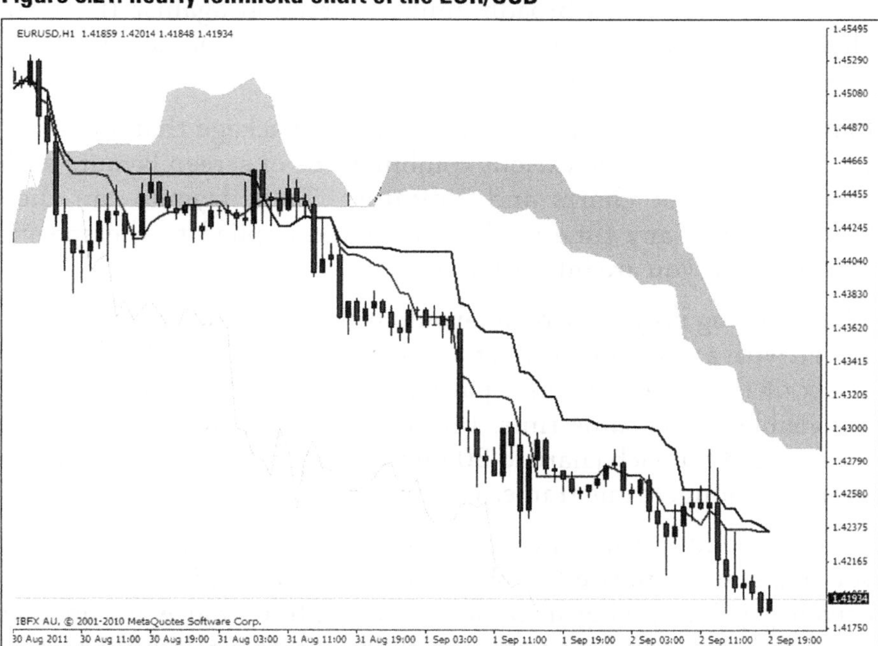

Source: MetaTrader 5, © 2001–2011 MetaQuotes Software Corp.

A basic understanding of the components that make up the Ichimoku chart is essential to effectively applying this trading method. The method was developed in the 1920s and released to the public in 1968 by Tokyo financial journalist Goichi Hosoda. It is believed that he employed over 10 000 university students to back test the indicators that make up the Ichimoku trading method.

Ichimoku charts are commonly used by many Japanese trading rooms because they offer multiple assessments of price action in many time frames and suggest trades with higher or lower probability for success. Traders new to the method may be confused by the 'busy' looking Ichimoku charts, but a basic understanding of the indicators reveals a method that is quite simple in its application.

Visit <www.ichimokucharts.com> for more information.

Currencies are often observed moving in unison

As you observe the currency markets, you will start to notice that for much of the time currencies tend to move in unison. These moves are often in a broadly unified direction against the USD, although sometimes the markets will move in relation to other major currencies such as the EUR or JPY.

Many trading platforms include a charting package that will allow you to set up and save various combinations of screen layouts with various different charts and indicators. These layouts can then be accessed at any time in the future and applied to the specific currency pair you are interested in.

When setting up your screen layouts it is a good idea to set up one screen with a selection of short-term (intraday) charts of either four or six of the larger currency pairs (the 'majors'), so that all charts are visible at the same time. Intraday traders may like to set the time period for each chart to 30 minutes initially, although slightly shorter or longer time frames can be used.

As you monitor this multi-currency screen throughout the day, you will start to notice the phenomenon mentioned above; that is, currency pairs moving in broad unison. Often, you will find that all of the pairs you are watching will lapse into a relatively narrow band of sideways congestion. When you see this type of activity, it is worth paying more attention and watching for signs of a breakout, which is usually the beginning of trending price action above or below resistance or support. One of the pairs on your screen will usually make the first move, followed by another, then another, and soon all pairs will be breaking out of their respective trading ranges. When you see this type of unified breakout attempt across several pairs, you should do a quick scan of the charts to determine which pair offers the best trading opportunity, then place your order accordingly.

Figure 8.22, a screenshot of 30-minute charts of four currency pairs, shows how they move broadly in unison. The first three charts (moving clockwise) show consolidation after a down trend, while the chart in the bottom left-hand corner shows the inverse—consolidation following an up trend. In general we would expect to see pairs such as AUD/USD, EUR/USD and NZD/USD moving in the same direction at the same time, unified by virtue of having USD as the 'terms' currency. Moving in the opposite direction would be a pair such as USD/JPY, which clearly has USD as the base currency. When one of these pairs acts in a way that does not fit with our expectations, it may be an indication that a tradeable move is getting under way.

Figure 8.22: currency pairs moving in unison

Source: MetaTrader 5, © 2001–2011 MetaQuotes Software Corp.

Trade the market, not your opinion of the market

When using the tools of technical analysis, it is important to remember that, whatever happens, the market is always 'right'. You must not become so caught up in your analysis that you continually trade against the market because you believe that your view is 'right' and the market has it 'wrong'. If the market is behaving in a manner that you were not expecting or that you feel is wrong, it may well be that there is an extra piece of information out there in the marketplace that you have either overlooked or not yet encountered. In such a situation, it is probably best to stand aside until things become clear to you once again.

You should also remember that old market saying, 'The trend is your friend'. Fighting the trend is likely to see a trader suffer many losses for each win that is achieved. Some traders have the capacity to withstand this type of trading environment, but most do not, so you are likely to fare better if you take trades that are broadly in line with the underlying trend.

A stop-loss order ('stop') is an order used to exit an open position. As its name suggests, its purpose is to limit the potential losses if the market turns against an open position. For example, if you have bought AUD/USD at 1.0660, you may place a stop-loss order at 1.0640. In theory, this will limit the risk that you face on this trade to just 20 pips provided the stop is executed at the nominated price. A stop-loss order can also be used to lock in profits once the market has moved in a favourable direction.

One of the major benefits of technical analysis is that it can help to quickly alert you to the possibility that your view of the market is wrong. Even some of the most basic tools, such as the identification of key support and resistance levels, can be used to help assess the risk to your position and the potential for a trade to move against you. Once these areas are identified, you will have a clear indication of where to place your stops. This is one vital piece of information that you will not be able to glean from fundamental analysis, especially for short-term trades.

In figure 8.23, the break of the technical 'support' line at 1.3373 by the long black candle (seventh from the right) gives a clear indication to those looking for a rally that their view has turned out to be incorrect. Placing stop-loss orders for long positions just below the support line (at, say, 1.3365 or 1.3360) protects longs from significantly greater losses; in this case subsequent falls saw trade probe below 1.3300.

Figure 8.23: support and resistance

Use of tools that require a figure for the daily close

Once trade in the global foreign exchange market gets under way in New Zealand each Monday morning, there is no actual cessation of trading until late on Friday afternoon in New York, some five and-a-half days later. This raises questions about the validity of using many of the tools and techniques of technical analysis that rely on the level of the daily close in their implementation (for example, figure 8.24, overleaf). If there is no 'close', what do we do?

Figure 8.24: daily FX chart requiring 'close' data

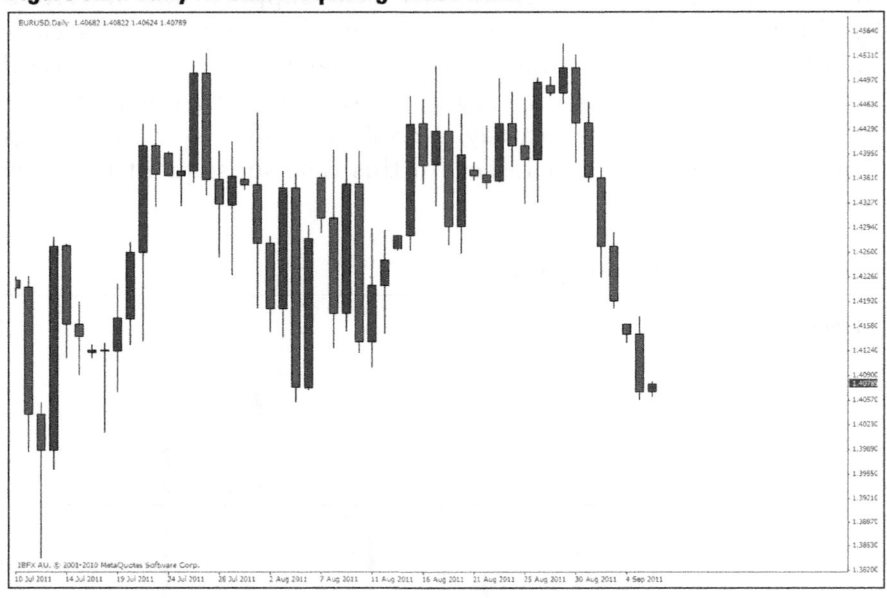

Source: MetaTrader 5, © 2001–2011 MetaQuotes Software Corp.

The simple solution, of course, is to use the arbitrarily selected time of 1700 (5.00 pm) New York time, which is generally accepted by market convention as being the 'close' of the foreign exchange day—and the start of the next. There is some validity to this given that this time is so widely accepted and many participants in the inter-bank market who wish to square up their positions by the 'end' of the day will use this time as their guide. This time is also widely used as the rollover time for open positions, although there is some variation in practice with times from 1500 to 1800 used by different institutions. On the other hand, many charting platforms are available that use midnight, or 0000 GMT, as the time to roll their charts from one day to the next. This also has some validity considering the volume of activity that flows through the London market.

As more markets head towards 24-hour-a-day trading, this issue is likely to gain more prominence. Informal discussions held between some of the world's pre-eminent technical analysts suggest that, provided you remain consistent in your selection of 'closing time', the results obtained will provide useful information. Therefore, whichever time we select to roll our charts from one day into the next, provided we remain consistent in the use of the selected time, we should still be able to observe valuable information on daily charts and indicators.

Identify the current type of market activity

Before selecting your trading strategy, it is a very good idea to take a look at a slightly broader time frame than that in which you intend to trade, in order to determine the dominant type of activity currently being experienced in that market.

As can be seen in figure 8.25, there is a significant difference between a market that is trending firmly and one that is chopping about in a trading range. Each of these phases offers good opportunities for the active trader, but different techniques are required.

Figure 8.25: market phases

Source: MetaTrader 5, © 2001–2011 MetaQuotes Software Corp.

Once we identify that the market is in a clear trending phase, such as the bull trend on the left side of figure 8.25, our strategies will be skewed towards identifying buying opportunities and using trailing stops. However, once we recognise that the market has become caught in a trading range, such as that on the right-hand side of this chart, we can start to look out for good opportunities to take both long and short positions as the market swings from end to end within the range.

While trend trading has clear potential to deliver the biggest gains for the lowest number of trades, markets do spend a significant amount of time caught in ranges, and it is important to be able to identify the opportunities that lie within them.

Start with the big picture

Trends have been compared to ocean movements, with the direction of the tide (rising or falling) representing the longer term trend, while waves represent the medium-term trend, and the ripples on the surface of the waves represent the shorter term movements or 'noise' in the market. Knowing whether the tide is rising or falling will help you gauge how far up the beach each wave is likely to travel. In the markets, knowledge of the direction of the longer term trends can help you gauge how far the shorter term moves are likely to travel and how much velocity and commitment is likely to be behind each move. Although there are always exceptions to the rule, having an idea of the underlying trend will help in your efforts to tip the balance of odds in your favour.

When starting your analysis of a particular market, it is a good idea to start with a longer term chart to ensure you get a feel for the broader underlying trends affecting the market you are looking at. It is a good idea to start with a weekly chart, then drill down through a number of successively shorter time frames, such as daily, then hourly, and possibly fifteen minutes or even five minutes, depending on your trading style. (This is shown in figure 8.26.)

Figure 8.26: examining multiple time frame views of a currency pair weekly/daily/one hour/five minutes

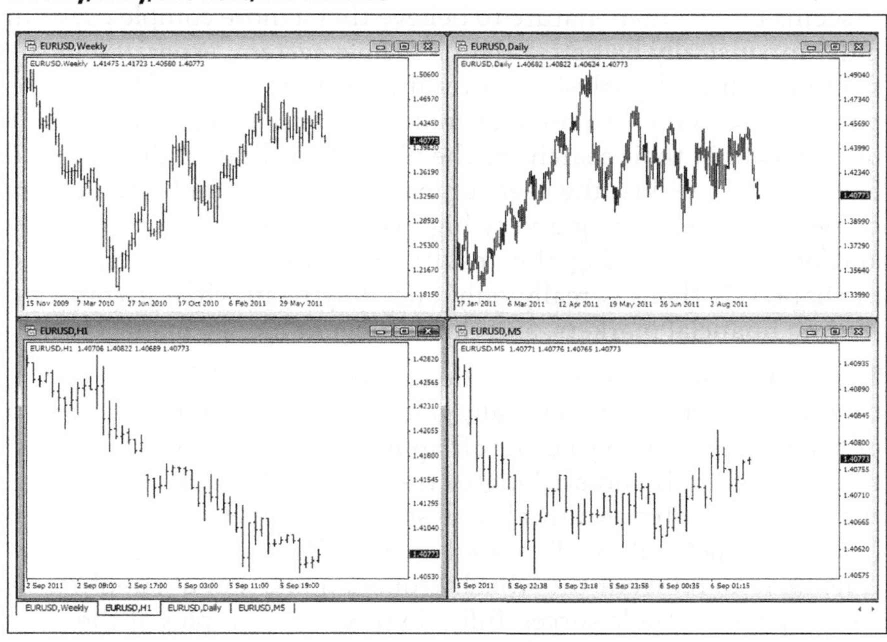

Source: MetaTrader 5, © 2001–2011 MetaQuotes Software Corp.

Volume

Remember, in the foreign exchange market there is no single source of reliable volume data. If your charts have volume for foreign exchange markets, you might want to investigate the source of that data. Some online margin FX providers may show a representation of the relative levels of volume passing through their platform, but they are more likely to protect the precise figures as it would be regarded as sensitive business information. Others may attempt to use volume data from the foreign exchange futures contracts traded on the Chicago Mercantile Exchange <www.cme.com>, but this is just a tiny fraction of the actual volume that flows through the broader global currency markets and may not necessarily be reflective of the activity therein.

Keep it simple

It seems to be human nature to believe that a more complex system must intrinsically be better than a simple system, especially in the field of technical analysis and trading system design. This can be observed in the custom-made indicators and systems that some users create in their search for the ultimate indicator, the so-called Holy Grail. In reality, the users of many of these complex indicators or systems are running a very high risk of using them incorrectly and/or misinterpreting the results. Remember, as we discussed in chapter 1, there is really only one Holy Grail when it comes to trading financial markets, and this is diligent money management.

Those who have the time, experience, patience and funding to test complex systems may eventually gain a small edge, but the majority of traders are probably better off applying the KISS principle (keep it simple, stupid) and sticking to the tried and trusted techniques that have benefited technical analysts and traders for many decades (some of which will be discussed in the following chapters). There is no need to reinvent the wheel. Proper application of simple tools will help you to trade successfully. Some good examples of the tools you may wish to use 'straight out of the box' are:

- moving averages
- relative strength index (RSI)
- Fibonacci retracements
- Ichimoku Kinko Hyo
- moving average convergence divergence (MACD)
- Bollinger Bands
- Elliott Wave (it is useful to have at least a basic understanding of this tool).

But always remember that a particular indicator should never be used in isolation. In fact, it is best if several independent indicators suggest the same direction for the market. It should also be remembered that indicators work at an optimum level when used to confirm price action; after all, 'price' is what will determine whether you end up with a profit or loss.

Chapter 9

FX fundamental analysis for traders

Having looked briefly at the scope and potential use of technical analysis of currency markets, it now comes time to consider the underlying fundamentals of this market.

How do we determine exchange rates?

Fundamental analysis attempts to measure the intrinsic or underlying value of a currency and how this intrinsic value may change under certain circumstances. In its practical application, a fundamental analyst forms this opinion by assessing how economic factors — such as inflation, interest rates, balance of payments and many others — have an impact on a theory or combination of theories of exchange rate determination. For information on such fundamental factors, it may be useful to refer to chapter 7.

Fundamental analysts who work in the inter-bank market are usually called upon to determine how a pending release of economic data may have an impact on a currency and are required to form an opinion as to the intrinsic value of that currency after the release has taken place. Based on this recommendation, trading positions may be taken up if the analyst considers the post-release intrinsic value to be different from the pre-release value. The interplay of all of the economic factors can be very complex and, in their detail, they are beyond the scope of this book. For the most part, fundamental analysts in the retail online sector (that is, most of us) use such analysis to understand the nature of pre-release valuations so we can assess the fundamental landscape and take a position as to whether we concur with or demur from the consensus forecasters.

A weakness that should be remembered in applying fundamental analysis is that it is very difficult to formulate a model to accurately predict intrinsic value. On top of this, fundamental analysts also generally assume that markets behave rationally. As experienced market players know, sometimes markets can behave irrationally, as there may be extemporaneous factors that come into play. We must always remember that a market is made up of many opinions of intrinsic value and that price is simply a consensus of those opinions.

Over the long term, economic fundamentals can have a profound effect on exchange rates. Relative rates of inflation, measures of national output and relative trends in the balance of payments, and its components, have great influence.

Interest rate differentials are generally accepted as having a great influence on exchange rates in the short term, although traders should also be aware that supply and demand have a short-term effect.

In this chapter we describe the most important theories of exchange rate determination and briefly look at some of the more important economic data releases and where the information may be obtained.

Theories of exchange rate determination

This topic serves as a brief introduction to how, theoretically, exchange rates may be determined. A working knowledge of these theories may assist traders to understand how changes in the factors that influence exchange rates may affect those currencies, enabling them to take appropriate action in the marketplace.

The law of one price

The 'law of one price' states that the same items sold in different countries will have the propensity to sell for the same price when expressed in one currency. For example, a loaf of bread that sells in Switzerland for 1.30 Swiss francs should sell in the US for 1.30 Swiss francs.

In reality, we know that this law does not hold. The reason is due to different taxes, trade restrictions, transportation costs and input prices in the two countries.

Purchasing power parity

Purchasing power parity (PPP) takes the 'law of one price' to the next level. 'Absolute' PPP is simply the law of one price applied to a representative basket of identical goods.

Under a theory of 'absolute' PPP, economists will assert that exchange rates will move into equilibrium when the purchasing power in the two countries is equivalent. Therefore, by simply dividing the price of the representative basket of goods in one country by the price of the representative basket of goods in another country will give a theoretical exchange rate. Obviously, changes to the set of prices in one country will have an impact on exchange rates. That means that if a country experiences a period of inflation, then the exchange rate of that country will depreciate.

Against the 'absolute' doctrine, the 'relative' version of PPP simply subtracts the *change* in price of the representative basket of goods (inflation) in one country by the *change* in price of the representative basket of goods (inflation) in another country, to arrive at a theoretical change in exchange rate. For example, if country A has an inflation rate of 1 per cent and country B has an inflation rate of 3 per cent, then country A's currency will appreciate by 2 per cent against country B's currency in an attempt to move towards purchasing power equilibrium.

As with the law of one price, different taxes, trade restrictions, transport costs, input prices and, in the case of the 'relative' PPP model, the inability to choose an *identical* basket of goods, makes the effective use of the PPP models, in our opinion (and that of most FX traders it has to be said), difficult.

The complications with the models do not mean that PPP should never be used, just that it should only really be used as an effective longer term 'rough' guide to determining exchange rates.

The Big Mac index

In 1986, *The Economist* magazine pioneered the use of a simple substitute for PPP—the Big Mac index. They dubbed the study of this index as 'Burgernomics' and it has subsequently given rise to other PPP substitutes, such as the Coca-Cola index and the Starbucks tall-latte index. The Big Mac index remains the most popular of all.

The Big Mac is possibly the best-known hamburger produced by the world's largest fast food retailer, McDonald's. They are made to the same standard in every McDonald's in about 120 countries. And, as most who have travelled the world will know, a Big Mac in the United States is a Big Mac in France is a Big Mac in Australia is a Big Mac in Slovenia, and so on. The similarity enables us to substitute a Big Mac for an identical basket of goods in PPP theory. In effect, it has become the layperson's PPP.

Note, after more than 25 years of use, the Big Mac index in July 2011 was adjusted to also include an enhanced, so-called 'GDP adjusted' version side-by-side the 'raw' version that has been used historically. It follows from the intuitive presumption that average prices should be lower in poor countries than in rich ones because labour costs are lower. Indeed, research by The Economist magazine shows a strong positive relationship between the dollar price of a Big Mac and GDP per person. The theory being that the difference between the prices predicted for each country, given its average income, and its actual price offers a better guide to a currency under consideration, be they otherwise under- or over-valued.

How does it work?

The Big Mac PPP is the exchange rate that would leave a Big Mac in a country costing the same as in the United States. Simply, the cost of a Big Mac in a country priced in the local currency is divided by the cost of a Big Mac in the United States in US dollars. For example, if a Big Mac in Australia cost A$4.56 and in the United States cost US$4.07, then you divide 4.56 by 4.07 to arrive at a US$ PPP against the A$ of A$1.12 (see table 9.1).

Table 9.1: the Big Mac index

The hamburger standard						
	Big Mac prices		Implied PPP[†] of the dollar	Actual dollar exchange rate July 25th	Under (–)/over (+) valuation against the dollar, %	
Country	In local currency	In dollars*			Raw index	Adjusted for GDP per person
United States‡	$4.07	4.07	—	—	—	—
Argentina	Peso 20.0	4.84	4.92	4.13	19	101
Australia	A$4.56	4.94	1.12	0.92	22	12
Brazil	Real 9.50	6.16	2.34	1.54	52	149
Britain	£2.39	3.89	1.70[§]	1.63[§]	–4	9
Canada	C$4.73	5.00	1.16	0.95	23	24
Chile	Peso 1 850	4.00	455	463	–2	58
China	Yuan 14.7	2.27	3.60	6.45	–44	3
Colombia	Peso 8 400	4.74	2 066	1 771	17	108
Czech Republic	Koruna 69.3	4.07	17.1	17.0	Nil	45
Denmark	DK 28.5	5.48	7.01	5.20	35	23
Egypt	Pound 14.1	2.36	3.47	5.96	–42	11
Euro area**	€3.44	4.93	1.18[††]	1.43[††]	21	36
Hong Kong	HK$15.1	1.94	3.74	7.79	–52	–43
Hungary	Forint 760	4.04	187	188	–1	57
India[§§]	Rupee 22 534	1.89	20.7	44.4	–53	–8
Indonesia	Rupiah 22 534	2.64	5 543	8.523	–35	24
Israel	Shekel 15.9	4.67	3.91	3.40	15	43
Japan	¥320	4.08	78.7	78.4	Nil	5
Malaysia	Ringgit 7.20	2.42	1.77	2.97	–40	2
Mexico	Peso 32.0	2.74	7.87	11.7	–33	13
New Zealand	NZ$5.10	4.41	1.25	1.16	9	29
Norway	Kroner 45.0	8.31	11.1	5.41	104	46
Pakistan	Rupee 205	2.38	50.5	86.3	–42	16
Peru	Sol 10.0	3.65	2.46	2.74	–10	63
Philippines	Peso 118	2.78	29.0	42.4	–32	33
Poland	Zloty 8.63	3.09	2.12	.80	–24	21
Russia	Ruble 75.0	2.70	18.5	27.8	–34	10
Saudi Arabia	Riyal 10.0	2.67	2.46	3.75	–34	–3
Singapore	S$4.41	3.65	1.08	1.21	–10	–6
South Africa	Rand 19.45	2.87	4.78	6.77	-29	24
South Korea	Won 3 700	3.50	910	1.056	-14	21
Sweden	SKr 6.50	7.64	11.9	6.34	88	85
Switzerland	SFr 6.50	8.06	1.60	0.81	98	63
Taiwan	NT$75.0	2.60	18.5	28.8	–36	–7
Thailand	Baht 70.0	2.35	17.2	29.8	–42	6
Turkey	Lira 6.50	3.77	1.60	1.72	–7	53

*At current exchange rates; [†]Purchasing-power parity; local price divided by price in United States; [‡]Average of Atlanta, Chicago, New York and San Francisco; [§]Dollars per pound; **Weighted average of prices in euro area, [††]Dollars per euro; [§§]Maharaja Mac

Source: © The Economist Newspaper Limited, London, 2011.

You then compare this figure with the current exchange rate, which may be A$0.92 (inverse of AUD/USD 1.0870). This suggests that the A$ is 18 per cent overvalued and one would expect that the valuation will move to equilibrium over time.

The most successful application of the Big Mac index was when the euro was launched. The Big Mac index showed that the euro was overvalued. This was contrary to popular opinion and was ultimately proved to be correct.

Unfortunately, this method breaks some of the rules of PPP in that the Big Mac is not traded between countries, some countries have beef trade barriers and subsidies, and the cost of non-tradeable goods and services distorts prices. Because of this, this index is at best a rough guide and should generally not be taken too seriously by FX traders.

Balance of payments

The balance of payments (BoP) is a record of all transactions between one country and the rest of the world. The transactions are divided between three accounts:

1 the current account
2 the capital account
3 the balancing account.

In theory, the current account should be the equal and opposite of the capital account. In practice, the balancing account is used to ensure balance between the two.

The current account

The current account is a record of all exports and imports of goods and services, unrequited transfers and income transfers.

It has four sections:

1 The balance of merchandise trade is the difference between the export and import of goods.
2 Net services is the difference between service credits and debits; for example, the cost of transporting goods overseas

would be classified as a service credit whereas the export of the goods would appear in the balance of merchandise trade section as an export.

3 Net income is the difference between income sourced from other countries by local entities and income paid to foreign entities; for example, a dividend paid by the Australian telecommunications company Telstra to a United States citizen.

4 Current transfers are transfers for which there has been no exchange of goods or services; for example, withholding tax and foreign aid.

The balance on current account is the sum of these four sections:

Balance on current account = (Exports – Imports) + (Service credits – Service debits) + (Income credits – Income debits) + (Transfer credits – Transfer debits)

This is shown in figure 9.1.

Figure 9.1: the current account

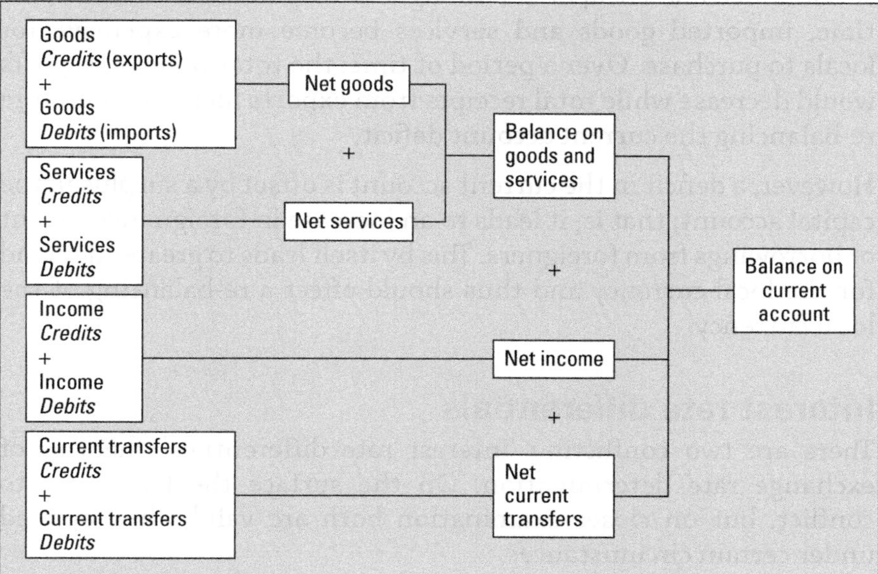

Note: debit entries are shown with a minus sign.

Source: Australian Bureau of Statistics.

The capital account

The capital account is, basically, a record of all foreign investment into a country and all investment made abroad. There are two sections to the capital account: net capital transactions by foreign entities and net capital transactions by local entities.

The difference between the two is known as the balance on capital and financial account, and is essentially the difference between capital inflows and capital outflows.

How does BoP affect foreign exchange?

The current account can have a significant impact on the foreign exchange rate. For example, an increase in the current account deficit may have come about by an increase in expenditure on imports and foreign services, and this in turn may have resulted in increased demand for foreign currencies and thus a greater supply of local currency. The outcome of this would be a decrease in foreign reserves and depreciation of the local currency in the short term. As a result of the lower value of the local currency, local goods and services become cheaper for foreigners to purchase. At the same time, imported goods and services become more expensive for locals to purchase. Over a period of time, the total value of imports would decrease while total receipts from exports increase, therefore re-balancing the current account deficit.

However, a deficit in the current account is offset by a surplus in the capital account; that is, it leads to an increase in foreign investment or borrowings from foreigners. This by itself leads to greater demand for the local currency and thus should effect a re-balancing of the local currency.

Interest rate differentials

There are two conflicting 'interest rate differentials' theories of exchange rate determination. On the surface the two seem to conflict, but on closer examination both are valid when applied under certain circumstances.

The first theory is based on the idea that changes in interest rates reflect changes in inflationary expectations. A rise in a country's interest rate relative to another country's reflects a loss of value of that country's currency due to inflation. Demand for the currency falls due to a perceived consistent loss of value, which results in a depreciation of that country's exchange rate. This theory holds when the deviation in inflation differential is large. For example, an increase in European Monetary Union (EMU) interest rates in a relatively high inflation environment reflects even higher inflationary expectations in the EMU. Investors will dump EMU assets due to a perceived consistent loss of value, which will subsequently result in a decrease in the EUR/USD exchange rate.

The second theory is based on the idea that changes in interest rates invite a global movement of capital that seeks the greatest return. Capital flows into the country with the highest interest rate return, resulting in greater demand for that currency. This results in appreciation of that country's exchange rate. The second theory holds when the deviation in inflation differential is small and is quick acting.

For example, an increase in British interest rates in a relatively low inflation environment will elevate the rate of return on British pounds above the rate of return on US dollars. Investors will transfer investments to British assets, which will result in an increase in the GBP/USD exchange rate.

There are other theories that combine variations of the two above, but they start to get into quite complicated derivations and, thus, are beyond the scope of this book.

Economic indicators

In this topic we will look at the reasons economic data releases are important and examine some of the more relevant ones.

Why are economic indicators important?

It is important for foreign exchange traders to have an understanding of the importance of economic indicators. Before an economic report is released, a multitude of analysts throughout the world postulate what the figures in the economic report may be. These analysts attempt to predict how these indicators, such as inflation, interest rates, balance of payments and many others, have an impact on a theory or combination of theories that they use to determine an intrinsic or theoretical value for the exchange rate. Many analyses may be written for the many players in the foreign exchange market. Thankfully, for smaller traders, quite a few of these reports are published and can be accessed through the internet. Websites where these reports may be obtained are <www.fxstreet.com>, <www.forexfactory.com> and <www.fxtimes.com>.

What we tend to find is that market participants generally arrive at a consensus about these figures and the market adjusts to a certain exchange rate prior to announcement based on consensus of the effect of the economic indicator on the exchange rate. A certain amount of speculative trading may take place based on a particular view that is out of step with consensus. Eventually, the market will find equilibrium before release of the economic indicator.

Once the figure is released, the amount by which the figure deviates and how it deviates from consensus determines the resulting short-term directional movement and volatility in the market. Traders may trade to bring their positions in line with the perceived effect the actual figure has on the exchange rate and speculators may trade to take profits or to cover losses.

Quite often you may find that, post-announcement, a market will move strongly in a particular direction before settling back, due to an effect known as the 'bandwagon effect'. The bandwagon effect occurs when traders become caught up in a group or herd mentality and the market tends to overrun what should be a comfortable value. Under such prevailing conditions, non-speculators can find it difficult to easily unwind their positions and this tends to push the market further than expected.

Economic indicator announcements are usually seen by hedge fund managers, who can build fairly large positions, as an opportune time to either take profits or to quickly cut losses. This dumping of the currency on the market may also tend to push the market excessively in a certain direction.

Economic reports

The most significant economic reports are looked at in the following pages. Traders need to be aware that they have an impact on their trade position.

Interest rate announcements

As you'll recall from chapter 5, central banks regulate short-term interest rates with the aim of achieving low and stable inflation in the medium term. The Federal Reserve in the United States ('the Fed') <www.federalreserve.gov> is the best known central bank. In the European Monetary Union, the European Central Bank (ECB) <www.ecb.int> Governing Council usually meets twice a month. At the first of the monthly meetings, the Governing Council makes monetary policy decisions. Following the first meeting, the President of the ECB explains the monetary policy decisions in detail at a press conference.

In China, the Monetary Policy Committee of the People's Bank of China (PBC) <www.pbc.gov.cn> meets approximately every three months and the Policy Board of the Bank of Japan conducts a Monetary Policy Meeting (MPM) once or twice a month <www.boj.or.jp/en/>. The Swiss National Bank (SNB) <www.snb.ch> sets a target rate for the Swiss franc following an assessment of its monetary policy in March, June, September and December each year. The Monetary Policy Committee (MPC) of the Bank of England <www.bankofengland.co.uk> meets monthly to set the official bank rate for the United Kingdom. In Australia, the Reserve Bank of Australia <www.rba.gov.au> meets every month except January to decide the target for the short-term interest rate, known as the 'cash rate'.

In the United States, the Federal Open Market Committee (FOMC) of the Federal Reserve meets eight times a year to formulate monetary policy. At the conclusion of the meeting, the FOMC announces the targeted federal funds rate and an explanation. The open market operations are the main tool by which the FOMC influences its targeted rate for federal funds, which is the rate at which banks lend excess federal funds to each other. Changes in the federal funds rate lead to changes in interest rates available to clients of financial institutions, and thus an effect is exerted upon aggregate demand within the economy and economic activity. The minutes of the FOMC meeting are published three weeks after the meeting and quite often provide a strong insight into the thinking of the Committee.

Figure 9.2 shows changes in the Federal Reserve federal funds rate over a 21-year period from 1990 to 2011.

Figure 9.2: Federal Reserve federal funds rate (per cent)

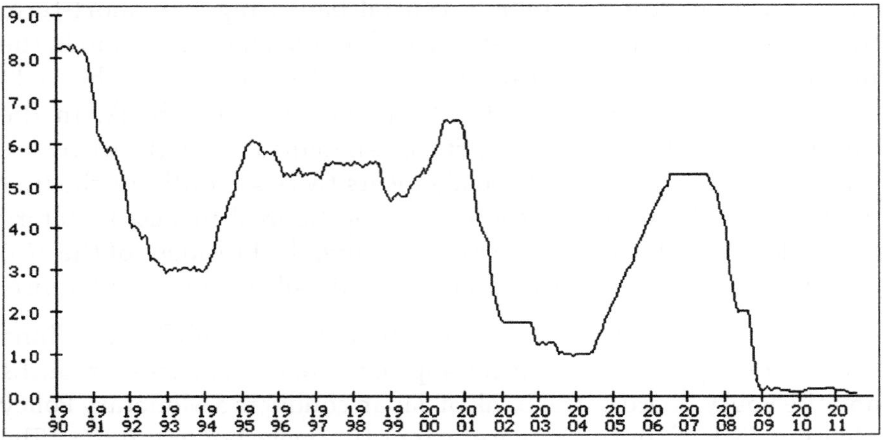

Source: <www.economagic.com>.

Quantitative policy

Quantitative policy is a tool rarely used by central banks to stimulate money supply when inter-bank interest rates are close to zero. A quantitative easing (QE) is effected when the central bank purchases bonds or mortgage securities from banks and financial institutions. Money supply is stimulated by the banks and financial institutions increasing reserves available for lending. The increase in demand for bonds leads to increased prices for them and thus lower yields and lower interest rates across the board. In theory, the increase in available credit at lower interest rates may increase aggregate demand and activity in the economy.

A quantitative easing policy was first adopted by the Bank of Japan in 2001. More recently, in the late 2000s the Bank of England, the European Central Bank (in a similar way) and the Federal Reserve with its famous 'QE1' and 'QE2' have implemented quantitative easing.

International trade in goods and services, BoP and the current account balance

The balance of payments is a record of all transactions between one country and the rest of the world, while the current account balance is a country's record of all exports and imports of goods and services, unrequited transfers and income transfers. Sometimes, in relatively small countries, such as Australia and New Zealand, the figures may be skewed by the purchase of very large and expensive items, for example, the purchase of a new fleet of jet aeroplanes.

Generally, international trade in goods and services figures are released monthly while the balance of payment and current account releases are made quarterly. The Census Bureau and the Bureau of Economic Analysis release the US international trade in goods and services data every month. United States international transactions are released quarterly by the Bureau of Economic Analysis <www.bea.gov>. Figure 9.3 shows the European Monetary Union current account transactions.

Figure 9.3: European Monetary Union current account transactions

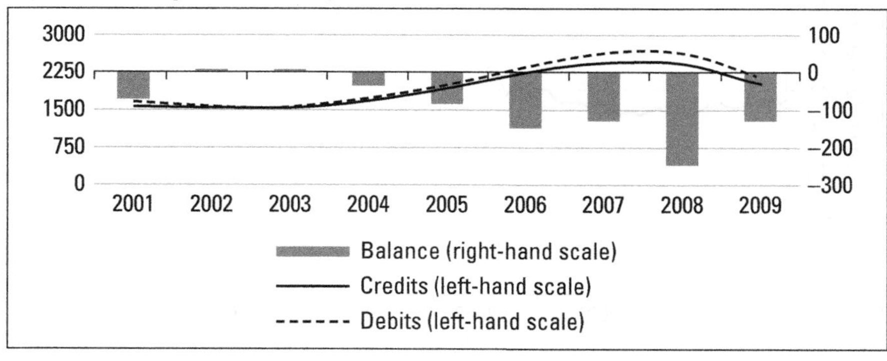

Source: © European Union, 1995–2011.

Employment and unemployment

Employment figures examine the number of people who have been involved in some form of work during a period, while unemployment figures examine the number of people who are without work, are actively seeking it and are available to do it.

In the United States, the national employment and unemployment figures are released every month by the Bureau of Labor Statistics <www.bls.gov>. The Australian Bureau of Statistics releases labour force figures every month in Australia. In New Zealand, employment figures are released every quarter by Statistics New Zealand, while in Switzerland, unemployment figures are released monthly and employment figures are released quarterly.

When comparing employment figures with the immediately preceding figure, it is important to look at the figure in a broader context. In figure 9.4, we can see that even though the current unemployment figure remains at high levels and is coming off a peak of over 10 per cent, the overall trend has begun to move down. This could affect the significance that some market players place on the current figures at high levels.

Figure 9.4: US unemployment rate (%)

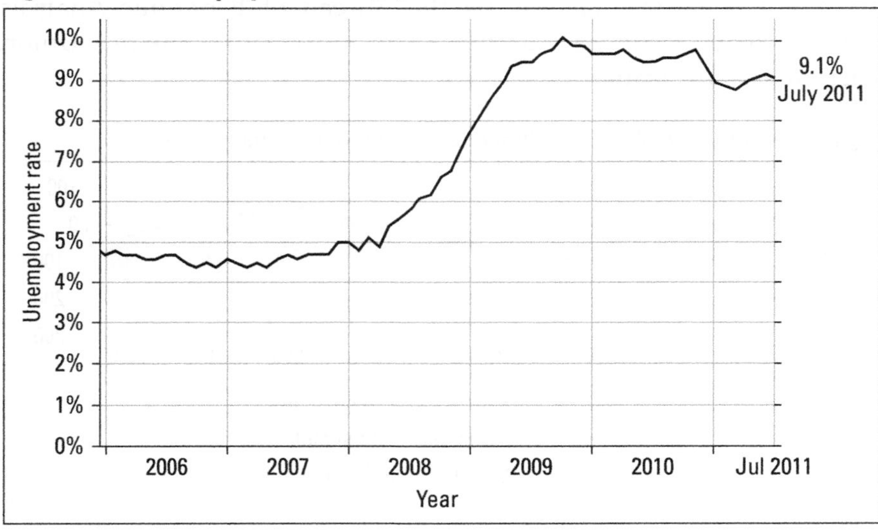

Inflation data

The best known inflation indicator is the consumer price index (CPI), which measures the change in value of a fixed basket of goods and services over a period of time. The producer price index (PPI), or the wholesale price index, measures the change in value of goods produced by a diverse range of manufacturers.

The US Bureau of Labor Statistics releases the CPI and the PPI every month in the United States. In Australia, the CPI is released quarterly by the Australian Bureau of Statistics. In New Zealand, the CPI is released quarterly by Statistics New Zealand, but in most major economies the figures are released monthly.

The chart in figure 9.5 shows the annual percentage changes in the harmonised index of consumer prices (HICP) for the European Monetary Union. The chart shows relatively stable inflation data from 2001 to 2008 and a very volatile period from 2008 to 2011.

Figure 9.5: HICP annual change, European Monetary Union

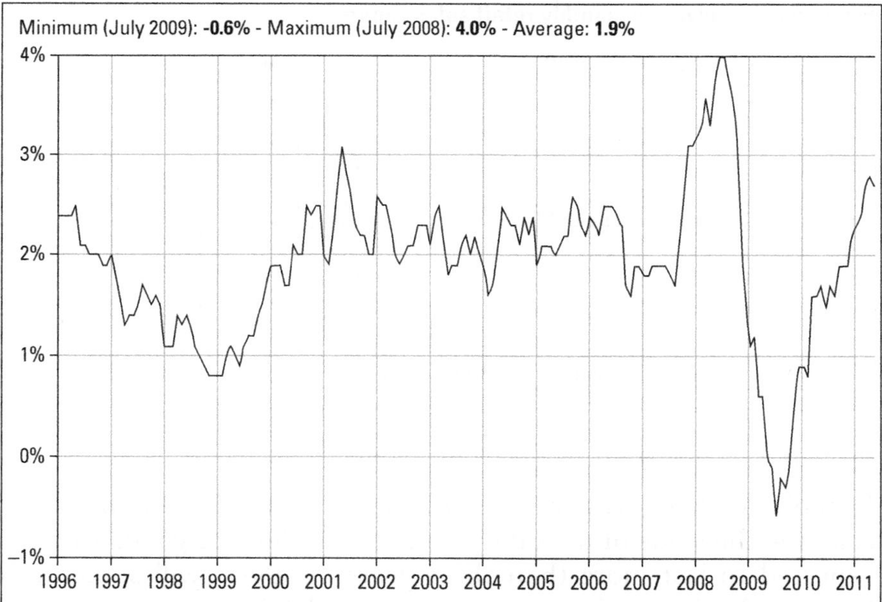

Source: © European Monetary Union.

Retail sales

Retail trade figures examine the value of goods sold by the retail trade to consumers. The US Census Bureau <www.census.gov> releases the US retail sales figures monthly in the United States. All of the other major currency countries also release retail sales figures every month.

These figures should always be viewed with caution. The monthly changes may often be erratic and the data may be subject to large revisions.

In the US advance monthly retail sales chart in figure 9.6, you can see that not only are total retail sales disclosed but also figures with some components excluded, which may skew the current figure. For example, you can see that the rise in total retail sales in the month of February was largely the result of greatly increased auto sales. Examining quarterly changes and trends in retail sales is also quite important when trading.

Figure 9.6: US advance monthly retail sales report

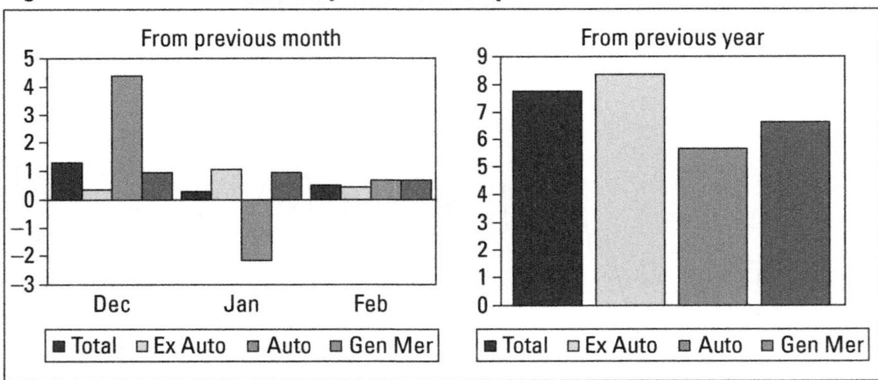

Durable goods

Durable goods figures are released in the United States only. They examine the value of manufacturers' new orders for goods that are expected to last more than three years. Analysts will sometimes focus on the data exclusive of transport and defence orders, as large orders for defence equipment and aircraft may skew the data. Non-defence capital goods orders may be used as a leading indicator of business investment in capital equipment.

The US Census Bureau releases the US durable goods figures every month. For example, figure 9.7 shows the month-to-month change in durable goods new orders from August 2009 to July 2010. Here we can see that durable goods orders picked up in July 2010 following two consecutive months of negative figures.

Figure 9.7: month-to-month change in durable goods new orders 2009–2010

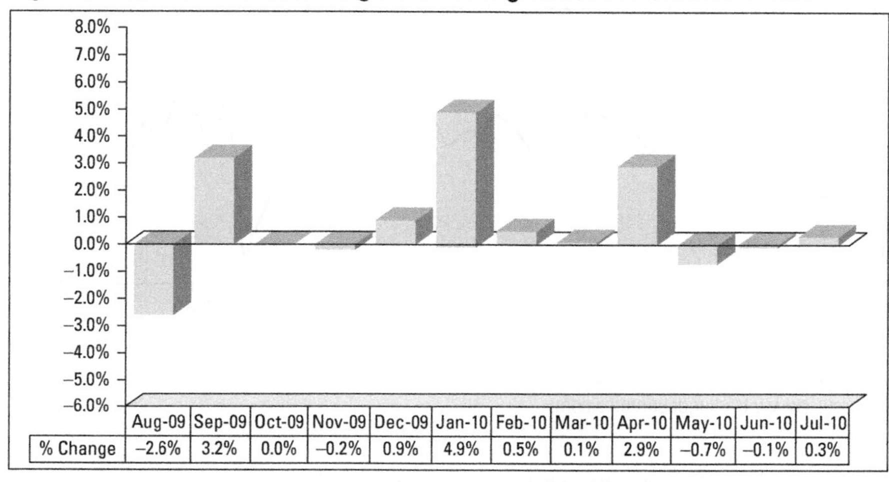

	Aug-09	Sep-09	Oct-09	Nov-09	Dec-09	Jan-10	Feb-10	Mar-10	Apr-10	May-10	Jun-10	Jul-10
% Change	−2.6%	3.2%	0.0%	−0.2%	0.9%	4.9%	0.5%	0.1%	2.9%	−0.7%	−0.1%	0.3%

Note: seasonally adjusted, month-to-month percentage change.

Gross domestic product

Gross domestic product (GDP) is often regarded as the best indicator of economic activity in a country. It examines the value of *all* goods and services produced by a country. Unfortunately, there is a considerable lag in the figures, which are only produced every three months.

Gross domestic product figures are released quarterly in all of the major currency countries. Figure 9.8 (overleaf) shows the annual change in real GDP in Japan. Real GDP is the inflation-adjusted value of GDP. It gives analysts an accurate measure of the volume of domestic output as opposed to the value of GDP given by the raw figure.

From figure 9.8 we can clearly see the cyclical nature of GDP and the economy as evidenced by well-defined peaks and troughs. We can also see that, at the end of the chart, even though GDP is negative and falling, the decline seems to have lost some downside momentum.

Figure 9.8: real GDP annual growth rate, Japan

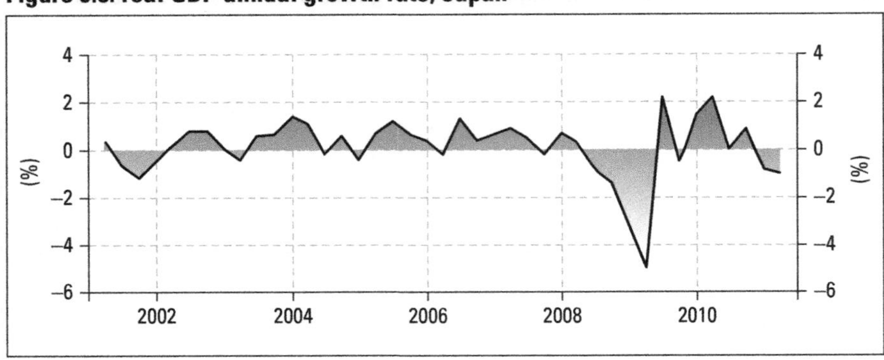

Note: annual GDP growth adjusted by inflation.
Source: <www.tradingeconomics.com>.

Economic reports schedule

Table 9.2 is a brief guide to the frequency of release of some of the more significant economic reports.

Table 9.2: schedule of frequency of release of significant economic reports

Economic report	Country/region	Frequency
Interest rates	USA	Eight times per year
	European Monetary Union	Monthly
	Japan	Once or twice per month
	United Kingdom	Monthly
	Switzerland	Quarterly
	Australia	Every month except January
	Canada	Eight times per year
	New Zealand	Every six weeks
International trade in goods and services	USA	Monthly
	European Monetary Union	Monthly
	Japan	Monthly
	United Kingdom	Monthly
	Switzerland	Monthly
	Australia	Monthly
	Canada	Monthly
	New Zealand	Monthly

Balance of payments	USA	Quarterly
	European Monetary Union	Quarterly
	Japan	Quarterly
	United Kingdom	Quarterly
	Switzerland	Quarterly
	Australia	Quarterly
	Canada	Quarterly
	New Zealand	Quarterly
Current account balance	USA	Quarterly
	European Monetary Union	Quarterly
	Japan	Quarterly
	United Kingdom	Quarterly
	Switzerland	Quarterly
	Australia	Quarterly
	Canada	Quarterly
	New Zealand	Quarterly
Employment and unemployment	USA	Monthly (jobless claims weekly)
	European Monetary Union	Monthly
	Japan	Monthly
	United Kingdom	Monthly
	Switzerland	Monthly (unemployment) and quarterly (employment)
	Australia	Monthly
	Canada	Monthly
	New Zealand	Quarterly
Inflation data	USA	Monthly
	European Monetary Union	Monthly
	Japan	Monthly
	United Kingdom	Monthly
	Switzerland	Monthly
	Australia	Quarterly
	Canada	Monthly
	New Zealand	Quarterly

(cont'd)

Table 9.2 ***(cont'd)*****: schedule of frequency of release of significant economic reports.**

Economic report	Country/region	Frequency
Retail sales	USA	Monthly
	European Monetary Union	Monthly
	Japan	Monthly
	United Kingdom	Monthly
	Switzerland	Monthly
	Australia	Monthly
	Canada	Monthly
	New Zealand	Monthly
Durable goods	USA	Monthly
Gross domestic product	USA	Quarterly
	European Monetary Union	Quarterly
	Japan	Quarterly
	United Kingdom	Quarterly
	Switzerland	Quarterly
	Australia	Quarterly
	Canada	Quarterly
	New Zealand	Quarterly

Sources of economic information

The following institutions and government bodies will be of great use to the retail FX trader. Fortunately, all of the information you will need to stay up to date with FX fundamentals is only a mouse click away. For information such as that outlined above and much more besides, look up the following sources:

- Central bank websites <www.bis.org/cbanks.htm>
- US Federal Reserve <www.federalreserve.gov>
- The European Central Bank <www.ecb.int>
- The Bank of Japan <www.boj.or.jp/en>
- The Swiss National Bank <www.snb.ch>
- The Bank of England <www.bankofengland.co.uk>
- Reserve Bank of Australia <www.rba.gov.au>
- Reserve Bank of New Zealand <www.rbnz.govt.nz>

- The People's Bank of China <www.pbc.gov.cn/publish/english/963/index.html>
- OECD Statistics <http://stats.oecd.org/Index.aspx>
- US Economics and Statistics Administration <www.economicindicators.gov>
- US Bureau of Economic Analysis <www.bea.gov>
- US Bureau of Labor Statistics <www.bls.gov>
- US Census Bureau <www.census.gov>
- European Commission EuroStats <http://epp.eurostat.ec.europa.eu/portal/page/portal/eurostat/home>
- Japan Statistics Bureau and Statistics Centre <www.stat.go.jp/english>
- Swiss Statistics—Swiss Federal Statistical Office <www.statistics.admin.ch>
- UK National Statistics <www.statistics.gov.uk>
- Australian Bureau of Statistics <www.abs.gov.au>
- Statistics New Zealand <www.stats.govt.nz>
- National Bureau of Statistics of China <www.stats.gov.cn/english>
- Financial Times <www.ft.com>
- The Wall Street Journal <www.wsj.com>
- International Business Times <www.ibtimes.com>
- Nikkei.com <http://e.nikkei.com/e/fr/freetop.aspx>
- The Australian Financial Review <www.afr.com.au>
- China Business News <http://cnbusinessnews.com>
- Economic Observer (China) <eeo.com.cn/ens>
- Bloomberg <www.bloomberg.com>
- Reuters <www.reuters.com>
- The Economist <www.economist.com>
- Economagic <www.economagic.com>
- Econoday <http://econoday.com>
- FX Street portal <www.fxstreet.com>
- Forex TV portal <www.forextv.com>
- Forex Factory <www.forexfactory.com>
- FX Times <www.fxtimes.com>

- [illegible] Bank of [illegible] Data <www.[illegible]/[illegible]/english/[illegible]>
- OECD Statistics <http://stats.oecd.org/Index.aspx>
- [illegible] Economics and Statistics Administration <www.esa.doc.gov>
- US Bureau of Economic Analysis <www.bea.gov>
- US Bureau of Labor Statistics <www.bls.gov>
- US Census Bureau <www.census.gov>
- European Commission Eurostat <http://epp.eurostat.ec.europa.eu/portal/page/portal/eurostat/home>
- Japan Statistics Bureau and Statistics Centre <www.stat.go.jp/english>
- Swiss Statistics — Swiss Federal Statistical Office <www.statistics.admin.ch>
- UK National Statistics <www.statistics.gov.uk>
- Australian Bureau of Statistics <www.abs.gov.au>
- Statistics New Zealand <www.stats.govt.nz>
- National Bureau of Statistics of China <www.stats.gov.cn/english>
- Financial Times <www.ft.com>
- The Wall Street Journal <www.wsj.com>
- International Business Times <www.ibtimes.com>
- [illegible]
- The Sydney Morning Herald <www.smh.com.au>
- China Business News <http://cnbusinessnews.com>
- Bloomberg (Australia) <www.bloomberg.com/[illegible]>
- [illegible]
- [illegible]
- [illegible]
- [illegible]
- [illegible]
- [illegible]
- [illegible]

Chapter 10

FX trading at the big end of town

Institutional foreign exchange is the big end of town when it comes to the FX market. This is the home of the inter-bank and wholesale market. Though bigger, it is by no means necessarily any more able in its ability to assess and profit from the FX market.

However, unlike the little person, what institutional investors can do as a group will sometimes have a large bearing on short to medium moves in the currency markets. Therefore, knowing who they are, what they do and why they do it will give retail traders (us little people) the chance to survive and hopefully thrive in what is an enormous sea of money trading on the inter-bank and wholesale markets across the globe in 100+ currency pairs. This chapter is designed to orientate our place in the broader landscape of this, the largest of the world's financial markets!

What is institutional FX?

Basically, institutional FX is the big end of town when it comes to foreign exchange. And don't forget, we are talking about a $4 trillion or more a day business, so to be 'big' in this business means huge amounts of funds being traded at the bat of an eye. While it is standard to trade $5- to $10-million parcels, very often $100- to $500-million parcels are quoted. Compare that with *your* likely trading position and you can quickly see that retail online traders are dwarves in a market for giants. But what is important (and comforting) to note is that even these guys are vulnerable to market moves and they too are subject to market volatility. What this means in a practical sense is that, because the market is simply too big, no one player can hope to control this largest of the world's financial markets.

Recall the discussion about George Soros. Soros's Quantum Fund, though famous for winning in the FX market against the Bank of England in 1992, has in its turn lost substantial amounts of money (many hundreds of millions of dollars) betting against the USD/YEN exchange rate in 1995. As even a man of this wealth and phenomenal trading expertise found out, he was not as big as the market. The lesson is a palpable one: no-one is bigger than the market—even the major global brand-name banks can't lay claim to being able to swing markets. Thus, so-called insider information is not only hard to come by, but it is also quite doubtful that even if someone did have such information it would be of anything but passing or very limited value.

The players

The players are the participants in the market who have a minute-by-minute commitment to and focus on the FX market and rates. This is where millions of dollars are in play (and at risk!) and for that reason they are very active participants in the markets, hence the term 'players'.

Banks

Whether big or smaller scale, banks participate in the currency markets both from the point of view of managing their own foreign exchange risks and that of their clients. They also speculate, should their dealer/traders have a particularly strong view of the market. What probably distinguishes them from other players is their unique access to the buying and selling interest of their clients. This knowledge can give them an insight to the likely buying/selling pressures on the exchange rates on a particular day or another small time frame.

Deals are transacted by telephone, with brokers (we will talk about these people later) or via electronic dealing terminal connection to their counterparty. The usual transaction time is somewhere between five and ten seconds, so the foreign exchange dealer requires good reflexes and decisiveness, particularly when we are talking about multi-million-dollar transactions.

Because of the tremendous sums of money involved, the foreign exchange dealing desk is invariably the hub of the banks' and other institutions' FX trading operations. The size of a bank's FX operation will, of course, be commensurate with the amount of money being traded through the organisation. Often, the larger the transactions, the larger the room and number of dealers, and thus the greater the ability of the firm to have specialist dealers in currencies or forward foreign exchange markets.

The ostensible role of the foreign exchange dealing desk in a bank or other financial company is to make profits by trading currency directly and in the managing of in-house and clients' trading positions. However, their roles will also include periodic hedging or arbitrage opportunities as part of their normal funding activities, especially if a bank or banking system needs funding beyond the abilities of their home country's depositers' capacity in deficit countries like Australia and New Zealand.

Brokers

The foreign exchange broker acts as an agent in the same way a stockbroker acts in the sharemarket. The slight difference is that they usually confine themselves to acting between inter-bank market participants and do not accept orders from corporate clients.

The broker firstly examines what is on offer from all potential participants. He or she then selects the highest bid and lowest offer, and combines them to establish the best two-way price 'the market' can provide, and displays or verbalises this for all to see and hear.

Brokers, through their extensive and direct electronic contacts with the banks, take and match currency buying and selling orders of their bank clients. They do this, of course, for a fee, but the value to banks using this service is that it is usually quick (orders can be placed and dealt in a matter of seconds) and it avoids the bank having to deal on a competitor's price (and thus pay a 'spread' on the transaction). A lot of the broking functions have been significantly computerised, cutting out the need for human handling of the orders.

How brokers work

Assume four banks provide the following quotes in the AUD/USD:

Bank A: 1.1020/25
Bank B: 1.1021/26
Bank C: 1.1019/24
Bank D: 1.1022/27

The broker selects the highest bid (bank D) and lowest offer (bank C) and combines them to establish the best two-way price 'the market' can provide.

Thus they show 1.1022/24.

Central banks

The majority of developed market economies have a central bank. The roles of central banks tend to be diverse and differ from country to country. In Australia, the central bank is the Reserve Bank of Australia and it is charged with the responsibility of maintaining an orderly market for the national currency, the Australian dollar.

In a practical sense, this involves the RBA monitoring and checking the prices dealt in the inter-bank market. Sometimes it even 'tests' market prices by actually dealing on them to check the integrity of quoted prices. In extreme circumstances, where the Reserve Bank feels prices are out of alignment with broad fundamental economic values, it may 'intervene' in the market to influence its level directly. The intervention can take the form of direct buying (to push the price up) or selling (to push the price down). Another tactic it adopts as often as the practical step of entering the market is that of 'jaw-boning'; that is, commenting in the media about its 'preferred' level for the currency.

In other countries, central bank regulation and sometimes intervention takes many forms and is a function of the type of currency regime that the particular central monetary authority would operate, as well its own acquired 'style' and historical policy of the country.

Since 1945 China, for instance, has had a policy that essentially was one of a fixed currency — even though it has 'allowed' narrow trading bands around this fixed rate, it is still essentially a fixed currency.

Japan comes closest in our region to a managed float. The yen is officially a free-floating currency; however, the Bank of Japan has intervened in the FX market periodically to influence the exchange rate — usually to contain its appreciation against the US dollar.

For currencies such as the Australian, US and New Zealand dollars which are relatively free floating regimes, their central banks still intervene (rarely) to influence their exchange rates according to dictates of policy circumstances. The bottom line is, regardless of the official currency regime, central banks around the world do play an active, if not regular, part in the dynamics of FX markets.

A case of this was shown quite recently where the export-led Japanese economy was seen as very vulnerable to a rise in the yen following the major earthquake and resultant tsunami of 11 March 2011. Immediately following the catastrophe the yen moved higher in anticipation that many corporations and individuals would repatriate their money in order to finance the significant rebuilding. Traders and speculators exacerbated the rise by buying yen. At this time of a rising yen the world's major central banks began coordinating their efforts. The Bank of Japan began by selling yen and was soon joined by the European Central Bank, followed by the Bank of England and then the US Federal Reserve and the Bank of Canada, an intervention that was seen as largely successful.

Centrals banks are not always successful in their efforts to stem or turn exchange rate trends by themselves (as shown by the failed Bank of England defence of the pound in 1992 against George Soros and other speculative funds), but when they cooperate and agree on a common aim or goal they tend to be far more effective. Central banks can and do talk and cooperate with each other to make their individual FX market interventions more successful.

In the aftermath of the 2008 financial crisis and into 2011, the dominant central bank strategy in both developed and emerging economies appears to be to mitigate currency pressures to rise against the US dollar and other currencies; that is, against each other. Depreciation of one currency automatically means an appreciation of another currency so not all currencies can appreciate against each other. This is a conundrum that the world's central banks currently face, where most famously both the US and China, the two largest economies of the world, are embroiled in a currency devaluation contest with countries favouring a weaker currency to bolster their own exports and import substitution industries, and, in the US's case, to try to wind back its yawning trade (deficit) imbalance with China. Bankers, fund managers and companies all tend to respect the opinions of the central banks (if not always agreeing), as their sheer financial power to borrow or print money gives them a huge say in the value of a currency. Their opinions and comments should never be ignored and it is always good practice to keep up with their comments, be it in the media or on their websites.

A central bank has other responsibilities that include managing the government's and the nation's foreign exchange reserves and interest rate policy, both of which can be powerful indirect influences on the currency's value at any particular point in time. Money and currency markets are very sensitive to rates of return being offered by various markets (that is, interest rates).

The CLS Bank

CLS stands for 'continuous linked settlement' and was founded in 2002 to mitigate the settlement risks that inter-bank traders have with each other; that is, the risk that your counterparty fails after you have paid them your side of an FX deal and they have not paid their side. This actually happened with the famous (in FX circles) collapse of the German Herstatt Bank in 1974, which right up until the day it was forced to shut by the German central bank, the Bundesbank, was busily selling US dollars to US banks (in European time) and accepting the US banks' deutsche marks in FX transactions only to close forever, never honouring its side of the bargain and leaving the US banks out of pocket.

Since then moves have been towards the establishment of a centralised clearing system, the CLS Bank, which eliminates that risk. More than 75 per cent of the world's FX trades occur under the aegis of the CLS Bank.

Originally composed of member banks and for only the top seven or so currencies, the pool of CLS currencies has expanded and now includes non-bank participants looking to mitigate their settlement risks. Even hedge funds ask to have their trade deals settled through the CLS system, bypassing banks that otherwise have direct access.

The CLS system officially does not 'trade' in the FX market. Nonetheless it is important to distinguish CLS cleared from non-CLS currencies as the FX market implicitly now differentiates between CLS and CLS currencies, and indeed between CLS members and non-CLS members. This increases the cost of dealing outside the scope of the CLS clearing system.You will probably not notice the difference except when you try to trade a non-CLS currency or compare a CLS cleared with a non-cleared FX provider.

The section at the end of the chapter lists CLS cleared currencies (member banks have not been included because they run into the many thousands).

Corporations

Corporations include companies and businesses of any size (from small to multi-billion-dollar enterprises) that are compelled by the nature of their business to engage in commercial or capital transactions that require them to either purchase or sell foreign currency.

These commercial transactions could be a function of these corporations selling goods overseas and being paid in foreign currency, or conversely companies may need to buy foreign currency to pay for goods sourced from overseas. Additional to their payment needs, they could also approach the foreign exchange markets with a view to either borrowing or lending foreign currency.

Traditionally, corporations have been divided between those that need to buy the local currency, known as 'exporters' (they have foreign currency to sell) and those that need to sell the local currency to buy foreign currency, known as 'importers'.

Corporations can and do operate on both sides of the market, often having foreign payables and receipts to deal with at different times. This constant, two-way flow ostensibly gave opportunities for corporations to actively manage and even speculate on exchange rate trends. However, since the early 2000s this has fallen out of favour among most conservative firms that have witnessed a few too many currency/derivative trading disasters in both banks and in other corporations. Since the introduction of the international hedge accounting standard IAS 39 and the US equivalent FASB 133 companies have tended to passively protect and hedge their currency risks, essentially keeping their FX transactions to a need-to-do basis.

Fund managers

Fund managers in the currency markets are basically international and domestic money managers. They tend to deal in the hundreds of millions, as their pools of investment funds are very large. And, because of their investment charters and obligations to their investors, they are constantly seeking the best investment opportunities. The opportunities of course may not all be found in Australia, nor are the fund managers necessarily domiciled in Australia. Accordingly, they seek out the best investment markets, and in order to access them they may need to use the currency markets. They invest money across a range of countries and classes of investments on behalf of a range of different clients, including pension funds, individual investors, governments and central banks.

Increasingly, this segment of the foreign exchange market is exerting a greater influence on currency trends and values, as fund managers tend to be very active and sensitive to market conditions.

Hedge funds

Hedge funds are a special class of fund manager. They are also now referred to by their more appropriate name of 'absolute returns funds'. These high-end funds are generally more concerned with managing the total risk of a pooled investment than just relative performance which preoccupies traditional fund managers. They tend to be more aggressive in their investment approaches and so will be found adopting investment strategies such as borrowing to realise leverage potential and using derivatives (though the extent of leverage has decreased since the 1998 Long-Term Capital Management debacle and more since the financial crisis of 2008). They are relatively small in comparison to traditional funds (though high in profile), but are continuing to grow at an exponential rate, with US$2 trillion now under hedge fund management according to the Reserve Bank of Australia's August 2011 statement of monetary policy.

By their 'alternative' investment nature, hedge funds tend to be a diverse bunch, with many having peculiar niche aims, styles and methods. Hedge funds in FX markets can range from pure currency funds (that speculate on exchange rate moves) to those that include:

- FX cash funds
- futures-based FX trading funds
- 'macro' funds that take economy or even regional wide 'bets' in FX markets
- 'carry trade' funds that borrow in low interest rate countries and invest
- arbitrage funds (we will talk about these a little later).

Even hedge funds not directly concerned with FX markets tend to have their own particular impact if their activities are of a cross-border nature; for example, borrowing in one country's markets to invest in another, picking up along the way a return in foreign currency trade.

Dealing centres

Major dealing centres do not necessarily reside in the one geographic centre. Indeed, the global FX clientele is quite dispersed and as a consequence so is the market as a whole. When it comes to FX, it is simply not possible, as is the case for the equities markets, for the market to be located on formal exchanges or at national centre points. In practice, the foreign exchange market is made up of a network of dealers and traders clustered in various hubs across the globe. They are linked via computer terminals, telex, fax, phone and the internet or internet-based dealing platforms to form a diverse global market where prices and information are freely exchanged. In other words, there is no single 'centre' in this market.

However, the foreign exchange market has prominent and major dealing centres roughly geographically located in London, New

York and Tokyo. We generally call these the major centres, not just because of the sheer size of the volumes and the number of market participants in their vicinity, but also because the happenings in these places tend to influence other dealing centres around the world. These other smaller centres include Sydney, Singapore, Hong Kong, Switzerland and Frankfurt, and they tend to take up the remaining balance of traded global flows. Thus, these three major and five minor centres are the regions that set the pace of currency transactions across the globe.

It is worth bearing in mind that the information mentioned above has practical implications for FX dealing, regardless of your level of sophistication. It forces everyone, including the small retail trader, to be aware of the most recent leading centre's trading activity. In the case of an FX trader in Australia, it means that at the start of the trading day looking to the US market action will give some clue about the likely direction of the local morning session. After this, a few hours into the session, it is normal to keep an eye on the course of action emanating from the Tokyo market (to our north), as it plays its part in influencing the course of Australian currency trading trends.

Don't forget, this applies not just to market activity, but also inactivity. If these centres are together or separately on holidays, don't be surprised if Sydney trading also tends to go quiet. Holidays have a bearing on the general flow of business and price activity (or lack thereof). Hence, it is a good idea to keep a calendar of major international holidays as part of your research, so you can recall these in planning particular trades.

Market makers and price discovery

What we mean by 'price discovery' is that the marketplace is the place where buyers and sellers want to trade their side of a transaction. Given that the 'grade' of their transaction is clear (their currency), all that the FX market really serves to do is provide a 'price'. This is where market makers come in. Market makers are almost always banks, and their job is to provide a price to the market. In that process, an FX currency price is revealed or, in other words, 'discovered'.

To be considered a market maker, a bank must be prepared to quote a two-way price (a bid and an offer). Their bid is the market maker's 'buying' price, and their offer price is their selling price to all other enquiring market principals, whether or not they are market makers in that particular currency. The price rates are quoted over the telephone, electronically via digital dealing platforms or, less frequently nowadays, by telex to dealers in other countries.

Being a market maker, reputation is important; they must be reliable and of the highest integrity, otherwise clients or other market makers will not deal with them. The people who actually buy or sell the currency are called foreign exchange dealers or traders. These traders make their money by the difference between their buying price and their selling price—their spread. These spreads are extremely fine for large inter-bank parcels; for instance, in the AUD on a parcel of, say, 10 million USD, it is only five fourth decimal places. In such a case, quoted as, say, 1.0005/10, the difference between the two prices adds up to US$5000 profit to the market maker. Not a bad profit if all they do is quote the price and people buy and sell off both sides, but still rather fine compared with those that existed in days gone past.

The following example of a typical Reuters terminal-based conversation shows how clipped the conversations sometimes are between inter-bank dealers. It may also look a little like jargon; however, it is not really that hard to follow once you understand the basic intentions of either side.

Inter-bank foreign exchange dealing at its most terse:

Bank A: oz 10
Bank B: 5–10
Bank A: big figure please
Bank B: 1.1005/10
Bank A: at 5
Bank B: that's done thks
Bank A: bibi fn

Briefly, Bank A in the above conversation is the price taker; that is, he or she is asking for Bank B's price in the Australian dollar versus the US dollar, simply by saying 'oz'. The amount that they wish to transact is A$10 million (as the base currency in the quote).

The answer that Bank B gives is simply the two-way price (as the last two decimal places). However, to avoid ambiguity, Bank A has asked for confirmation of the big figure of the price. Bank B responds with 1.1005/10, the long form of the price.

At this point Bank A states what 'side' it would like to deal: 'at 5', meaning the bid side. We now know Bank A wants to sell A$10 million at 1.1005 US per Australian dollar. Bank B confirms the deal as 'done'. Bank A simply says 'bye bye for now'.

Currency arbitrage

Arbitrage is something you will hear mentioned a lot in FX circles. However, for the small retail investor, it is usually something that is talked about a lot more than it is actually practically taken advantage of. Mostly, it happens at the big end, and when it does it is extremely swift and often very profitable.

Let's have a look at an example.

Assume you are a dealer quoting USD/JPY in the currency market and your current price is 85.00/10. This means you buy US dollars at 85.00 and are willing to sell dollars (for yen) at 85.10. You notice one of your competitors is quoting 85.03/13; that is, they are willing to bid (or buy) at 85.03 and willing to offer (sell) at 85.13.

Now let's further assume that you are worried that the USD may fall. To avoid people selling to you (you buying at 85.00), you lower your price to, say, 84.85/95. Now look what happens.

At this point, a third-party bank notices the price you are now quoting (based on your fears of a fall) and the other, less-worried bank's price at 85.03/13. In a *flash*, the third-party bank will have taken your offer (bought USD from you at 84.95) and will be simultaneously selling the USD back to the other bank still quoting a bid of 85.03.

Bingo! This third-party (who we will now call an 'arbitrager') will have just succeeded in making a riskless profit from you and your competitor's lazy pricing.

Implications and limitations of arbitrage

To prevent 'arbitraging' of a market maker's price, all market makers endeavour to keep their price spread overlapping their immediate competitors. And widening a spread is regarded as 'poor form' for a market maker. Thus, the competitive discipline forces market makers to have the same spread; any wider and basically no-one in the know will ever deal with them on their risk-averse pricing.

As can be seen in this example, because of the pressures of time and the sensitivity of foreign exchange rates changing at any moment, it is in the interests of an arbitrager to ensure both parties transact almost immediately. Thus, the above transaction would normally take all of about 15 to 20 seconds. This is not a place for the indecisive!

Clearly, for the market maker, this price-making function is not a risk-free exercise. The risk of course is that they may give or be 'taken' on their price and may subsequently be forced to sell at lower, or buy at higher, levels. Indeed, this risk is not just a theoretical risk, it is a very real risk and a not unlikely occurrence that prices move against the dealer. To mitigate this somewhat, the prices set by market makers are constantly adjusted to reflect either their risk or their view of the market (while at the same time not providing a price that may otherwise lead to an arbitrage).

As the previous example of arbitrage shows, FX dealers have to be very quick to ensure they are never too far away from the market, even if they have a particularly strong view on the currency.

Note also that in the practical environment of the dealing room and inter-bank currency trading desk, the task of speaking to clients and that of making prices is usually separated; that is, one person will be considered a specialist in charge of 'making prices', usually the chief FX dealer, assisted by another spot FX dealer. This person or team tends to occupy a central place within a dealing room environment so that they are accessible to everyone, easily and quickly (usually to give out prices).

The benefit of this is that when clients contact a bank, they will receive its most up-to-date price direct from its original source. If you were to ring another dealer at the same time, you would get the same price. (Note, though, this is not to say you will necessarily get the same price if you ring another bank.) As some banks and market makers have found out, it is all about ensuring consistency of pricing, mixed with a judicious degree of risk management.

Don't forget that the banks are not charities; they are there to make a profit and will seek to do so whenever a market opportunity presents itself. An example could be if a particular institution has a large individual order to buy AUD, and on the basis of this order it also seeks to accumulate AUD to mitigate its newly acquired risk. Crucially, banks will not necessarily be in a position to tell other clients of this reasoning (mostly for ethical, privacy and commercial reasons). So on this basis, FX traders should generally take it as a given that market makers have access to more information than they do and may not always be in a position to — or be willing to — pass it on.

In the post-2008 financial crisis world, a significant number of financial institutions (at least temporarily) have become financially impaired, so credit is more expensive because of its relative scarcity. This has the effect of restricting major FX trading banks from potential opportunities as credit rationing forces major market players to be more discerning in what markets and geographies they trade in, and when to trade.

The 21st century generation of FX broking and trading

One of the great challenges to the institutional foreign exchange market has been the emergence of the internet and internet-based trading platforms. These changes have challenged the very domain of institutional investors and how they conduct their foreign exchange business.

On the electronic broking side, systems such as EBS (short for 'electronic broking system') and Reuters are providing computer platforms where bank dealers and traders can input their prices directly to the computer without the need for a human broker to take their prices down. This includes the process of collecting prices from all contributing banks automatically. And, because of the instantaneous response of these platforms, prices are not just indicative, they are the actual dealing prices. This has, in turn, significantly speeded up the process of price discovery and also contributed to the market's overall transparency, while at the same time reducing the costs to participating banks.

There is an ongoing rationalisation in the industry that will continue as computers increasingly take over tasks once done purely by employed brokers and give rise to new types of traders and platforms.

High-frequency and algorithmic traders, and dark pools

Labels such as 'dark pools' and 'algorithmic trading' sound ominous to those not familiar with the latest innovations in trading platform technology and the peculiar subset of hedge funds called 'high frequency'.

High-frequency trader and trading (HFTs for short) relate to highly mathematically oriented traders (and funds) that employ computerised algorithms to analyse real-time market data, and then order and execute proprietary trading strategies at nanosecond speeds. As is implied, HFT traders and funds are very sensitive to the processing speeds of markets as well as the type of access to the market that they obtain in order to operate.

These traders are not long-term holders of trading positions. They very often hold the positions for less than a few seconds and seldom carry a position at the end of the day. They are likely to trade several hundred times a day in extreme situations.

In the US it is estimated 70 per cent of equity trades are likely to be of HFT origin, with evidence it is rapidly gaining popularity in Asia and Europe and acceptance in currency markets as well, with only advances in technology determining its rate of uptake.

Algorithmic traders are a subset of HFTs. Entering trading orders is done with a computer algorithm deciding aspects of the trading order, such as when, the price and the quantity of the order, without necessarily any human intervention. Algorithmic trading is used by banks to hedge risks or clear positions automatically in an efficient manner and to reduce their risks. For investors and other participants it is used to execute their strategies, whether to break up trades, to reduce impact or indeed to identify arbitrage opportunities across a range of price points or market makers. It is estimated 40 per cent of all FX trades are initiated this way, where it was estimated to be only 30 per cent in 2007.

Algorithmic traders are attracting the attention of market regulators such as the International Council of Securities Associations and the Australian Securities and Investments Commission (ASIC) which, while broadly supportive of technological innovation in the market, are committed to risk managed as well as efficient exchange trading institutions.

While these algorithmic traders are more 'famous' in working the world's more advanced equity traded exchanges, they also operate in the foreign exchange markets. It is these types of traders that have been blamed for the 'flash' crash of 6 May 2010, where the Dow Jones index fell around 900 points or about 9 per cent towards the end of the trading day, only to recover those losses within minutes. A lot of the blame for the 'crash' was directed at HFTs and algorithmic traders who were found to have withdrawn from the market for a time, only to return on the rebound.

Dark pools are where large trades by financial institutions are offered and exchanged away from public exchanges (and gaze) so that trades are anonymous. The fragmentation of financial trading into separate and competing platforms and markets, as well as the rise of electronic trading overall has allowed the creation of dark pools. They are normally accessed through private exchanges or directly between market participants. The advantage of dark pools to institutional investors is that it offers many of the efficiencies associated with trading on the exchanges' public limit order books, but without showing their actions to others, so by being anonymous they avoid the commercial disadvantage of people knowing their identity and their intentions.

While FX markets are in the main over the counter or direct counterparty markets, the issue of dark pools is less of a concern here historically than in equities markets. Nonetheless, the rise of electronic (and virtual) exchanges and broking services has presented the big end of town with even more choices and challenges of which to avail itself in foreign exchange at nano speeds.

Institutional online portals and the rise and rise of electronic brokers

As if the changes in the FX broking industry were not enough, increasingly the task of customer/order matching is being automated. This has led to the human element of the brokering process being virtually dispensed with altogether. This does not mean humans do not decide to put orders on or take them off, but the number of people involved when an order is put to the trading system and when it is dealt and matched by a counterparty is being reduced by technology. The system is called 'straight through processing'—the automatic processing of an order as soon as it becomes 'live'.

FX internet portals perform this automated processing and, in doing so, they have made FX trading available to a much wider audience of traders (and not just bank traders either). Indeed, because of the competitive pressures of the marketplace, FX participants of all types are being given a choice of available trading and processing systems (on all scales of transaction). Some of these new trading platforms include FXall, FXconnect, Atriax and hotspotfx.com. (All of these are easily available on the web for your further research.)

Generally speaking they fall into three types of platform—a single bank, multi-bank, or an official 'exchange' platform. These platforms tend to service major participants who have specific requirements. For instance, a bank or fund manager may choose a multi-bank platform as a single method of trading and to handle the relationships with multi-bank and counterparty relationships. Others may prefer a single-bank-run platform for ease and quality services, an aspect that gives rise to the dark pool concept we discussed earlier.

In regards to exchange-based trading, despite assumed regulator support, the FX market remains an OTC-traded market where the sheer volume and multicountry nature of participants makes it difficult for exchanges to meet the needs of real money clients who need actual delivery of cash and flexible forward value dates.

Some of these portals did not survive the crisis of 2008, with the failure of major FX participants such AIG and smaller bankrupticies such as Irish FX software firm Cognotc focusing market participants on the risk controls and quality of organisations that offer these automated services.

Regardless, these portals provide a crucial step for the retail trader: they allow foreign exchange market participants (importantly, including the corporations and fund managers) to bypass bank dealers in being able to directly access the market for foreign exchange. This cuts out the middleman and the associated costs. The theory behind such operations is that prices will be 'finer'; that is, traders will receive a narrower buy/sell spread, and thus the rates will be more competitive compared with those available through the traditional bank-operated access to the FX market.

Indeed the hypercompetitiveness of the foreign exchange market, though by no means always perfect, is constantly using cutting edge technological advantages to seek not only finer prices, but also ways to best execute trades at lower and lower costs. Much of this is driven by (high end) customer demand, with FX providers now able to offer 'pegged' or time sliced and even discretionary orders to a level that only a few years ago was the preserve of algorithmic traders in the marketplace. In the past the high cost and complexity of different types of orders forced FX service providers to have a human dealer to perform the task of order handling and management. Now the technology is there to accelerate the process to nanosecond time frames, just like the high-frequency traders.

It is only a matter of time before the retail trader gains access to this trading functionality — so stay tuned!

These platforms are undeniably still evolving and because of this they exhibit a large diversity of available structures. For example, a bilateral FX platform is usually managed by a bank, but the prices that are displayed are those of its customers. Conversely, a multilateral system has no managing bank or agent and is purely an unofficial foreign exchange trading system. Naturally, there are regulatory and privacy issues in dealing with these innovative platforms and their offerings, but they have emerged as a fact of market life that is probably here to stay. One thing is certain though: the marketplace for foreign exchange has changed irrevocably and continues to evolve. The little person (you, the retail FX trader) has to be aware that as these institutional changes are taking effect, they will ultimately dictate and influence what eventually becomes the reformed way to trade FX.

The differences between the small trader portals and the systems available to larger players are actually not all that large (assuming you don't want to trade nanosecond time frames!) and are more to do with the (dollar and time) scale of each operations rather than the method or quality of trading. In fact, there is no fundamental difference between systems available to the inter-bank market and those offered to retail traders, other than the efforts each makes to exclude the other and represent a technological improvement on previous foreign exchange price discovery systems.

The big guys are just like us—only bigger

We have looked at the various large-scale FX participants, such as the banks, hedge funds and fund managers. These are the big players, but they are not necessarily the controllers of global currency markets. Though their scale is huge compared with that of the average retail FX trader, their concerns are actually not dissimilar to those of the small-time speculator. Whether a price maker or price taker, both want to make a profit out of being involved in the FX market, while at the same time avoiding unnecessarily large downside risks.

The big end of town is not immune to the technological changes afoot in the industry, with a lot of inter-bank dealing now brokered electronically, usually through various platforms. Indeed, the technology and trading infrastructure now exists to dispense with the need for bank intermediaries altogether, which will certainly make the future of the foreign exchange market an interesting one!

CLS currencies

In August 2011 the following 17 currencies were in the global CLS FX clearing system tied in respective central bank currency accounts:

- Mexican peso
- Canadian dollar
- Pound sterling
- Israeli shekel
- Japanese yen
- South Korean won
- Danish krone
- Euro
- US dollar
- Hong Kong dollar
- Singapore dollar
- Norwegian krone
- Australian dollar
- New Zealand dollar
- South African rand
- Swedish krona
- Swiss franc

Chapter 11

Introduction to FX trading strategy

In this chapter we look at a tiny sample of the many thousands of methods and techniques that you can employ when trading in the foreign exchange market. One or two are really just explanations of technical tools, while others are more detailed. Before employing any strategy in real life, though, it is important to ensure that you understand the correct way to implement that system and that you are able to confidently interpret any output it may generate.

Although strategies come in all shapes and sizes, they mostly fall into just a handful of categories. While there may be some overlap, these categories can be broadly described as:

- trend following strategies
- range trading strategies
- breakout strategies
- mean reversion strategies.

For each type of strategy, certain types of trade orders will be particularly useful. For example, with a breakout strategy, it is very useful to be able to place stop-entry orders, which may also be known as buy stop and sell stop orders. This will allow you to place your orders, then lie in wait for prices to break out of the range.

For a mean reversion strategy, you might find buy limit and sell limit orders useful for catching extreme moves that are not expected to last. More advanced strategies may call for one cancels other (OCO) or even one cancels all (OCA) grouping of orders.

Some traders never place a trade without placing a corresponding stop-loss order at the same time. A variation on this is the trailing stop loss, which will be automatically adjusted as prices move in your favour. On some platforms, it is possible to attach both types of stop to a single trade.

The point to take away from this is that there are numerous types of orders that can help you to implement your trading strategies and achieve your goals. It is up to you to find out exactly which order types are available on your platform and then to ensure that you know how and when to use each of them.

Trend following

Many strategies aim to help the trader catch and ride an emerging trend. You don't need to catch the absolute low point or the absolute high point of a trend. In most instances, taking a chunk out of the middle is sufficient.

As with any market, one of your most important tasks is to determine which time period you are going to focus on. Are you going to take a longer term position, a medium-term position or a short-term one? What do the longer and shorter time periods tell you about the trend in the period you have selected?

Once you have decided which period to trade, determining the trend is much the same as it is in any other market. Basic price data should be your first starting point. A series of higher highs and higher lows will indicate an upward trend. A series of lower highs and lower lows will indicate a downward trend (see figure 11.1). You may also choose to use basic tools such as moving averages to help determine trend, or you might elect to use something more complex such as the directional movement index (ADX).

One thing that you will notice when trading currencies is that trends can remain in place for a long time. Once a trend takes hold in a given currency pair, it has the potential to be of a greater magnitude and duration than you may be used to if your prior trading experience is limited to equities. Once global fundamentals are set on a particular course, they can continue to push prices in one primary direction for months. If you have taken a long-term position and have managed to pick the direction correctly, such a move can be extremely profitable.

Figure 11.1: daily chart of USD/CHF showing an extended downward trend

Source: MetaTrader 5, © 2001–2011 MetaQuotes Software Corp.

Range trading

As the name suggests, a range trading strategy involves trading a market as it swings from end to end within a trading range. The first challenge is to identify the trading range. The daily EUR/GBP chart in figure 11.2 (overleaf) shows a period between July and September 2011 during which prices were contained within a range of approximately 0.8650/55 to 0.8880/85.

In its simplest form, a range trading strategy involves selling as prices reach the upper end of the band and buying as prices approach the lower end of the band. You might place your orders inside the band to ensure that you don't miss trades when price swings fall short of either end of the band. In this example, you might place buy orders around the 0.8680 region and sell orders around 0.8850.

As we will examine in the next section, prices do eventually break out of trading ranges. Accordingly, a good range trading strategy should also include a contingency plan to accommodate such a breakout.

Although trading ranges look easy to identify in hindsight, it can be difficult to accurately determine the upper and lower limits of a range in real-time. Often, by the time you determine that a tradeable range exists, it is nearing a breakout.

Figure 11.2: daily chart of EUR/GBP showing a trading range

Source: MetaTrader 5, © 2001–2011 MetaQuotes Software Corp.

Trading the breakout from a tight range—straddling the market

If your online margin FX platform allows you to use 'stop' orders to enter into new positions, you may find opportunities in which you wish to attempt straddling the market, with a stop-entry order on either side of a range. The basic idea is that when the market breaks out of its trading range, it will trigger either your stop-buy order (on a break higher) or your stop-sell order (on a break lower).

The first step in using this strategy is to identify a trading range on the chart. Take a look at figure 11.3, a 60-minute chart of USD/SGD, overleaf. You can see that trade has been caught in a band of 1.1997 to 1.2048 for several days. While the preceding trend was bearish, bounces from support that has emerged in the 1.2000/1.1997 region may give bears cause for concern. Rather than staking everything on a one-way directional play, you can straddle the market with stop-entry orders that will open a new position for you when the market breaks out of the range.

Figure 11.3: a 60-minute chart of USD/SGD

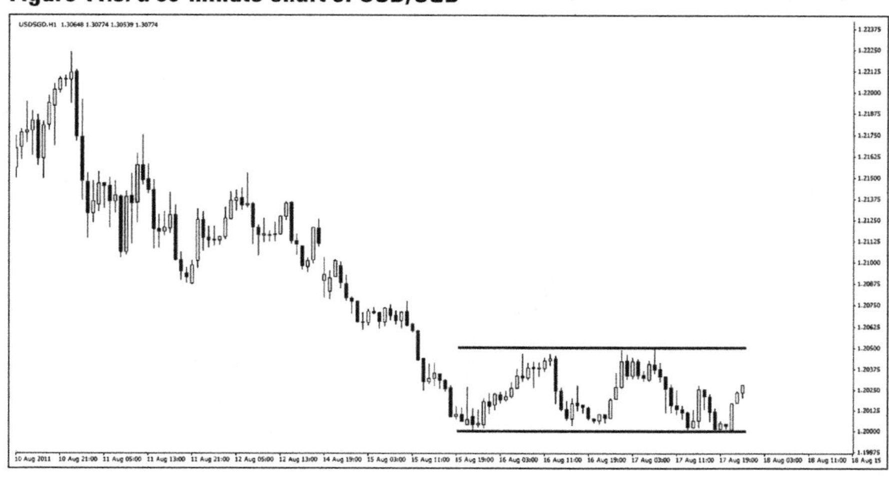

Source: MetaTrader 5, © 2001–2011 MetaQuotes Software Corp.

So, with a range of 1.1997 to 1.2048, you may decide to place a stop-buy order above the range at 1.2055 and a stop-sell order below the range at 1.1990.

If the market rallies and breaks above 1.2048 to hit 1.2055, your buy order will be triggered and you will be long at 1.2055 — assuming that the order is executed at the stop level; in other words, without slippage. While the buy order is triggered, the stop-sell order remains in place. Depending on your trading platform and your preferred method of trade management, you may then either leave this order in place as the stop loss for the long position, or replace it with a stop-loss order tied to your long position. Either way, having this sell order in place will provide a certain level of protection against a sudden reversal in the market, limiting losses to the difference between the original entry and the subsequent stop-sell exit.

However, as we can see in figure 11.4 (overleaf) in this particular example the market pushed firmly through the upper end of the range and triggered our stop-buy order, leaving us with a long position at 1.2055 (if there was no slippage) and a stop-sell order acting as our initial stop loss at 1.1990. As the trade progressed, this initial stop-sell order would have been replaced with a trailing stop, locking in profits as the market rallied towards 1.2150 and beyond.

Figure 11.4: stop-buy order triggered

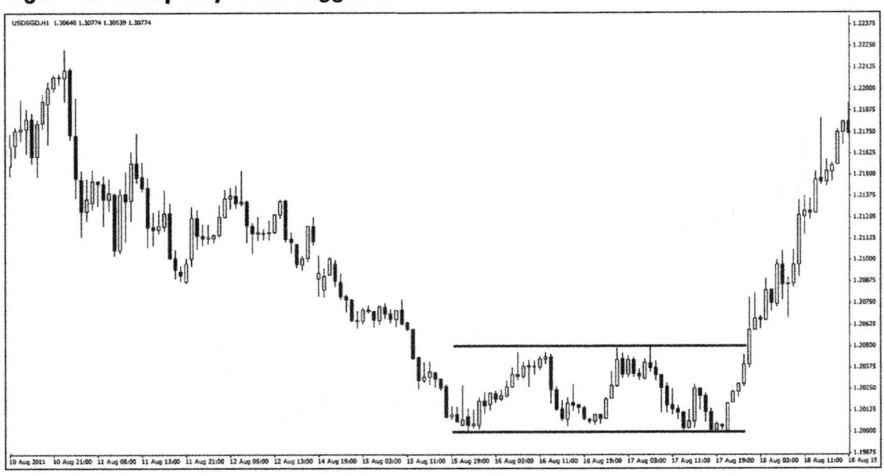

Source: MetaTrader 5, © 2001–2011 MetaQuotes Software Corp.

One of the dangers with this type of straddle strategy lies in correctly identifying the trading range. If you believe that the range is narrower than it actually is, you may find that your stop-entry orders are placed too closely together. For example, consider a situation in which you have identified the upper limit of a USD/JPY range as being at 85.65 and subsequently place a stop-buy order at 85.70. If, in fact, the upper limit of the band was closer to 85.70/72, you may find that one last push to the upside triggers your buy order shortly before the market collapses through the bottom of the range, triggering your sell order on the other side of the range. While you are happy to see the sell order triggered, it is because it is acting as a stop loss to your inadvertently acquired long position rather than because it has delivered you a short position in a falling market, as desired.

Slippage

There is another important point to make about this type of strategy. When orders are executed on stop, there is no guarantee that the order will be filled at the stop level. In most instances, once the stop level has been triggered the stop order is executed at the next available price. Often, this will indeed be the selected stop level, but in times of high market volatility and/or reduced liquidity, the level at which a stop order is executed may be significantly different from the actual stop level. This is known as 'slippage'.

Slippage can be a significant factor to consider if attempting to execute this type of trade at the time of the release of important economic or statistical data. Many traders note the tight trading ranges that develop in the half-hour or so prior to the release of data such as US non-farm payrolls, and the dramatic breakouts that often occur within seconds of the release of this data. These moves can see trade break from a congestion band that may be just 5 to 10 pips wide, with subsequent rallies or falls frequently delivering moves of 50 to 100 pips or even more. Stop orders that are triggered by the break from a tight trading range may suffer slippage of 5, 10 or even 20 pips, depending on market conditions. If the interbank market is very thin (low liquidity) then online margin FX providers that pass trades through to the interbank market will have trouble laying off the positions of their clients and slippage may be exacerbated.

These comments are not intended to scare you away from using this strategy, but instead to ensure that you are aware of the risks you may face if you attempt to use this strategy to capture data-related breakouts.

Mean reversion

When prices move too far, too fast, there is often a return towards what are regarded as more 'normal' prices, perhaps around a moving average. This is known as reversion to the mean.

Consider a situation in which the gap between current prices and the 55-day moving average is the largest it has been for 12 months. This may be taken as a warning signal that prices and the 55-day moving average will soon converge.

Somewhat more reliable signals can be obtained using a tool such as Bollinger Bands. These bands reflect the volatility of a given security or currency pair. Explaining Bollinger Bands and strategies that make use of them in detail would fill a book of its own, so this section will just cover some of the key basics.

Bollinger Bands are constructed around a simple moving average. Bands are plotted either side of the moving average. The upper band is plotted two standard deviations above the moving average with the lower band plotted two standard deviations below the moving average (see figure 11.5). The beauty of the bands is that the width between them adjusts automatically in response to price volatility, as measured by the standard deviation calculations.

In a normally distributed data set, readings that fall one standard deviation either side of the mean should account for about 68.2 per cent of the whole data set. Two standard deviations either side of the mean encompasses 95.4 per cent, while three standard deviations either side of the mean should contain 99.7 per cent of data.

Figure 11.5: EUR/USD 30-minute chart with Bollinger Bands

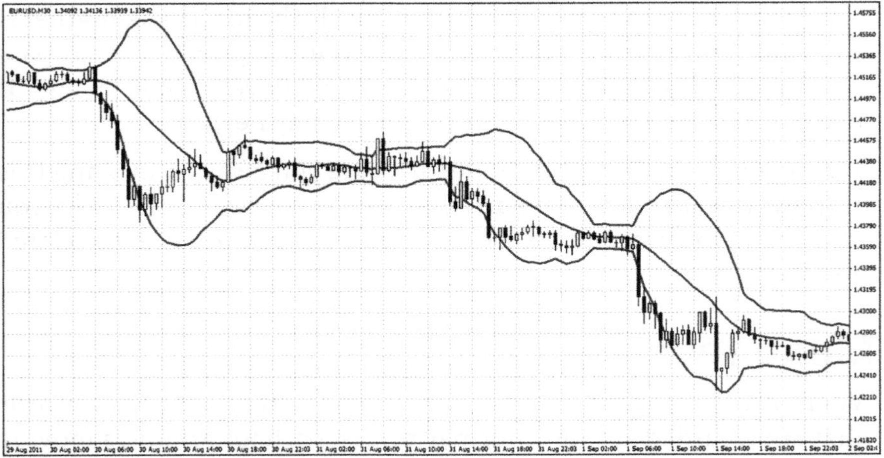

Source: MetaTrader 5, © 2001–2011 MetaQuotes Software Corp.

In the section on Bollinger Bands in chapter 8, we noted that a bullish move above the upper band or bearish move below the lower band suggests that the price action is very strong and is likely to continue in that direction — subject, of course, to confirmation.

However, if a price move outside of the Bollinger Bands coincides with a clear reversal signal given by another tool or indicator, there is a greater than usual chance that the reversal signal will be a valid one. Bollinger outlined this concept in his presentation at the annual conference of the International Federation of Technical Analysts (IFTA) in Tokyo in 2001. He used the example of a 'karakasa' (paper umbrella) candlestick and observed that when this reversal candle appeared on or outside of the Bollinger Bands, it greatly improved the reliability of the candlestick pattern. Further information regarding this use of Bollinger Bands can be found on the website <www.bollingerbands.com>.

John Bollinger has created a number of spin-off indicators based on his eponymous Bollinger Bands. One of these is known as '%b' (see figure 11.6). It is given this nomenclature in recognition of the stochastic indicator as the calculation is very similar. In a nutshell, %b is an indicator that shows how prices are moving in relation to the Bollinger Bands. When this indicator probes outside of the Bollinger Bands, indicated by horizontal lines drawn at 0 and 1, and then displays divergence in relation to price action, it is a good indication that there may soon be a price reversal. As always, you should look to other indicators to provide confirmation.

Once you learn to use this tool, it can be a very powerful early warning device and can form the basis of a strategy based on catching a trend reversal and reversion to the mean. Some people use it to enter new positions while others use it as a warning to take profits on existing open positions.

If using %b to enter a trade, remember that you are initially taking a counter-trend trade. You are trying to catch the proverbial falling knife (if buying). If you get it right, you should see positive results fairly quickly. However, if you get it wrong and prices continue trending against you, think very carefully before adding further trades.

Figure 11.6: EUR/JPY daily chart with Bollinger Bands and %b indicator

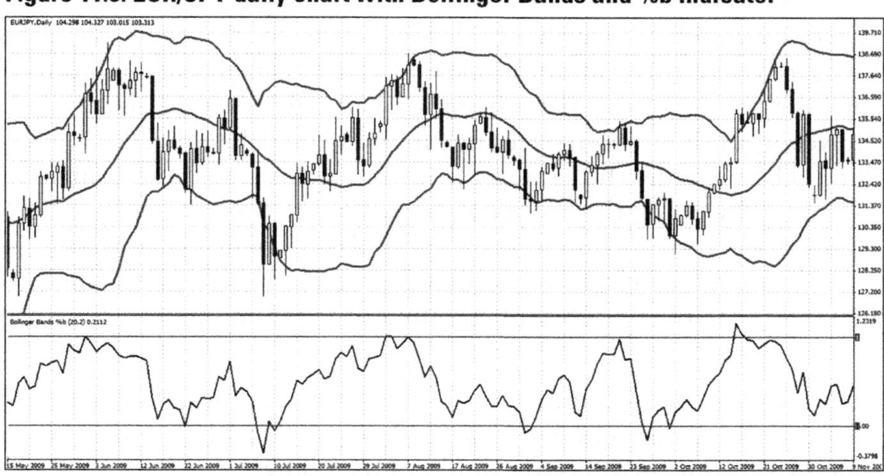

Source: MetaTrader 5, © 2001–2011 MetaQuotes Software Corp.

Pivot points

Pivot points are a fairly simple tool that you may not have come across before unless you have had exposure to the foreign exchange or futures markets. The levels used are fairly easy to calculate and have been a favourite 'rough guide' for floor traders and institutional foreign exchange traders for many years.

In a nutshell, pivot points make use of yesterday's high, low and 'close' to project five levels of potential intraday support and/or resistance for the current day's trading activity. Provided you have yesterday's high, low and close, you can work out the five levels.

We can calculate the five levels as shown below:

Yesterday's high = H
Yesterday's low = L
Yesterday's close = C

The first level to calculate is the pivot point itself. This sits between the other four levels, of which two are support and two are resistance.

Pivot point = $(H + L + C) \div 3$
Resistance 1 = $(2 \times \text{Pivot point}) - L$
Support 1 = $(2 \times \text{Pivot point}) - H$
Resistance 2 = $\text{Pivot point} + (H - L)$
Support 2 = $\text{Pivot point} - (H - L)$

If you are familiar with this tool from the futures market, you may be used to a slightly different method of calculating the pivot point, including the 'open' of the current day and dividing the result by 4. However, in the foreign exchange market the value of today's open should be virtually the same as yesterday's close, so there is little to be gained by doing this, other than weighting the data towards the 'close' price. It's also important to note that there is no ironclad rule as to how the calculation for pivot points should be performed, so you may wish to try different combinations for yourself to see what you find most useful.

Let's look at an example. If we noted the range for EUR/USD yesterday included a high of 1.21940, a low of 1.21250 and a close of 1.21510, our pivot points would be as follows:

$$
\begin{aligned}
\text{Pivot point} &= (1.21940 + 1.21250 + 1.21510) \div 3 \\
&= 1.21570 \\
\text{Resistance 1} &= (2 \times 1.21570) - 1.21250 \\
&= 1.21890 \\
\text{Support 1} &= (2 \times 1.21570) - 1.21940 \\
&= 1.21200 \\
\text{Resistance 2} &= 1.21570 + (1.21940 - 1.21250) \\
&= 1.22260 \\
\text{Support 2} &= 1.21570 - (1.21940 - 1.21250) \\
&= 1.20880
\end{aligned}
$$

Each of these five levels can then be plotted as a horizontal line across an intraday chart of the current day—a 30-minute chart, for example.

As the market approaches each of these levels, it can act as a level of resistance if approached from below, or a level of support if approached from above. Unless there has been a sharp move in the early hours of the current day, it is likely that trade will initially start out the day between the first support (S1) and first resistance (R1) levels.

There will, of course, be days where the market moves quickly away from the pivot point levels projected from yesterday's range, and on these days the pivot point indicator will be of little use to you. However, there will be many more days on which market advances and retreats do indeed appear to be influenced by the proximity of the projected pivot point levels. If you have been considering a purchase of a certain currency pair and you notice that the market is nearing the first resistance level, you may well find that you would be better off delaying your entry.

Forward rolls, forward points and carry trades

It is not the purpose of this book to delve too deeply into topics such as forward foreign exchange contracts or currency swaps, or longer term strategies such as the 'carry' trade, but being aware of the existence of these will help you to paint a more complete picture of the foreign exchange landscape. We will cover these issues in just enough detail so that you may decide for yourself whether you wish to investigate each area in more detail.

Forward rolls

As mentioned several times, interest rates have a significant impact on the foreign exchange market. Foreign investors pay particular attention to the absolute (real or effective) interest rates in specific countries, as well as to the relative levels of interest rates in different countries. This is partly because the interest rate differentials will determine whether a trader holding a position 'overnight' receives a financing benefit or faces a financing cost.

For any given currency pair traded:

- If a trader has bought the currency with a higher underlying yield, that trader will earn interest.
- If a trader has bought the currency with a lower underlying yield, that trader will incur an interest expense.

The calculations for this are relatively simple and we will look at an example. However, in reality, most trading platforms will automatically roll open positions from one day to the next, with any adjustments for interest rate differentials made automatically by the system. Many retail traders would probably be entirely unaware of the process and might only realise something is going on in the background when they notice that their account statements reveal small amounts of interest being added to or deducted from their account. Being aware of the process should help to ensure you are not caught unprepared when you read your account statement.

Let's assume a world in which Australian interest rates are at 4.75 per cent and interest rates in the US are at 0.25 per cent. A trader buys $1 000 000 AUD/USD at 1.06250 (which would require a margin of A$2500 assuming leverage of 400:1 was in use).

Although adjustments to the trader's account will reflect the net result of the interest differential between AUD and USD, he or she will in effect be earning interest on the currency bought and paying interest out on the currency sold.

Therefore, for the AUD leg ($1 000 000 bought) our trader will receive:

$$A\$1\,000\,000 \times (0.0475 \div 365) = A\$130.14$$

For the USD leg (US$1 062 500 sold), our trader will pay out:

$$[US\$1\,062\,500 \times (0.0025 \div 360)] \div 1.06250 = A\$6.94$$

In summary:

In	AUD 130.14
Out	AUD 6.94

Therefore, the net result of interest movements on this trade when held overnight will be: 130.14 – 6.94 = A$123.20.

So, given these specific interest rates and AUD/USD exchange rate, an overnight roll of a 1 000 000 AUD/USD position results in a credit of A$123.20 being received by the trader who has bought this position.

You may have noticed above that we used a different annualising factor for these two currencies. One night of interest in AUD was calculated as 1/365th of 4.75 per cent, while for the USD we calculated 1/360th of 0.25 per cent. Most countries use the 360 days method but many Commonwealth countries use 365 days. It is worth speaking to your online margin FX provider to find out the exact method they use if this is of specific interest to you.

It is important to understand that the value (or settlement) date for a spot FX deal is two days forward. However, the value date for a deal done on (or rolled forward into) Thursday (FX time) is Monday. Because Thursday trade starts when it is 5.00 pm on Wednesday in New York, trades that are held open prior to this time and rolled forward until after this time will attract triple swap. Thus the rollover benefit or charge is three times larger than on any other day. It would be a good idea to work out what time it is in your location when it is 5.00 pm on Wednesday in New York and keep in mind the potential impact of rollover. If there is a public holiday on the Monday in one of the countries concerned, the swap benefit or charge may be extended to four days.

Individual margin FX providers have different ways of calculating the rollover, or swap. Many will do it with reference to the relevant swap rate. The actual sum paid or received will rarely be precisely as outlined above. You should consult your chosen provider directly if you want full details regarding this calculation.

Forward points

Forward points are unlikely to be encountered when trading regular (spot) FX with the majority of providers. However, if you are trading 'forward' contracts it is useful to understand how they work. In either case, having a little knowledge will broaden your overall understanding of the foreign exchange market.

The impact of interest rates on the future level of exchange rates relative to the current spot price is reflected in the forward points, also known as forward pips or forward margin. The forward points are either added to or subtracted from the spot price to give the forward price. The longer the period to delivery of the forward contract, the greater the impact of any interest rate differential between the two currencies being traded.

Forwards form a major part of the world of inter-bank currency trading, but are less likely to be encountered by the average retail trader who, in most instances, will be more concerned with spot prices. As mentioned earlier, forward prices are arrived at through the addition or subtraction of forward points/pips from that starting base of spot prices. Forward prices are therefore moving constantly in response to changes in the spot prices and changes in interest rates in the short-term money market. Inter-bank traders will negotiate a forward price that is acceptable to both parties and therefore they need to be able to calculate forward points effectively. However, retail traders are price takers and on those platforms that do offer trading in forwards, the forward price will simply be presented as a bid and ask representing the forward adjusted spot price.

In a situation where the underlying interest rate of the base currency is higher than the underlying interest rate of the terms (variable) currency, the forward points will be subtracted from the spot price and the forward price will therefore be lower than the spot price. In this instance, the base currency is said to be trading at a 'forward discount'.

Obviously then, in a situation where the underlying interest rate of the base currency is lower than the underlying interest rate of the terms (variable) currency, the forward points are added to the spot price and the forward price will therefore be higher than the spot price. In this instance, the base currency is said to be trading at a 'forward premium'.

Let's look at a simplified example. Say you wanted to trade $1 000 000 AUD/USD with a forward settlement date that is six months in the future, or 180 days, rather than the usual spot settlement date of two days after execution. To work out the forward price (see table 11.1), we need to know the current spot price and the relevant interest rates for AUD and USD.

In this example:

AUD/USD spot price = 1.0625
Australian interest rates = 4.75%
US interest rates = 0.25%

Table 11.1: calculating the forward price on a trade with six months' settlement date

Date	AUD	Rate	USD
Today	A$1 000 000	1.0625	US$1 062 500
	1 000 000 × (0.0475 × 180/365)		1 062 500 × (0.0025 × 180/360)
	A$23 424.66		US$1 328.13
180 days	A$1 023 424.66	1.0395	US$1 063 828.13

By projecting forward the impact of the interest rates on each currency, we determine the future value of each side of the spot trade. So, we can see that in 180 days our A$1 000 000 would be worth A$1 023 424.66 given a rate of 4.75 per cent, and the US$1 062 500 would be worth US$1 063 828.13 given the rate of 0.25 per cent.

When we compare these future amounts, we can determine the forward exchange rate. It is simply a matter of dividing the USD amount by the AUD amount (terms currency divided by base currency): 1 063 828.13 ÷ 1 023 424.66 = 1.0395. This figure of 1.0395 is the price for a six-month (180 day) forward for AUD/USD given the parameters outlined.

To calculate the forward points, we simply take the forward price that we have calculated and subtract the original spot price. In this instance, the forward price is lower than the spot price, so the forward points are shown as a negative number; in this instance it is −230 (10395 − 10625). Note that the decimal point is not used for ease of quotation. You may encounter quotes for forwards that are given either as forward prices, such as 1.0395, or they may be simply quoted in terms of forward points, such as −230 in our example.

It is important to remember that the forward prices do not reflect an expectation of the movements of one currency against another;

they simply represent the impact of the interest rate differential between the two currencies during the period between the spot date and the forward date (maturity date).

Carry trades

Carry trades exist in many forms in many markets. The basic concept involves borrowing funds in a lower interest rate environment and reinvesting those funds in a higher interest rate environment. When executed correctly, the revenues received from your investment activities will exceed the cost of borrowing the funds and you end up with a profit. Traders looking for a carry trade opportunity usually seek a currency pair with a wide difference in underlying interest rates. Recently, this has included pairs such as AUD/USD as interest rates remain relatively firm in Australia while they are at historically depressed levels in the US. In the past, it was USD/JPY that provided many traders with a carry trade. Obviously, the numbers look out of place in today's market, but in this section we will examine the basic mechanics that once drove the USD/JPY carry trade.

Official interest rates in Japan, as represented by the central bank discount rates, were at just 0.5 per cent in 2000, before falling to 0.1 per cent by September of 2001. Obviously, with rates scraping just above 0 per cent, Japan was seen as a good place to borrow money for reinvestment elsewhere—provided there were no adverse currency movements. (These days, it is nearly as cheap to borrow funds in the US as it is in Japan.)

In the US in late 2000, official rates set by the US Federal Reserve were at 6.5 per cent. International investors were able to borrow funds in Japan, then convert the funds into USD by buying USD/JPY and invest in US markets (via bonds for example) at significantly higher interest rates.

Conceptually, the yen carry trade is like buying USD/JPY and allowing the position to be rolled forward (overnight) again and again and again. Because the trader has bought the higher yielding currency (USD) and sold the lower yielding currency (JPY), each rollover will see the trader earning an amount determined by the interest rate differential.

For example, on a US$1 000 000 USD/JPY trade with USD/JPY at 120.55, US rates at 6.5 per cent and Japanese rates at 0.5 per cent, the interest income per day would be:

Interest received	=	$1\,000\,000 \times (0.065 \div 360)$
	=	US$180.56
Interest paid out	=	$[120\,550\,000 \times (0.005 \div 360)] \div 120.55$
	=	US$13.89
Net result (profit)	=	US$166.67 per day (per rollover)

Traders that used the yen carry strategy during the two-year period from early 2000 through to early 2002 not only enjoyed a financing benefit on their trade, they also saw their long positions in USD/JPY rally from the 100/105 region all the way up to highs of 135.00.

However, as we can see in figure 11.7, a weekly chart of USD/JPY, from early 2002 onwards there was a significant weakening of the USD against the JPY. The losses incurred by those holding USD/JPY long positions over this period would have exceeded any benefit they may have been receiving as a result of the yen carry trade and this specific strategy lost its attractiveness in early 2002.

Figure 11.7: weakening of the USD against the JPY, early 2002

Source: MetaTrader 5, © 2001–2011 MetaQuotes Software Corp.

This fall in USD/JPY serves to highlight the fact that simply because one currency offers greater yield earning opportunities than another, it does not automatically follow that the currency with the higher yield will remain stronger than the currency with the lower yield. This is because of the vast tapestry of interrelated events that determine exchange rates. In the case of USD/JPY, there were significant issues facing the USD at this time, starting with the bursting of the dotcom bubble followed by broader stock market weakness, the terrorist attacks of September 11, the constant stream of accounting and investment house scandals, and a series of interest rate cuts. All of these factors had an impact on market sentiment and reduced the attractiveness of investing in the US at the same time that other regions of the world (such as South-East Asia and Eastern Europe) were starting to recover after rough patches of their own.

As noted earlier, the carry trade is not restricted to USD/JPY. Any two currencies with sufficiently different underlying interest rates will offer the potential for a successful carry trade. Just remember to buy the currency that offers the greater yield and remain alert to the risk of an adverse move in the actual exchange rate.

Readers with long enough memories may recall the foreign currency loans that caught the headlines in Australia in the mid to late 1980s. Borrowers sought to bypass high interest rates in Australia by borrowing funds offshore, frequently in Swiss francs (CHF), where interest rates were at about half the rate of those in Australia at the time. Conceptually, there is nothing wrong with this strategy. However, as it turned out, the late 1980s saw a notable decline in the value of the AUD, which meant that more and more Australian dollars were required to service the foreign debt. Many borrowers faced financial ruin as the repayments required on their supposedly 'cheap' loans grew larger and larger. This saw many of the borrowers take action against the domestic banks that had promoted and facilitated these loans, and the whole mess ended up in the courts, in the newspapers and on our televisions.

Unfortunately, one of the outcomes of all this was that the average person in the street was left with the impression that dealing with foreign currencies was excessively dangerous and should be avoided at all costs. In reality, it was the failure to adequately hedge against the risk of adverse currency movements that caused these borrowers to suffer such heavy losses.

Options

Only a handful of retail trading platforms currently offer the ability to trade FX options. If you have not traded options previously, it would be wise to test your skills extensively on a demo platform before committing real money. While the following information provides a broad outline of this segment of the market, successful trading of FX options really does require specialist knowledge and skills which will require more extensive study.

On some trading platforms you can trade options over currency pairs just as you may already be doing with equities or futures. Many of the option types that we examine below will be familiar to equities and futures traders; however, in addition to the usual types of options there are a few more exotic, currency-specific options that we will briefly mention as well. Firstly, though, we'll deal with some of the terminology that surrounds options.

As with most other financial instruments, a trader may either buy or sell options. Slightly different terminology is sometimes used, with an option buyer known as the 'taker' of the option and the option seller known as the 'writer' of the option.

In addition to identifying whether an option is being bought or sold, we must also identify the type of option being traded, that being either a 'put' option or a 'call' option. As well as the regular put and call options and strategies that go along with them, you may come across somewhat more exotic currency options that include digital options and barrier options, such as one-touch options, no-touch options, double one-touch options and double no-touch options. Some of these may also be known as knock-in or knock-out options. Even more exotic are Bermuda options, lookback options, ladder options and even rainbow options, to name a few.

Most important is the definition of an option: the party that buys the option has the right but not the obligation to either sell (put option) or buy (call option) the underlying security at a price determined at the time the option trade takes place.

The fee paid by the option buyer to acquire this right is known as the 'option premium'. This is a sunk cost for the buyer of the option, meaning that it cannot be recovered. However, if the buyer of the option subsequently sells that option prior to expiry, he or she will collect a premium from whoever buys the option. If the value of the option has increased and this premium received on the sale of the option exceeds the premium paid out on the purchase of the option, the trader will make a profit. Obviously, the reverse is also true — if the premium received on the sale of the option is less than the premium paid out on the purchase of the option, the trader will incur a loss on the trade.

The price at which the underlying security may be exchanged is determined at the time of the initial transaction and is known as the 'strike price'.

When trading options, it is also worth ensuring that you know whether you are trading American-style options or European-style options. The buyer of an American-style option may exercise his or her right to exchange the underlying security at the strike price at any time up to the expiry date of the option. In contrast, the buyer of a European-style option may only exercise that option on the actual expiry date. In practice though, many option positions are squared up well before the expiry date and are therefore never exercised.

One other factor to consider is 'time decay'. This means that as the expiry date of an option draws nearer, the value of the option will start to decay at an accelerated pace as there is less and less potential for the market to move prior to expiry. Time decay works against the buyer of an option and, conversely, works in favour of the option seller.

For example, if you have bought a call option, you will profit if prices of the underlying market rise sufficiently, while your downside risk is limited to the amount you paid out in premium. Any time prior to expiry there is always the possibility that prices will rally substantially, thus delivering an even greater profit. However, this potential diminishes as the expiry draws nearer, and the ultimate value of the option becomes a function of the difference between the strike price of the option and the market price of the underlying security less the premium paid. In other words, as the buyer of an option your downside risk starts out and remains fixed at the amount paid in premium, while your upside potential is theoretically unlimited. Time decay works to reel in this unlimited upside potential.

For the option seller, it is the profit portion of the equation that is fixed. You cannot earn more from an option than you have received in the form of premium. However, the downside is potentially unlimited. If you sell a call option and prices rally strongly you will lose. The same applies if you sell a put option and prices fall. Time decay serves to reel in the potentially unlimited downside risks, as each day that passes reduces the potential for the worst-case scenario to unfold.

The 'Greeks'

For those serious about undertaking options trading, it would be worth undertaking further study into the 'Greeks'. These are additional measures that indicate such things as the implied volatility and the rate at which the value of the premium will change for a given change in price of the underlying instrument. They are called Greeks because they are named after letters of the Greek alphabet:

- *Delta:* Measures the impact of a change in price of the underlying instrument on the change in price of the option.
- *Gamma:* Represents the impact on delta for each change in price of the underlying instrument.
- *Lambda:* The percentage change in the option price for a percentage change in the price of the underlying instrument.
- *Theta:* Measures the impact on the price of the option as time closes in on the expiry date—a measure of time decay.
- *Rho:* Represents the impact on the price of the option if there is a change in interest rates.
- *Vega:* Measures the change in price of an option as its volatility changes.

Option pay-off diagrams

The diagrams that follow represent the potential pay-off that various strategies will generate for given exchange rates along a sliding horizontal price scale. Unlike equities, which can only fall to zero, the price scale here is unbounded on the downside (to the left). The profit or loss is represented by the vertical axis, as shown in figure 11.8.

Figure 11.8: pay-off diagram

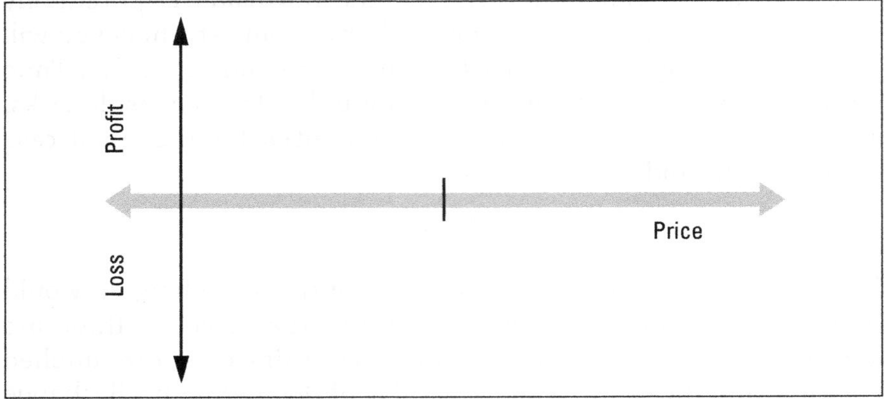

Let's have a look at some of the different buying and selling combinations.

Long call option

You would profit through buying a call option if prices of the underlying security were to rise. Once prices rise above the strike price by more than the amount you have paid out in premium, the trade starts to move into profit.

Maximum profit: Unlimited

Maximum loss: Restricted to the amount paid as premium

Reading the pay-off diagram for this strategy (see figure 11.9), we can see that the break-even point will be reached where the pay-off curve crosses the 'price' axis, at a price slightly above the 'strike' price, which in this example is at 0.7800. Any further gain in price from this point on will lead to increased profits. The maximum loss on this strategy is met when prices fall to the strike price. Below this price, the loss suffered by the holder of this option is equal to the premium paid for the option.

Figure 11.9: long call option

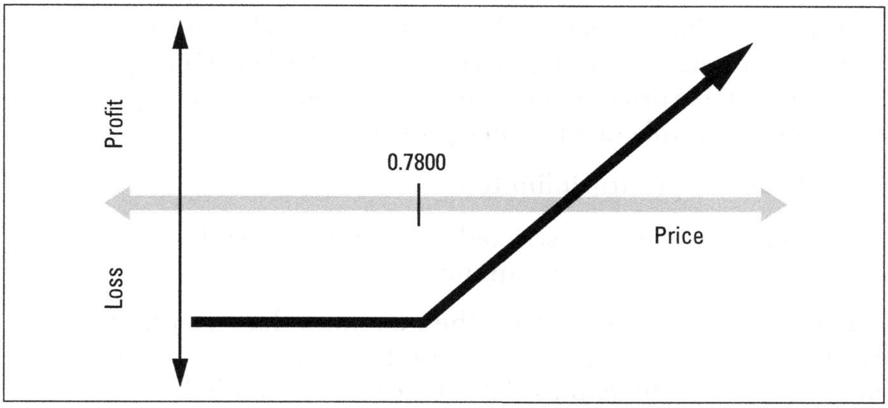

Long call option — showing the impact of time decay

The different curves shown in figure 11.10 represent the pay-off curve for this option at different points in time. The solid lower line represents the situation on the expiry date, with the higher lines representing periods in time successively closer to the date on which the option was traded.

Figure 11.10: long call option — showing the impact of time decay

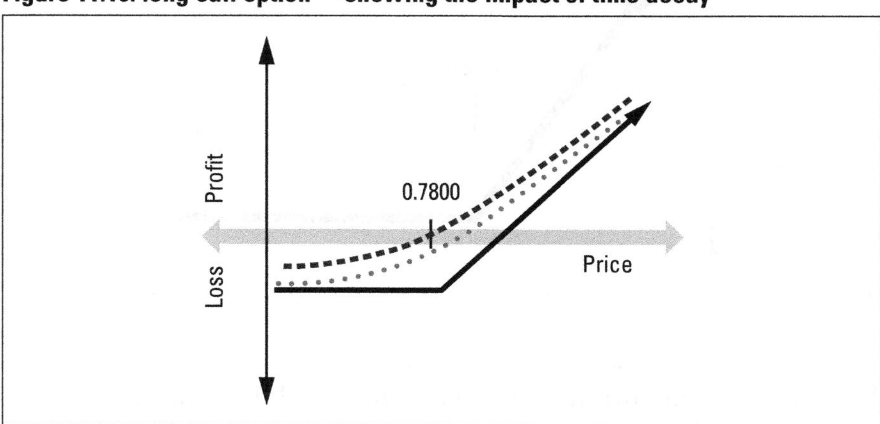

Long put option

In this scenario, a trader would benefit through buying a put option if prices in the underlying security were to fall. Once prices fall below the strike price by more than the amount you have paid out in premium, you will start to make profits on the trade.

Maximum profit: Unlimited

Maximum loss: Restricted to the amount paid as premium

The pay-off curve shows that the maximum loss you face on this trade will be realised if the market is trading at or above the strike price on the expiry date. Once prices fall below the strike price, your financial situation starts to improve, with break-even achieved at a point below the strike price that is sufficient to cover the cost of the premium you paid out to buy this option. As price continues to fall below this point your profits continue to grow, as shown in figure 11.11.

Figure 11.11: long put option

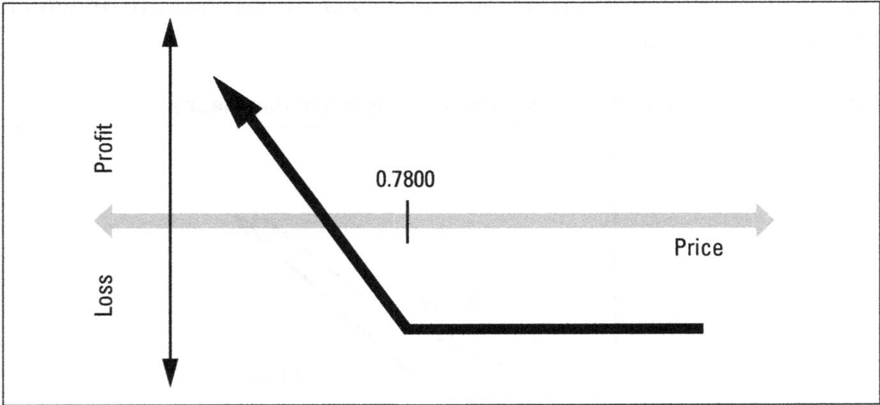

Short call option

With a short call option (as shown in figure 11.12), the seller of the call option collects the option premium but will lose money if the price of the underlying security rises above the strike price by more than the amount collected in premium.

Maximum profit: Restricted to the amount received as premium

Maximum loss: Unlimited

Maximum profit is achieved for the seller of a call option while prices remain below the strike price. Any move above this starts to erode profits, and once the pay-off curve crosses the price axis at a point that reflects the amount of premium initially collected on the sale of the option, the strategy starts moving into negative return territory. Losses will continue to mount as prices continue to climb.

Figure 11.12: short call option

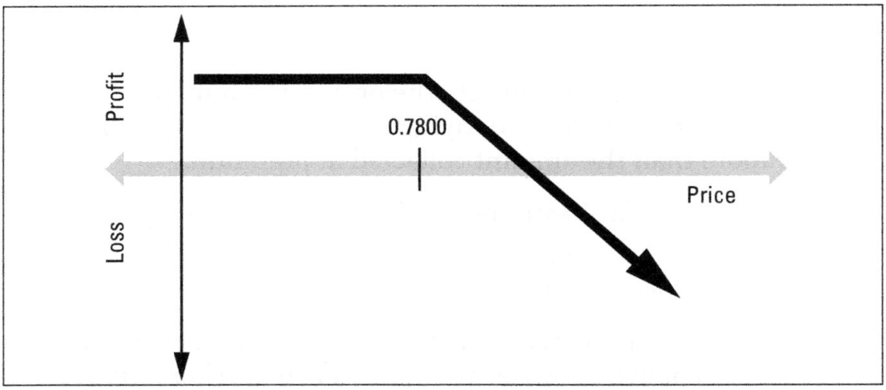

Short call option — showing the impact of time decay

Once again, we can see a simulation of the effect of time decay by plotting the pay-off curves for several different points of time on the one diagram (figure 11.13, overleaf). In this instance it is the upper (solid) curve that represents the pay-off for the short call option at expiry. As noted, maximum profit is achieved when this option expires with prices at or below the strike price. If the price is above the strike price at expiry, maximum profit will not be achieved (by the writer/ seller of the option). The point where prices rise sufficiently to erode the entire premium received on the sale of the option is represented by the pay-off curve dropping below the horizontal line we have marked as 'price', which divides profitable territory from loss-making territory. Prior to expiry, the pay-off curve is precisely that: a curve. The lower the curve, the longer the duration to expiry.

Figure 11.13: short call option—showing the impact of time decay

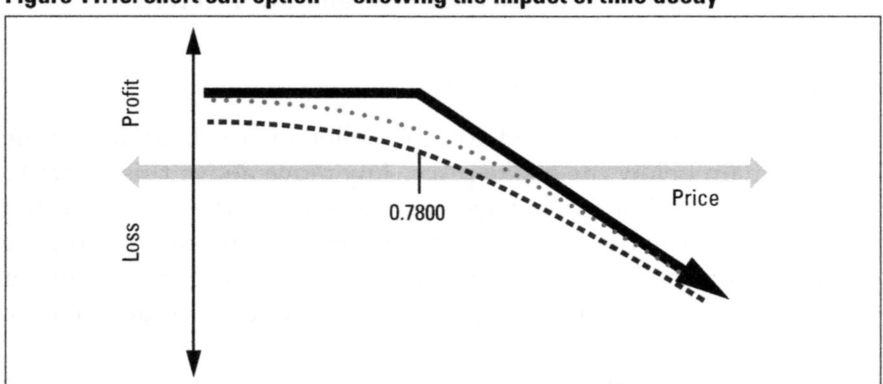

Short put option

The seller of a put option collects the option premium but will lose money if the price of the underlying security falls below the strike price by more than the amount collected in premium.

Maximum profit: Restricted to the amount received as premium
Maximum loss: Unlimited

Maximum pay-off is achieved for the seller of the put option when prices are at or above the strike price. Any fall below here will start to erode the value of the option. Again, break-even occurs at the point at which the pay-off curve crosses the price axis. Below here the losses will continue to grow as prices continue to fall (see figure 11.14).

Figure 11.14: short put option

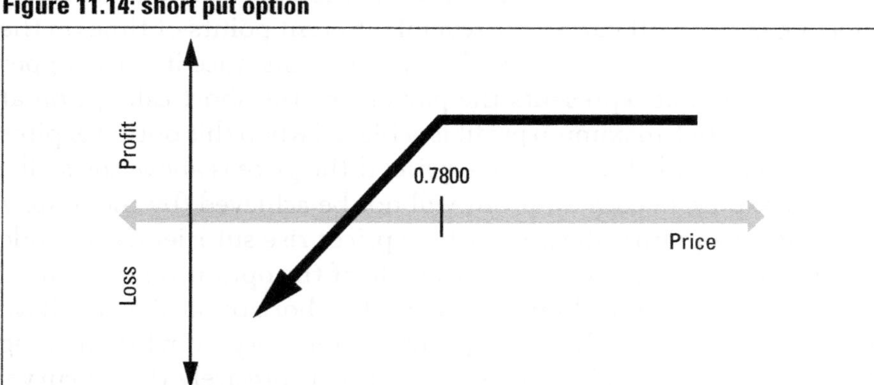

Multiple option strategies

In addition to using options as part of a strategy for trading a market in which you have a clear directional bias, multiple options can be combined to create strategies that will profit from either an increase in volatility and a significant move in price of the underlying security, or a fall in volatility and stability in the price of the underlying security. Some of the simpler strategies are shown in the following pages.

Long straddle

This is a long call and long put both at the same strike price. A trader using a long straddle strategy (as shown in figure 11.15) will profit from an increase in volatility and the associated move in price of the underlying security, regardless of which direction the market moves, provided it moves far enough to cover the cost of the double premium that has to be paid out to establish this position.

Maximum profit: Unlimited
Maximum loss: Restricted to the amount of premium paid for the two options

The maximum loss faced by the buyer of this option strategy is equal to the sum of the two option premiums paid out, as represented by the dotted line on this pay-off diagram. Break-even may be achieved at a level either above or below the strike price, once prices move enough to compensate for the premiums paid. Once prices rise or fall far enough to move the market beyond the break-even level, potential profits are unlimited on both the upside and downside.

Figure 11.15: long straddle

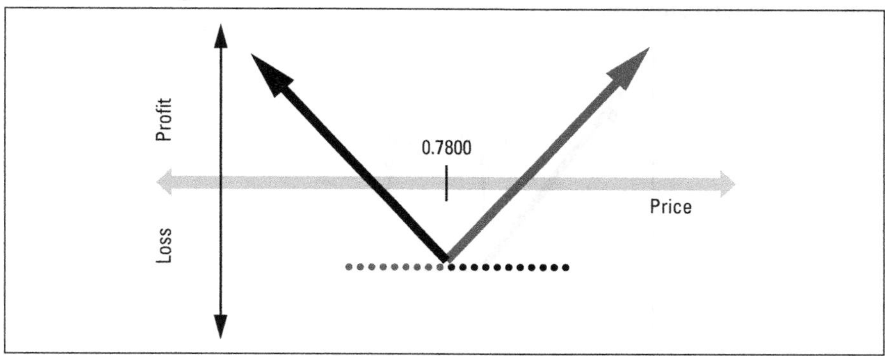

Long strangle

A long strangle is a long call and long put with the long put at a lower strike price than the long call. As with the long straddle, a trader using a long strangle strategy will profit from an increase in volatility and the associated move in price of the underlying security, regardless of which direction the market moves, provided it moves far enough to cover the cost of the double premium that has to be paid out to establish this position. The market has more room to move before this trade becomes profitable, due to the different strike prices. However, because one of the strike prices will be further from the market than the other, the premiums to be paid out on this strategy should amount to less than the premiums required for the long straddle.

Maximum profit: Unlimited
Maximum loss: Restricted to the amount of premium paid for the two options

Once again, the dotted horizontal line on this pay-off diagram represents the maximum loss faced by the buyer of a strangle strategy. It is equal to the two option premium amounts paid out to establish the position. As figure 11.16 shows, price movements between the two strike prices will not improve the theoretical pay-off situation. For the financial position of the holder of this strategy to improve, prices need to either rise above the upper strike price or fall below the level of the lower strike price. Once price has moved sufficiently above the upper strike price or below the lower strike price, the strategy will achieve break-even and any further move away from the strike prices will deliver potentially unlimited profits.

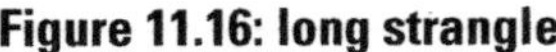

Figure 11.16: long strangle

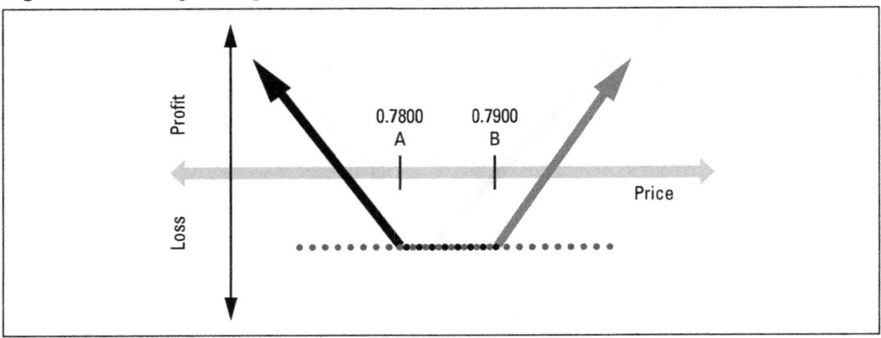

Short straddle

A short straddle is a short call and short put both at the same strike price. A trader using a short straddle strategy will profit in an environment of low or falling volatility in which prices remain close to the strike price. The seller collects a premium on two options, and will enjoy a profit so long as price movements away from the strike price do not exceed the amount collected in premium. If there is a significant move in price, the short straddle has the potential to deliver unlimited losses.

Maximum profit: Restricted to the amount of premium received for the two options
Maximum loss: Unlimited

Figure 11.17 is simply the reverse of the long straddle. Maximum profit is achieved when price is equal to the strike price at expiry. Any move away from the strike price will diminish profits, with losses being potentially unlimited as prices continue to move away from the strike price.

Figure 11.17: short straddle

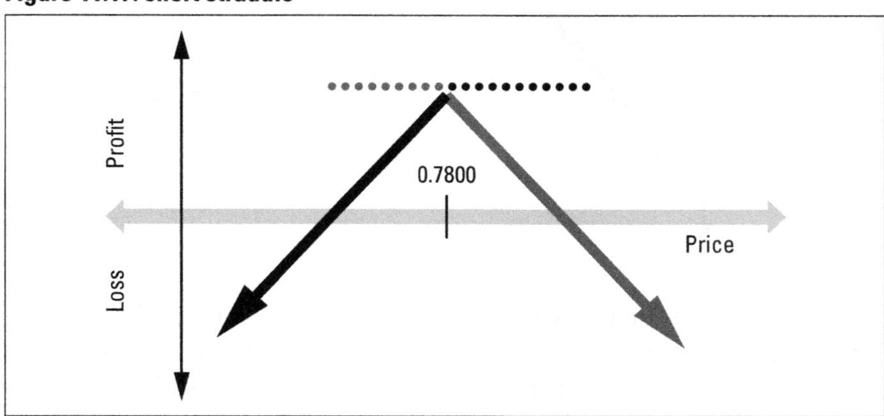

Short strangle

A short strangle is a short call and short put with the strike price of the short call at a higher strike than the strike for the short put. As with the short straddle, the trader employing a short strangle will receive premium on each of the two options and will benefit if volatility remains low or falls and prices remain relatively steady. There is room for slightly more movement in prices due to the different strike prices, but if prices move too far in either direction losses are potentially unlimited.

Maximum profit: Restricted to the amount of premium received for the two options
Maximum loss: Unlimited

Figure 11.18 shows that profits are maximised while price remains caught between the strike prices of the two options that have been sold. Once price moves above the upper strike price or below the lower strike price, the returns on this strategy start to diminish. As price continues to move away from the range defined by the two strike prices, losses become potentially unlimited.

Figure 11.18: short strangle

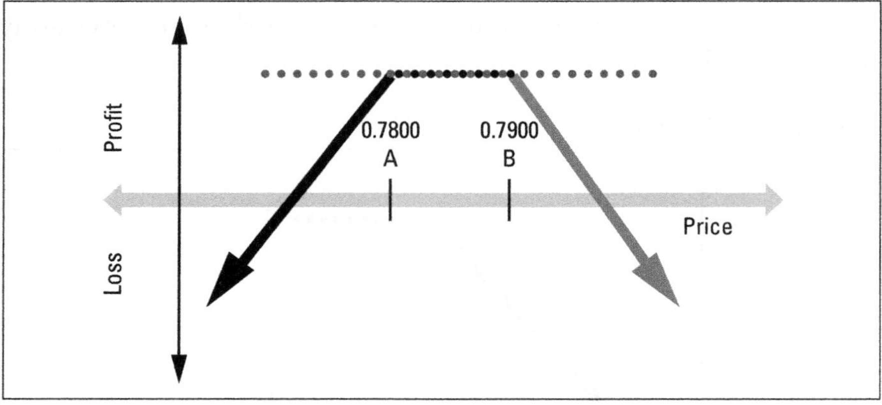

The option strategies outlined above are just the tip of the iceberg. Using different combinations of two or more options, it is possible to create many more strategies with names such as the call ratio back spread, condor, butterfly and Christmas tree, to name a few.

Chapter 12

Money management—the fundamentals

Yes, it's been a while coming since chapter 1, but finally, having covered most of the basics and a fair bit beyond, we can return to that most important of subjects for FX traders: money management. For many newcomers to trading, the field of money management is often given only a cursory glance, if that. People prefer to immediately search for that elusive pot of gold and jump right into devising systems that will guide them towards the best trade entry signals. Then, as they advance, they might start to consider the optimal time to close out their trades, whether they be winning trades or losing trades. Ultimately, though, those that achieve long-term success with their trading activities develop a stringent set of rules that relate to considerations such as:

- how much of their trading capital they will allocate to each trade
- how much of their trading capital will be placed at risk of loss on each trade (different from the amount allocated)
- how they will react to a long string of losing trades
- how and if they will add to winning positions
- what they will do with their losing positions.

Together these considerations amount to a stringent set of money management rules unique to each trader and they must be followed unfailingly. In the cumulative experience of the authors of this book, this is the one common thread for all successful traders, no matter what methods they use for generating entry and exit signals. The specific money management techniques used by traders are, however, wide and varied. A search of the internet will direct you to many resources, and you will quickly discover that money management methods range from the relatively simple through to the extremely complex. While it is true that the more complex methods may improve your overall performance over the long term, implementing even the simplest of systems will place you well ahead of the majority of traders who either ignore or are not aware of the importance of money management.

In the world of inter-bank trading there are considerably more factors to be considered, with issues such as settlement risk, pre-settlement risk and credit risk adding to the broader and more obvious market risk. The techniques employed by inter-bank traders to guard against these risks and the methods they use to achieve successful money management would fill a book of their own. For our purposes, it will suffice to say that inter-bank traders too are concerned very much with limiting the risk they face on each trade.

In the following pages, we outline one of the most popular and relatively simple methods of money management—the fixed fractional method.

The fixed fractional method

Firstly, you need to identify the amount of funds you have allocated to your trading activities. Usually, this is a simple matter of checking the balance of your trading account. The next step is to decide upon the level of risk that you are willing to accept on each trade. In other words, what percentage of your trading capital are you willing to lose on each trade? A commonly used figure by many in the markets is 2 per cent, which is why this method is also sometimes known as 'the 2 per cent rule'. Although we will run with the figure of 2 per cent for the examples that follow, there are many views on what this percentage should be.

Let's assume you currently have US$30 000 available for trading. If we use the 2 per cent figure, this means you are willing to accept a loss of 2 per cent of US$30 000, or US$600, on your next trade. When you have determined the dollar amount you are willing to risk, you need to look at your intended trade and work out how much risk you are facing in terms of pips. To do this, simply work out the difference between your entry price and the stop-loss price.

Let's say you decide to sell GBP/USD at 1.61250 with a stop loss at 1.61550. In this instance, you would be risking 30 pips. In the current example, selling one standard lot of GBP/USD is equivalent to selling £100 000 and buying US$161 250, assuming we get the rate of 1.61250. The profit or loss per pip is US$10.

So, having identified that the intended trade will deliver 30 pips of risk, if you trade a standard one lot contract you will be risking US$10 per pip, which equates to US$300 risk (30 pips × US$10). Earlier, you determined that you were willing to accept risk of 2 per cent of your US$30 000 account, or US$600. Therefore, it is a simple calculation to work out that you could, under these circumstances, trade two contracts on this particular trade and remain within the predetermined risk parameters.

Trading in varying currencies

The situation is slightly different if you are trading a currency pair in which the terms currency (the one on the right) is different from the currency in which the account is denominated. Let's assume the account in this example is denominated in GBP rather than USD. Pay close attention to the currencies of the following figures. If you assume an account balance of £30 000 and again use 2 per cent as the fixed fractional risk level, you will calculate that you can risk £600 on the next trade. At a GBP/USD rate of 1.61250, £600 is a significantly larger amount than US$600. Accordingly, you will be able to take a larger position.

Using the same details as above, the intended trade is presenting you with 30 pips of risk. And, because the terms currency in the GBP/USD pair is USD, this risk equates to US$10 per pip for each standard-sized one lot contract of £100 000 that is traded. Having determined that the risk on this trade is 30 pips, each lot traded results in US$300 worth of risk. At a rate of 1.61250, this is the equivalent of £186.05.

So, if your margin FX provider required you to trade only in multiples of 100 000 currency units, you would be able to trade three whole lots, or £300 000. This is determined by dividing the maximum risk allowance of £600 by the risk per contract of £186.05. However, if you are using a platform that allows you to trade smaller parcels, you may be able to trade 3.22 lots, or £322 000.

The process becomes more complicated when the currency in which your account is denominated is different from both of the currencies being traded. Consider for example a situation in which your account is denominated in AUD and you wish to trade EUR/USD. Let's assume this time that you have a trading account containing A$50 000. Using the 2 per cent figure once again, simple maths reveals you will be willing to risk a loss of A$1000 on your next trade.

If you are trading EUR/USD, your profit or loss will once again be derived in USD, but you will also need to know the AUD/USD rate so that you can convert the USD profit or loss back into AUD and compare this against your predetermined level of risk.

Consider an example in which you buy EUR/USD at 1.41450 with a stop loss at 1.41200. The risk on this trade is 25 pips.

Once again, on a standard-sized contract of €100 000, the profit or loss will be US$10 per pip. For this trade, your risk is therefore US$10 × 25 pips per standard contract, or US$250. Assuming an AUD/USD rate of 1.06780, this equates to A$234.13 per standard contract. As you have already determined that you can risk up to A$1000 of your A$50 000 account on this trade, it is now simply a matter of dividing A$1000 by the amount of risk per contract to determine the number of contracts to be traded. So, A$1000 ÷ $234.13 = 4.27. If you can only trade whole lots, you could trade up to four lots, or €400 000. If your platform allows trading in partial lots, you could take a slightly larger position, trading 4.27 lots, or €427 000.

Fixed fractional summary

Let's summarise the basic elements of the fixed fractional method of money management as applied to foreign exchange trading:

1 Identify the total value of funds you have available for trading.

2 Calculate the percentage of your trading account you are willing to risk on each trade and apply this to the current balance of your trading account to arrive at a dollar figure of acceptable risk.

3 Look at your intended trade. Determine the amount of risk as represented by the number of pips between the entry price and the stop-loss price.

4 Divide the amount you are willing to risk by the number of pips of risk associated with your intended trade. The result will reflect the amount you are willing to risk per pip of movement.

5 Divide the result of the above calculation by the value per pip of movement of a standard contract of the pair you intend to trade. If the per-pip value is not in the same currency as your underlying trading account balance, you will need to convert it before performing this division. Round down the result of this calculation to the nearest whole number to arrive at the number of whole lots that can be traded.

For example:

1 Trading funds available = A$50 000.

2 2% risk = A$50 000 × 0.02 = A$1000.

3 Risk in terms of pips, using the prior example with long entry at 1.41450 and stop loss at 1.41200: risk = 1.41450 – 1.41200 = 25 pips.

4 Divide dollar risk by pip risk: A$1000 ÷ 25 = 40.

5 Per-pip movement of a standard contract of 100 000 EUR/USD = US$10. Converting this to AUD at an AUD/USD rate of 1.06780 = A$9.365.

So, we now take the result from step 4 and divide it by A$9.365: 40 ÷ 9.365 = 4.27. This represents the amount we are willing to risk per pip, divided by the value of each pip.

As you can see, the calculations produce a figure of 4.27, which indicates that for the given account size, risk parameters and intended trade you can trade four standard-sized contracts.

An alternative to steps 4 and 5 is to simply divide the amount you are willing to risk, from step 2, by the result of the number of pips of risk from step 3, multiplied by the value per pip, converted into currency in which the account is denominated:

A$1000/[25 × (US$10/1.06780)] = 4.27.

It is interesting to note here that if the EUR/AUD rate were 1.3247, an account balance of A$50 000 would be the equivalent of €37 744.40. The full-size trade of €427 000 in the example above utilises leverage of slightly more than 11:1. This is considerably less than the 500:1 and 400:1 leverage available from many providers and is also less than the 50:1 cap in the USA and the 25:1 cap in Japan. This highlights the fact that when using disciplined and realistic money management techniques, it is rare that you will fully utilise the margin that is made available to you. Leverage of 100:1 is considerably more than most successful traders will ever need.

The method outlined above is very basic but, as mentioned, even the use of a simple money management plan such as this will help put you well ahead of most traders who never consider such things. As mentioned at the start of this chapter, the figure of 2 per cent is one that is widely used by many traders, although some would actually consider that even this figure is a little too large for their liking. There are many traders who aim to restrict the risk on each trade to no more than 1 per cent of their underlying trading account balance, and these traders would regard any risk of more than 2 per cent as being real 'gunslinger' territory. For example, one global currency fund manager recently published figures that show a maximum risk per trade of 0.005 per cent for intraday trades. On the other hand, some suggest that those with small accounts will take a long time to build their account if they limit their risk to just 2 per cent. These people would advocate using a higher percentage; perhaps 5 per cent, or even 10 per cent in extreme cases.

While it may indeed take longer to build up your account balance if you are risking smaller amounts of capital, when it comes to trading, slow and steady wins the race. Once you have more experience, you may wish to try out different levels of risk, but for starters you are probably best to stick with no more than 2 per cent if using this method of money management.

Risk management with open positions

In the examples above we have assumed that we are able to simply use the current value of a trading account balance for computation of the amount of risk you are willing to be exposed to on each trade. This is fine if you do not currently have any open positions and your account balance is a true reflection of all of the funds currently available to you. But what if you already have an open position, or several open positions? These open positions would have resulted in a reduction in the capital available in your trading account, by an amount equal to the margin requirements if trading margin FX.

Thus, if you simply use your current account balance as the basis for determining the amount of funds you are willing to risk on the next trade, each subsequent trade following the first will be of an artificially smaller size due to the fact that the available funds reflected in your account balance have been reduced by the amount of margin required to fund your existing open positions.

One way around this problem is to calculate the current value of your open positions if they were liquidated at the prevailing market price, and then add the freed-up margin, adjusted for the relevant profit or loss, to the current account balance. For example, you may have an available account balance of A$25 000 plus an open position of three lots, or A$300 000, in AUD/USD that is showing a profit of 55 pips. If you simply took your available account balance of A$25 000 and multiplied it by your chosen risk factor, say 2 per cent, you would arrive at a figure of A$500, meaning you would only be able to risk A$500 on the next trade. However, if you included the current value of your open position in this equation you would arrive at a higher figure, thus allowing more risk through either a larger position or a wider stop loss. A profit of 55 pips on this trade would be equal to US$1650 (or 55 pips × US$10 × 3 contracts). If AUD/USD were trading at 1.0443, this US$1650 would be equal to A$1580. This profit and the freed-up margin requirement of A$3000 can now be added to the available account balance for the purpose of determining how much you are able to risk on the next trade.

Adding up these various amounts, you have A$25 000 + A$1580 + A$3000 = A$29 580. This is the theoretical balance that you would have if you liquidated your open position at the current market price. Using this higher figure to determine your risk, you would end up with a figure of A$591.60, or 2 per cent of A$29 580. This extra A$91.60 of risk capital (or US$95.66 at AUD/USD 1.0443) would allow you to use a stop that was 9.5 pips wider on a A$100 000 position than would have been possible with only A$500 of risk capital.

On the surface, this may seem like a good way to squeeze extra mileage from your trading funds, but there is significant danger in using open positions in this way, especially if you are including the value of unrealised profits. If the market happens to turn against the original position, any other positions entered on the basis of the unrealised profits in that position would now be larger than you would like them to be, and your risk may suddenly exceed the level that you had previously selected.

To avoid this problem, you can modify the approach slightly and only include that portion of your open positions that is protected by a stop-loss order. In theory, the stop-loss order gives you a reasonable idea of the minimum amount that you can expect to recover from a trade if it is stopped out. If the trade is in profitable territory you will receive your margin plus the profit achieved between your entry price and the stop-loss price. If the trade has moved into negative territory, you will receive back your margin less the amount lost between your entry price and the eventual exit price achieved on the stop-loss order.

This method of using stop-loss–protected open equity is slightly more conservative than simply using open equity, but it should protect you from making decisions based on the shifting sands of unrealised equity.

If this whole field of analysing the potential risk that each trade poses to your account balance is new to you, it might be a good idea to make a conscious effort to alter the way you look at your trades. Before you start thinking of ways to spend the profits of your next trade, pause for a moment and ask yourself this very important question: 'If I am wrong about this trade, how much damage will it do to my account balance?' The answer should be within the risk parameters you have set for yourself, whether it be 2 per cent of stop-protected equity or some other measure.

The vital thing is to ensure that you adhere to your plan and do not allow the trade a little extra leeway in the hope that a loser will come good again. Tardiness in executing stops and cutting losing trades will eventually cost you a great deal of money.

Bear in mind, also, that this chapter barely scratches the surface of the field of money management, though hopefully it has awakened you to the idea that this is a crucial component of your trading activities which cannot be ignored. It is highly recommended that you take the time to discover more about this topic and find a method that suits your personal style and individual risk portfolio.

FX risk calculator

To simplify the whole process of calculating the most favourable position size and its approximate impact on your underlying account balance, regardless of which currency pair is being traded, you may want to try out the free FX Risk Calculator available from <www.alexdouglas.com>, as shown in figure 12.1.

By entering a number of variables—including your account balance, entry price, target price, stop-loss price and relevant exchange rates—the calculator will give an indication of your potential profit and loss figures, converted back into the same currency as your trading account balance along with the value per pip and reward/risk ratio.

Figure 12.1: risk calculator

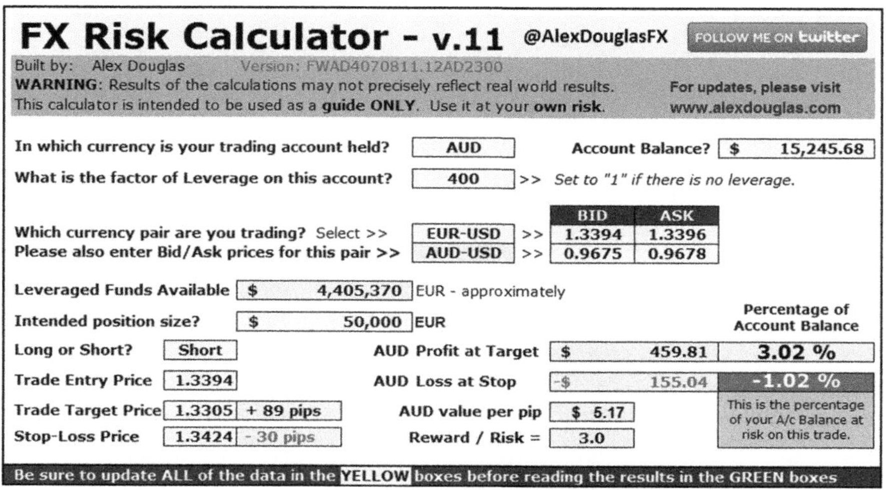

Chapter 13

(Your) Wealth on the global stage

By now you are probably convinced that there is some value in having an interest in the foreign exchange markets, but perhaps not that convinced that you should devote a lot more of your time or your own hard-earned money to it. Let us challenge your thinking by saying that quite a lot of you are already putting far too many eggs in one basket.

Accept you live in a currency volatile world

Currency volatility continually affects us in various direct and indirect ways. Accepting this paves the way to asking how to measure the likely impact of currency volatility on you, your portfolio and family. With currencies rising and falling, there are both opportunities and risks. A lot of these risks and opportunities will be involuntary. If we look at the recent volatility of the Australian dollar against the USD, for example, since 2000 the Australian dollar has risen from 47.7 US cents to 98.70 in mid 2008, then almost halved to 60.20 by the end of 2008, to trade back in the middle of 2011 more than US$1.10. In US dollar terms, the Australian dollar has doubled and halved and doubled again.

Even if you never intend to go to America and buy and spend in USD, you are still exposed to this capricious volatility. In recent years, many global investors in the face of the US dollar's persistent weakness and very low interest rates have sought comfort in buying gold; hence its stellar rise from $250 an ounce lows in the mid 1990s to more than US$1700. Very open and vocal discussions about the future (diminished) role of the US dollar challenges people, both professional and amateur, to think about ways to protect and enhance their wealth — and more importantly, think more creatively about what currencies to invest in. Some say the Chinese yuan, or at least a basket of our neighbours' currencies, should replace the US dollar in our region. Others say the euro is the way to go. Others suggest commodities, like gold and silver. But we haven't an answer or agreement yet, so the choices remain unresolved.

For those of us in sophisticated and advanced economies such as Singapore, Hong Kong, Japan, Australia, New Zealand and Malaysia, the default position is to sit in our own domestic economies. However, many recall the abrupt and disruptive nature of FX on wealth as well as currencies during the regional financial turmoil of 1997–98, something Europe and America have also recently discovered.

Even if we are wealthy and developed in our financial institutions our own personal plans are still subject to this overarching risk. We need to move away from the naïve comfort in our domestic wealth and investment asset allocations because we are taking a big gamble just sitting where we are.

The triple bet

In financial circles it is commonly acknowledged that investors have an overwhelming 'home country bias'. It means we tend to be heavily biased to investing exclusively in our home country (in some cases, home town), in its industries, real estate, and stocks and bonds, with a natural aversion to and suspicion of foreign markets.

Now emotionally there is a lot of sense in this. We tend to like to invest in what we can see, touch and, more importantly, 'understand'. Here we are making a virtue out of ignorance, which is great for emotional security, but bad risk management from a cool-headed investor's point of view.

In Australia and many other countries in Asia there is clearly significant currency risk for investors. It is called the triple bet on currency.

The first part of the triple bet is that the cost of living in Australia is largely not determined in Australia.

The US and Europe have huge economies that produce just about all the goods and services that anybody can possibly want. Most countries of the Asian region are heavily integrated. We don't produce all we consume in our country; we import an enormous amount.

The fundamental costs of living are not determined in your home country. The price of just about everything you put in your house, including the building materials and all the white goods, are not determined in Australia. The price of bread, for instance, is determined every day on the Chicago Board of Trade. Wheat, fish and meat all have global prices. Every time you put petrol into your car, take a holiday, buy a car or buy pharmaceuticals you are paying a global price.

The second part of the triple bet is the volatility of currencies around the world, specifically against the G7 major currencies like the euro and US dollar. How much our dollar, the yuan, yen, peso, won, ringgit and rupiah trade for is influenced by a variety of circumstances, including the current preferences of central banks around the world wanting to diversify away from US and European currencies. Major currency crosses such as the EUR/USD have been known to trade as low as 0.824 to as high as 1.48 in the space of one or two business cycles. Currencies are volatile and your money's buying power is too. You are carrying that risk every day, whether you want to acknowledge it or not.

The third part of the triple bet is that most of us have too many assets as a proportion of our wealth in our own country, so in constructing a long-term or more robust portfolio we need to think about diversifying into offshore investing. The big private and government funds adopted this strategy long ago and the better funds have significant offshore allocations, but the portfolio of the average wealthy Australasian does not. You cannot avoid the foreign exchange market; it is already in your pocket affecting you and your wealth and transactions day to day.

The mismatch of assets and life's liabilities

Investors with domestically focused assets face other risks or issues that need to be addressed in constructing a long-term portfolio. We can describe this as the mismatch of assets to life's liabilities.

Let us start with the cost of living. For most of us, the largest component in our spending is housing, which is largely the actual cost of construction. Then there is the household's goods and contents, as well as what we eat and drink, and the other things that we do.

Many people think that with a property and equity portfolio they are hedged to an extent to the inevitable rising cost of living. What is less appreciated is that often the stock index of a country may not be an adequate description of the true cost-of-living risks. The Australian stock market index, for instance, is a particularly stark example of this because it is concentrated in just two sectors, financials and materials (that is, mining). The Hong Kong stock exchange has bank and property sectors. Compare this with an investor in the US and you'd see an index that has different components. The London stock exchange and its index has completely different components again. The point is that it is too simplistic to regard investing in the long-term index as a good way to maximise your returns or hedge your cost of living. The Australian stock market and our region's stock exchanges are relatively small and skewed by our very industrial specialties. Investing in only one or two sectors is a pretty dangerous focus for hedging your long-term cost of living.

The next aspect of the mismatch of our assets and liabilities is life expectancy risk. Male life expectancy in 1950 in the developed world was 60; it has increased to 79. On average women will live two years longer. The healthy and wealthy live even longer, so if you look after your health and you're wealthy you need to plan for at least 25 or 30 years in retirement.

How much is enough to account for these long extra years? The amount you'll need in retirement depends fundamentally on your requirements. However, you can calculate the amount that you need to retire by working out the cost of living on the day you intend to retire, then multiplying it by 20. The figure you work out should enable you to withdraw enough money every year to leave enough capital gain to match the expected increase in the cost of living over the 20 to 30 years.

The challenge for contemporary investors is that they face cost-of-living volatility as a direct result of the globalised and integrated supply chain. We cannot run away from cost-of-living volatility; it is a fact of life. This volatility also affects the value of your accumulated wealth and that wealth is overwhelmingly concentrated against your future needs.

Because we are all living longer (and the wealthier we are, the longer we live) the capital we have will have to last longer and work harder and smarter for us. So what can we do?

Wealth creation, protection and transfer in the international setting

Knowing what they need and want is sometimes the hardest thing for investors. Too many of us focus on the day-to-day of our income activities and family pressures and responsibilities, but more needs to be considered.

Many holistic investors and family heads appreciate the need to plan their wealth creation, its protection and transfer in the international setting.

Protection is foremost. Affluent investors seek to diversify out of their local currencies to preserve their wealth. This is not always easy (or indeed locally legal), but the ingenuity of humans gives rise to ways to hedge out of currencies deemed weak or likely to weaken sharply. In local settings this is evidenced by people buying physical assets like land, buildings and jewellery as a way of 'selling' the local currency. Where legally allowed, buying foreign currency and assets is another way.

For those of us able to legally invest in foreign exchange, risk is more of a concern. Investors must work out their asset allocation, and where and how much to deploy wealth outside their normal currency of operation as a way to both protect and enhance wealth, a process that involves crossing political and currency borders.

For instance a Singaporean family wishing to educate their children in Australia may seek to hedge their exposure by buying an apartment near the intended school or university as a way to accommodate the physical needs of the child (and maybe the needs of the family to have a place to stay when they visit). Buying a property is a currency investing bet at its most basic. Aside from convenience, this is a wise investment if the family believes that the value of the apartment (or rents) will go up in Singaporean dollar terms in the future *faster* than if they kept their money in Singapore.

Buying an AUD asset is a definite weighting of the family's portfolio in favour of the Australian dollar to get domestic and currency related capital gains, while at the same time hedging the local (Australian) risk of rising rents that may hurt the family's cash flow, but also accommodates their future holiday/visiting needs.

Another example is a Hong Kong or Australian based investor who buys a Japanese ski lodge to accommodate their skiing hobby. In such a case, the investment both covers the accommodation requirements of the investor when skiing in Japan while hedging a portion of their assets into Japanese yen. Personal needs aside, this type of decision only makes sense if the price of the apartment (or rents) will go up in Hong Kong or Australian dollar terms in the future *faster* than if they kept their money at home.

First step — knowing your needs

Knowing their needs is sometimes the hardest thing for investors to come to grips with. As a good and trusted adviser will tell you, the investor should know what they want and need, as well as acknowledging their concerns, before any effective financial planning can be done. Alas, too many financial discussions talk about the risks and rewards of portfolio diversification as if it is purely a mathematical exercise. Working out the risks and rewards is partly arithmetic, but that is not the whole process. Financial professionals have fine-tuned but market-fallible means to best achieve the financial goals of a client, but will never tell the investor what they should have, want or need. That is best defined by the client.

The investor's needs could be about better wealth-enhancing investments and markets (here or internationally), protection of assets both here and abroad, or how to manage their assets in preparation for their incapacity or mortality; or it could be a combination of all three.

In simple terms the investor's needs could be as simple as deciding where to live — in Australia or in Bali?

If the investor wants to live in Bali, they will need a place to live and an income (if they don't intend to work) in the form of a rupiah-based cash flow, which means bank accounts. Do they want to repatriate their money to Indonesia now, later or never? If they don't want to repatriate their money, where and in what currency(ies) do they want to keep their investments? Is this consistent with their view of rupiah currency risks? Are they comfortable with the possible volatility of their capital and income in rupiah terms? Have the tax consequences been taken into consideration? What about residency and medical insurance? If the investor has children, what schools will they go to and how much will it cost? The questions and answers go on and on.

Many questions spin off the decision to relocate and lead to portfolio choice, not the other way.

While it is useful to think of wealth management in terms of maximising returns, there is more to consider when contemplating multinational wealth management. The investor should rule their investment portfolio, not the other way around.

Benefits of wealth management

Wealth management is actively assessing and enhancing the mix of your assets and investments (and liabilities), taking account of your changing needs in the context of the market (foreign currency) volatility, as well as other financial market trends and conditions.

Enhancing wealth is an important consideration for investors. In the context of foreign exchange, enhancing wealth is about what currencies and type of returns you are looking for. Many factors, such as geographical, legal, linguistic (you cannot converse in or understand the language of your target investment), tax and transactional cost reasons may lead to the default position of investors 'staying home' and investing only with the familiar.

While being able to do it yourself gives you a sense of control, it also helps sometimes to have a fully managed investment service in cases where you cannot necessarily be expected to run your own investment portfolio or know what markets to invest in, those to avoid and those that plainly don't fit your needs.

The need for support in wealth managing becomes paramount when you move away from your familiar environment and markets. Seldom does an investor, particularly when they are new to the art of investing, become an instant expert in foreign stocks, bonds and currencies just because the whim takes them, even when they accept the notion that in international markets, we don't know that much to begin with.

Many people may think they are as good as or better than investment professionals when it comes to wealth management. Aside from the risk of investor overconfidence, the self-directed investor also has the additional hazard of 'concentration risk'. You may hate the idea of giving the management of your money to just one adviser and relying on the wisdom and chance of one manager's performance, deeming it too risky, but you end up doing the same thing if you decide to do it all yourself.

Managing your wealth across borders is one thing, but it is always good to have more than one trusted adviser around you besides yourself (we mean a more substantial adviser than just the internet).

Protecting your wealth is as important a skill as being able to pick the markets correctly. It is not just about insurance, although this is important too. Protecting your wealth demands you plan and implement a set of strategies that provides protection for your assets against market disruption, legal or political risks, dissipation, divorce, litigation and third-party claims.

We are essentially talking about risk management. The most obvious (financial) risk for people with cross-border personal balance sheets is currency risk.

The diversity of assets (and liabilities) in a portfolio may be part of risk managing your portfolio. Take the case of the Australian-based investor in a Japanese ski lodge mentioned earlier. While the investor clearly has an exposure to the A$/yen rate with respect to his yen-priced asset (the lodge), this may be what the investor wants. Alternatively, this asset may be matched off with, say, a yen-based loan that means the investor's net A$/yen risk is mitigated by the complementary, like-priced yen loan. Of course he also has a choice of how to service the loan — does the investor pay with his A$ cash flow converted to yen, or does he do it with some other foreign cash flow? The choices can be endless and part of the attraction of thinking outside your home market.

One of the more obvious risk management measures you could undertake to avoid the dissipation of your wealth is appropriate tax planning. It is a good idea to prepare your assets and investments so that they form part of your tax planning provisions. It has been one of the banes of investors that investments into 'safe' developed economies markets tend to offer lower returns than emerging, higher risk markets (which is often where the affluent have made their money), compounded by the double drag of usually higher taxation levels, made even worse when penalty non-residency rates are applied. This is an important consideration when crossing borders with your investments

Lastly, with the responsibilities of wealth comes the need for discretion on the part of your financial services advisers and partners. Placing and managing your assets should be carried out while maintaining privacy. Discretion is a protection in itself.

Wealth transfer is planning the transfer of wealth. We may spend a lifetime accumulating and protecting wealth, but we do not live forever, so the transition to more sedate stages in life, such as retirement, needs to be managed effectively. When planning retirement you will need to decide where you want to live and travel, and what currencies you are going to spend. You will need to organise and manage your pensions and other retirement provisions, and in many cases you will want it to do it in several currencies.

Often affluent people have the choice of locations to 'rotate' their abodes, which they may do for weather or seasonally related reasons, or family, religious or school holiday events. If these abodes are in different countries then foreign currency and assets will be needed. Some countries have programs that actively encourage wealthy retirees to live at least part of their retirement in that country, provided they furnish a minimum amount of repatriated capital as well as appropriate character criteria. In our region, for instance, both Malaysia and Singapore have such programs which grant temporary residency (usually a minimum of five years) to financially qualified persons and families to settle, which may also carry with it tax and cost-of-living benefits for those who do choose to retire there. In Malaysia, the scheme is called Malaysia My Second Home (MM2H) see <www.malaysia-my-second-home.com>. Other plans are also available.

Another aspect of wealth is estate planning for when you are no longer around to provide for your partner, dependants and loved ones, or even to bequeath to philanthropic causes. Estate planning is more than about having a will (even though most people don't have one). It is also about planning for your incapacity and death.

Estate planning at the international level can be exceedingly complex and can have unintended consequences with respect to legal and tax issues that may give rise to cross-border and currency risk issues. Anyone who has dealt with international inheritances would vouch for the time and costs associated with settling affairs across borders, so estate planning should be addressed while you are healthy and have the capacity to address the issue.

Where to now? The checklist

Investors (and borrowers) with cross-border commitments must first identify actual or potential foreign currency exposures.

- Do you have foreign investments (or loans)?
- Do you have foreign exchange income (or expenses)?

If you answer yes to either of these questions, then you probably need a foreign exchange bank account for the non-local currencies that you will pay in or receive.

- Do you have a foreign exchange bank account?
- Where do you want that account to be?
- You may need a foreign currency credit or debit card as well. Have you considered this?
- Do you intend to live, work, invest, retire or study outside your normal country of residence?
- Do you care about the risks and opportunities of foreign exchange rate movements?
- How do you intend to manage the volatility of currency values of your wealth and cash flows?

Will it be by:

- speculating outright in the markets?
- hedging your transactional needs? If so, with what derivatives?
- invoicing in your revenues against the currency of your expenses?
- offsetting your foreign assets with foreign liabilities?
- having a ready reserve of foreign cash handy?

- Will you bother at all?

Now it is time to consider monitoring strategies:

- Will you have a stop-loss order or call trigger level with your broker or banker?
- Will you self-monitor (do you have time?), or not monitor at all and let God sort it out?

Finally of course, don't forget the non-financial aspects of your global wealth. Have you checked off the following?

- Do the legal structures around your wealth or assets provide adequate protection and allowance for your transfer instructions?
- Have you planned your finances for maximum growth? For income or capital appreciation?
- Have you adequately diversified across currencies, regions, assets and sectors to manage the overall portfolio risks?
- Have you made use of the tax planning opportunities that come with a global balance sheet?
- Have you started thinking outside the box of your local choices?

Some final points

We live in a currency volatile world. The currency market is a very important factor in determining the value of your wealth, which is usually far too heavily concentrated in your home country — the triple bet.

Your portfolio of assets may not match your current cost of living, nor your future liabilities. Having an internationally focused wealth plan to enhance, protect and prepare for the transfer of your wealth in the international market better integrates your needs with a more appropriate investment portfolio. We are not just talking about returns, but also about ways to mitigate and manage the inherent foreign exchange risks you carry generally, as well have as the risks specific to you.

For your wealth plan to be relevant and effective you need to first know what your needs are and that includes considering not just international investing, but a complete audit of where you want to live, work, invest, retire or study outside your normal country of residence. Working this out may be complex, as well may be the solutions, but it does not necessarily have to be so. The vast range of choices and potential rewards, as well as the safety of having a more integrated investment plan cannot be underestimated and should be considered, regardless of the ultimate choices you make.

Chapter 14
New technology

The only constant is change, continuing change, inevitable change, that is the dominant factor in society today. No sensible decision can be made any longer without taking into account not only the world as it is, but the world as it will be.
Isaac Asimov (1920–1992)

At its core, profitable trading is fairly simple. You just need to ensure that the price at which you buy is lower than the price at which you sell. While that may be easier said than done, it is a truth that has remained unchanged for thousands of years. However, nearly every other facet of trading has changed dramatically since the days when merchants travelled the ancient trade routes.

In the mid 1980s, major corporations would still use physical cheques delivered to a local bank branch for daily settlements. Charts used for technical analysis were still largely drawn by hand.

In the early 1990s, foreign exchange deals between global banks were confirmed via Telex messages. The first electronic foreign exchange brokers for the inter-bank market were still in development. Voice brokers sat around desks quoting prices down dedicated lines directly into the dealing rooms of participants in the inter-bank market, manually matching buyers and sellers.

By the mid to late 1990s, faxes had largely replaced Telex machines, and people were starting to discover the world wide web and the benefits of email. Around this time, the early adopters among retail traders started placing their trades on electronic trading platforms.

When we wrote the first edition of this book in 2005, the online retail foreign exchange market was growing in popularity but was still largely the domain of sophisticated traders and those with market experience. Back in 2001, the retail segment of the foreign exchange market was estimated to be responsible for turnover of less than US$10 billion per day according to LeapRate, an independent research and advisory firm. By 2007, the estimate by UBS for daily retail FX trading was US$50 billion. In September 2010, Forex Magnates published an estimate of US$165 billion per day. Just a few months later, in December 2010, LeapRate published a report estimating that daily foreign exchange trading volume by retail traders was in the region of US$200 billion.

Trading platforms

This phenomenal growth owes much to improvements in technology. Trading platforms have become increasingly sophisticated and reliable. Most now offer free charting tools to rival systems that once cost hundreds of dollars. Complex order types are also widely available, providing traders with greater control and ability to manage their risk.

Trading platforms continue to evolve. Although it can cost millions of dollars to build a new platform from scratch, many providers perceive there is a benefit in spending this money to provide traders with the latest tools and technology. No doubt we will continue to see brokers releasing new and updated trading platforms in the years ahead.

We are also likely to see more retail FX providers offering their clients trading platforms provided by specialist third party software companies. These companies are usually not involved directly in the 'broking' side of the FX business and instead focus solely on the front-end trading technology. Perhaps the most widely encountered company of this type is MetaQuotes Software, the provider of the popular MT4 platform.

Over the past couple of years there has been a notable increase in the number of providers offering MT4 to their clients. For some, especially for newer FX providers, this is an economic decision. However, it appears that some established providers have found demand for MT4 to be so strong that they have been compelled to add it to their product line-up.

A great many add-ons have been created by FX providers and other software companies to enhance the usability of the front-end of the MT4 platform. Some of these include one-click trading and the ability to place complex order types.

Although the MT4 front-end looks very similar from one FX provider to the next, there can be major differences in the back-end technology used to drive the platform. We discuss some of these differences in the next section.

In 2005, we could not have foreseen the development of today's smart-phones and tablet computers, or the speed with which they have been adopted. Trading platforms developed for these devices have finally seen the arrival of truly mobile trading. We can only imagine what kind of new trading platforms will be developed as technology continues to evolve in the years ahead.

Back-end technologies

Changes to the front-end of trading platforms are always the most obvious. However, changes on the back-end can have the greatest impact on your trading.

As the speed of execution has become more important for more and more traders, many FX providers have made significant investments in technology to improve performance in this area. As well as improving the actual back-end architecture, many have taken steps to ensure that their trade servers are located as close as possible to the banks they deal with in the inter-bank market. Moving trade servers can shave hundreds of milliseconds off execution times, resulting in a better trading experience for clients. Some providers now show average server-side execution times of just two milliseconds.

Many retail FX providers have also invested heavily in reducing the rates of trade rejection that their clients experience. While there can be many reasons for a trade to be rejected, providing fast execution times will help to reduce the likelihood of such an event. Cascading execution technology with multiple liquidity providers can further reduce rejection rates.

Virtual private server (VPS)

The majority of trading platforms simply cease managing your orders if your computer is turned off or goes off-line for any reason. This can be a significant risk for many traders.

One solution is to make use of a virtual private server (VPS). While some FX providers offer an in-house VPS solution, you can also use independent providers. A VPS is simply another computer in a remote location on which you can run your trading software. They are usually housed in a dedicated data centre with round-the-clock monitoring, back-up power systems and guaranteed 'up time' of 99.9 per cent (for example).

In addition to the peace of mind offered by the reliability of a VPS, there is often a speed advantage as well. If you use a solution provided by your broker it is likely to be located very close to the trade servers that your trades will be executed on. This is of special significance to traders making use of trading algorithms, or trading robots. For those using MT4, these are referred to as expert advisors (EAs).

There may be latency of a couple of hundred milliseconds between your computer and the trade server of your FX provider because of your geographic location. By using a co-located VPS, you may be able to cut this latency back to almost nothing. Even though the total difference in execution time may be less than half a second, this can have a notable impact on the results achieved by a trading robot (or EA).

Algorithmic trading

One of the major advantages of algorithmic, or robotic, trading is that once your algorithm is in place, it will continue to monitor and trade the market twenty-four hours a day, five and a half days a week.

Although you may not have tried algorithmic trading yourself, there has been a substantial increase in trading volumes attributed to this type of trading in recent years.

In September 2011, the independent research and advisory firm Aite Group published a report titled *Algorithmic Trading in FX: Ready for Takeoff?* The report indicates that while algorithms accounted for 7 per cent of FX trade volume at the end of 2010, they anticipate this figure will rise to 25 per cent by 2014 (see figure 14.1).

Figure 14.1: projected adoption of algorithms, 2007 to e2014

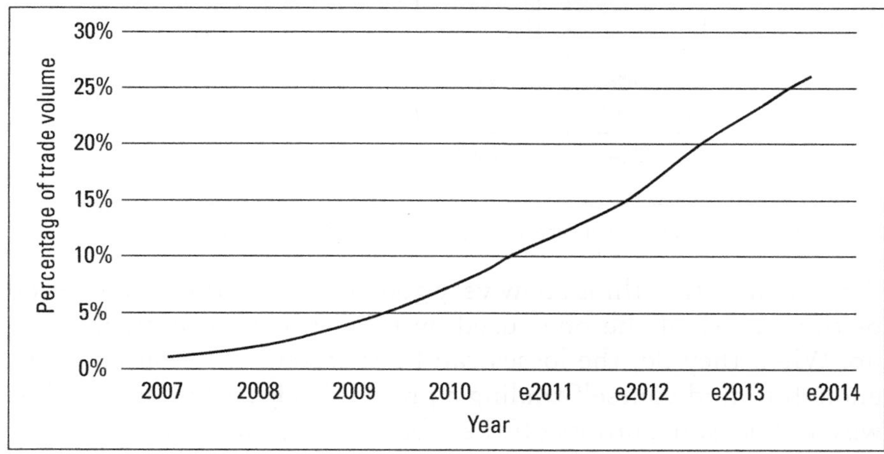

Source: © 2011, Aite Group, LLC.

On the institutional side, the growth of algorithmic trading has been even faster. The Bank for International Settlements (BIS) *Quarterly Review* of December 2010 included a special feature on the growth of the FX market. In this report BIS quoted research from the world's largest institutional FX broker, EBS, showing that 45 per cent of trade through EBS was attributable to algorithms in 2010. This figure was up from 28 per cent in 2007 and just 2 per cent in 2004 (see figure 14.2, overleaf).

Figure 14.2: share of manual versus algorithmic trading on EBS, 2004 to 2010

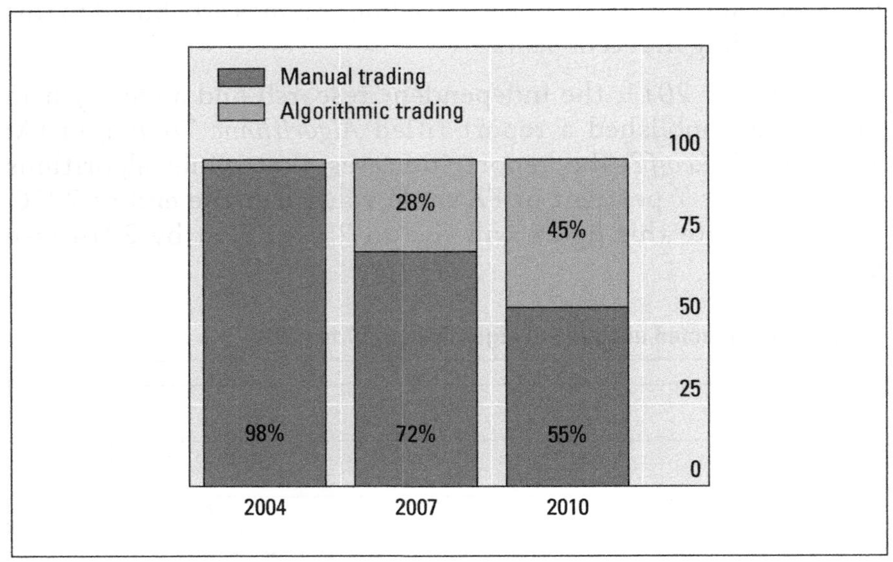

Source: Bank for International Settlements, *Quarterly Review*, December 2010.

While many algorithms show very good rates of return for a period of time, most of the ones used by retail traders eventually blow up. When they do, the losses can be spectacular. If you are lucky enough to find yourself trading a profitable algorithm, it would be wise to take some profits off the table on a regular basis in order to quarantine them from any unexpected drawdown in the future.

In both the institutional and retail FX markets, it is highly likely that we will see more and more automated algorithmic trading tools appear in the years ahead.

Social trading networks

Social trading networks are where trading meets Facebook. Several of these sites have emerged over the last few years. Although they are all slightly different in the way that they operate and the way that traders interact with them, there are some common threads.

All these services aim to bring together successful traders and those who want to follow them and/or copy their trades. Some require you to subscribe to a particular system (or algorithm) and some allow you to have trades copied directly into your own trading account. Others allow you to freely follow other traders, copy their trades and even 'like' them as you would on Facebook.

The future

Given the rate at which people are signing up to social trading networks, they are likely to play a growing part in retail FX trading in the future, as are platforms that allow for automated algorithmic trading.

There is no doubt that technology will deliver newer, smaller and faster devices in the years ahead that could be used for trading. However, we may not actually use them for trading to any great extent. Although traders are currently eager to have trading platforms on their smart-phones, the majority of trading still takes place on traditional desktop and laptop computers, with smaller mobile devices used more frequently for monitoring prices.

While they won't be so obvious to traders, improvements in back-end technology are also likely to continue at a rapid pace. This will provide traders with further improvements in the speed and reliability of execution.

If current trends continue, global foreign exchange turnover will continue to expand and the retail segment will make up an increasingly large portion of trade, albeit from a small base. This, in turn, should result in a further improvement in trading conditions for retail traders.

Conclusion and next steps

Alex mentioned at the start of this book's journey that an understanding of risk and the new trading technology is not something to be avoided but embraced. By now, in these final few pages, you know these are not the only challenges you will face when entering the marketplace. At the start of the second decade of the 21st century, the global economy is faced with a patchwork of threats as well as opportunities; still-recovering and troubled developed world financial markets cohabit with impatient emerging mega-blocs in the eastern hemisphere. Hitherto 'safe' currencies are under question as uneven borrowing and lending financial flows, contoured by jaggedly varying currency regulation and institutions, are stressed to find stable homes for savings and investment flows. Foreign exchange markets have become the early signaller of troubles ahead.

In crisis there is opportunity. In risk, there is reward. To the vigilant there are pearls of value. The FX market is truly a global stage and is wide enough to encompass our wildest visions of profitable opportunity. Your first task is to set limits on how much time and capital you want to give it. You need to sleep to avoid being swallowed by the FX market.

Investing in the FX market is a long-haul game, so have patience and pace yourself. You will not be able to read all the useful websites in a day, nor retain them instantly. With the closing of the back cover of this book comes the start of the challenge of coming to grips with the ebb and flow of foreign exchange markets and their trends. All of us, both amateur and professional, newly entered and hardened veterans, are constantly learning to adapt to its ruthless disciplines.

The FX market is eternally evolving and fascinating. It may even be a harsh teacher and task master too, as many of you will find. The acquired wisdom, as well as being rewarding, will make you a stronger, sharper and hopefully richer person for the effort.

Peter Pontikis
September 2011

Appendix: World currency codes

AED	United Arab Emirates dirham
AFN	Afghanistan afghani
ALL	Albania lek
AMD	Armenia dram
ANG	Netherlands Antilles guilder
AOA	Angola kwanza
ARS	Argentina peso
AUD	Australian dollar
AWG	Aruba guilder
AZN	Azerbaijan new manat
BAM	Bosnia-Herzegovina convertible marka
BBD	Barbados dollar
BDT	Bangladesh taka
BGN	Bularia lev
BHD	Bahrain dinar
BIF	Burundi franc
BMD	Bermuda dollar
BND	Brunei Darussalam dollar
BOB	Bolivia boliviano
BRL	Brazil real
BSD	Bahamas dollar
BTN	Bhutan ngultrum
BWP	Botswana pula
BYR	Belarus ruble
BZD	Belize dollar
CAD	Canada dollar
CDF	Congo/Kinshasa franc
CHF	Switzerland franc
CLP	Chile peso
CNY	China yuan renminbi
COP	Columbia peso
CRC	Costa Rica colon
CUC	Cuba convertible peso
CUP	Cuba peso
CVE	Cape Verde escudo
CZK	Czech Republic koruna
DJF	Djibouti franc
DKK	Denmark krone
DOP	Dominican Republic peso
DZD	Algeria dinar
EGP	Egypt pound
ERN	Eritrea nakfa
ETB	Ethiopia birr
EUR	Euro member countries
FJD	Fiji dollar
FKP	Falkland Islands (Malvinas) pound
GBP	United Kingdom pound

GEL Georgia lari
GGP Guernsey pound
GHS Ghana cedi
GIP Gibraltar pound
GMD Gambia dalasi
GNF Guinea franc
GTQ Guatemala quetzal
GYD Guyana dollar
HKD Hong Kong dollar
HNL Honduras lempira
HRK Croatia kuna
HTG Haiti gourde
HUF Hungary forint
IDR Indonesia rupiah
ILS Israel shekel
IMP Isle of Man pound
INR India rupee
IQD Iraq dinar
IRR Iran rial
ISK Iceland krona
JEP Jersey pound
JMD Jamaica dollar
JOD Jordan dinar
JPY Japan yen
KES Kenya shilling
KGS Kyrgyzstan som
KHR Cambodia riel
KMF Comoros franc
KPW Korea (North) won
KRW Korea (South) won
KWD Kuwait dinar
KYD Cayman Islands dollar
KZT Kazakhstan tenge
LAK Laos kip
LBP Lebanon pound
LKR Sri Lanka rupee
LRD Liberia dollar
LSL Lesotho loti
LTL Lithuania litas
LVL Latvia lat
LYD Libya dinar
MAD Morocco dirham
MDL Moldova leu
MGA Madagascar ariary
MKD Macedonia denar
MMK Myanmar (Burma) kyat
MNT Mongolia tughrik
MOP Macau pataca
MRO Mauritania ouguiya
MUR Mauritius rupee
MVR Maldives (Maldive Islands) rufiyaa
MWK Malawi kwacha
MXN Mexico peso
MYR Malaysia ringgit
MZN Mozambique metical
NAD Namibia dollar
NGN Nigeria naira
NIO Nicaragua cordoba
NOK Norway krone
NPR Nepal rupee
NZD New Zealand dollar
OMR Oman rial
PAB Panama balboa
PEN Peru nuevo sol
PGK Papua New Guinea kina
PHP Philippines peso
PKR Pakistan rupee
PLN Poland zloty
PYG Paraguay guarani
QAR Qatar riyal
RON Romania new leu
RSD Servia dinar
RUB Russia ruble
RWF Rwanda franc
SAR Saudi Arabia riyal
SBD Solomon islands dollar
SCR Seychelles rupee

SDG Sudan pound
SEK Sweden krona
SGD Singapore dollar
SHP Saint Helena pound
SLL Sierra Leone leone
SOS Somalia shilling
SPL Seborga luigino
SRD Suriname dollar
STD Sao Principe and Tome dobra
SVE El Salvador colon
SYP Syria pound
SZL Swaziland lilangeni
THB Thailand baht
TJS Tajikistan somoni
TMT Turkmenistan manat
TND Tunisia dinar
TOP Tonga pa'anga
TRY Turkey lira
TTD Trinidad and Tobago dollar
TVD Tuvalu dollar
TWD Taiwan new dollar
TZS Tanzania shilling
UAH Ukraine hryvna
UGX Uganda shilling
USD United States dollar
UYU Uruguay peso
UZS Uzbekistan som
VEF Venezuela bolivar fuerte
VND Vietnam dong
VUV Vanuatu vatu
WST Samoa tala
XAF Communaute Financiere Africaine (BEAC) CFA franc BEAC
XAG Silver
XAU Gold
XCD East Caribbean dollar
XDR International Monetary Fund (IMF) Special Drawing Rights
XOF Communuate Financiere Africaine (BCEAO) franc
XPD Palladium
XPF Comptoirs Francais du Pacifique (CFP) france
XPT Platinum
YER Yemen rial
ZAR South Africa rand
ZMK Zambia kwacha
ZWD Zimbabwe dollar

Index

absolute returns funds *see* hedge funds
algorithmic trading 1, 195–197, 256–258
amount to trade with 232–236
announcements, influence on FX markets *see* data releases
arbitrage, currency 4, 6, 189, 192–194
Asia *see also* individual countries
— central banks 56, 57, 101
— 1997–98 currency crisis 64, 65, 99, 100, 103
ask price *see* bid/ask price
asset prices, influence on FX markets 95
assets and liabilities, mismatch of 243–246
Australia 74, 82, 92, 96, 99, 104; *see also* Reserve Bank of Australia
Australian dollar (AUD) 10, 18, 23, 24, 55–56, 96, 103, 185; *see also* Reserve Bank of Australia

back-end technologies 255–256
balance of payments (BoP) and FX 91–92, 164–167, 171
Bank of Canada 185
Bank of England (BoE) 64, 82–83, 93, 169, 170, 185
Bank for International Settlements (BIS) 6–7, 15, 21, 24, 26, 60, 61
Bank of Japan (BoJ) 10, 56, 93, 169, 170, 185
banks, central *see* central banks
banks, investment 4, 52
banks, trading 4, 5, 52, 54
banks and FX 4, 54–55, 182–183, 191–192
base (commodity) currency 41–42
bear markets 47–48
bid/ask price 32, 34, 37–39
— decimal places 33–35, 36, 39
— spread 27–28, 39–41, 70 77–78, 86
bid quotes 5–6
big figure 35–36
Big Mac index 162–164
big trades, influence on FX markets 105–106
Bollinger Bands 145–146
borrowing *see* carry trades; margin; leverage
Brazil 95, 96
breakout strategies 204–207
Bretton Woods Accord 9, 11
brokerage *see* ticket fee
brokers, FX 1, 4, 5, 65, 73–74, 183–184, 197–199
bull markets 47–48

Canada 95
Canadian dollar (CAD) 26, 28
candlestick charts 146–149
carry trade 189, 211, 216–218
central authority, none in FX 5–6
Central Bank of China (PBoC) 15,16, 17, 93, 169, 184–185, 186
central banks 6–7, 10, 11, 14, 18, 19, 52, 55–57, 66–67, 92–93, 101, 169–170, 184–186; *see also* names of individual banks
CFDs (contracts for difference) 58, 65
chart patterns 132–139
—double and triple tops and bottoms 135–137
—flags 137–138
—head and shoulders reversal 133–135
—inverted 48
—triangles 138–139
charts *see also* Bollinger Bands; candlestick charts; Ichimoku Kinko Hyo charts; long-term charts; MACD (moving average convergence indicators); momentum oscillator indicators; short-term charts; trend following indicators
—information sources 115
—patterns 132–139
—types 121–132
—using 150–158
Chile 95, 96
China 15–17, 57, 94, 100–101, 184–185
Chinese yuan (renminbi) (CNY) 15–17, 20, 21, 54, 186
clients of wholesalers 57–65
CLS (continuous linked settlement) Bank 186–187, 200
closing time 153–155
codes for currencies 23, 24, 41
collinearity trap 118
commission 84, 86; *see also* fees and charges; ticket fee
commodity bloc 95–97
commodity (base) currency 41–42
commodity prices and FX 95–97
contract size 76–77
cooperation, economic 11–12
corporations and FX 54, 61–62, 187–188
costs, trader 34
counterparties 5, 31–32, 69–70; *see also* price maker; price taker
CPI (consumer price index) and FX 108–109, 173
CRB (Commodity Research Bureau) Spot Index 96
credit ratings and FX 98–99
crosses 27, 243
currency controls and FX 100–101
currency pairs *see* pairs, currency

daily swap *see* rollover
dark pools 195–197
data releases and FX 78, 106–113, 159–160, 167–168, 169–178
dealing centres 189–190
debt management, national 59–60
deflation and FX 94–95
Denmark 14
derivatives 53–55, 188
durable goods orders and FX 110, 174–175

EBS (Electronic Broker Services) 5–6, 34–35, 194–195
—pricing model 71, 72–73
ECN (electronic communications network) 37, 84
economic fundamentals and FX 89–113, 159
economic indicators and FX 167–168

economic information, sources of 178–180
economic reports 169–178
Elliott Wave 158
employment figures and FX 111–113, 171–172
environment and FX 103–104, 185
equilibrium at a glance charts 149–150
European Central Bank 11, 20, 21, 92, 169, 170, 185
European euro 10, 13–15, 19–20, 21, 23, 24
European Union 11–15, 20
euro zone 14
exchange rates, determining 159–160
—economic indicators 167–169
—economic reports 169–180
—theories of 160–167
execution of trades 5–6

Federal Reserve, US 18, 56, 92, 169–170, 170–171
fees and charges 32, 46, 73, 77, 84–87
Fibonacci retracements 131, 132, 158
Financial Conduct Authority (UK) 83
fiscal policy, and FX 97–98, 99
fixed fractional method 232–236
flash crash 196
foreign exchange, defined 3–4
foreign reserves 59, 61, 166
forward points strategies 213–216
forward rolls strategies 211, 212–213
forwards market 52, 53, 55
free-floating currencies 8, 9–10, 100, 185; *see also* managed float
fundamental analysis for FX 159–180
fund managers and FX 4, 62–64, 188; *see also* hedge funds
Future Fund, Australia's 59
futures 32, 47, 53, 74, 76, 83, 157, 189, 210, 219

Germany 15, 186
GFC and following 17–19, 56, 185–186, 194
global considerations 241–246
gold 8–9, 14, 20
government 10, 52, 55–57, 59, 60, 65, 90, 93; *see also* central banks
—budget and fiscal policy and FX 97–98, 99
—credit rating 20, 98–99
—currency controls and FX 94, 100–101
Great Britain *see* United Kingdom
Great British pound 10, 23, 24, 64, 185
Greece, debt crisis 20, 98, 99
Greek measures 221
gross domestic product (GDP) 15, 16, 20, 162, 175–176
Group of Eight countries (G8) 11, 12, 26
Group of Twenty countries (G20) 11–12, 18, 21

handle 36–37
harmonisation, international 11–12
hedge accounting standard 188
hedge funds 62–64, 188–189
hedging strategies 54, 55, 62, 62–64, 188, 218, 244, 245–246
high frequency traders (HFTs) 1, 63–64, 195–197, 198
history of FX market 8–12
hitting the bid 38
home country bias 242–243
Hong Kong Monetary Authority (HKMA) 17, 57, 100

Ichimoku Kinko Hyo charts 149–150
industrial production (IP) and FX 110
industrial unrest and FX 103–104
inflation and FX 94–95, 172–173

influences on FX markets 89–113
institutional FX 181–200
—defined 181–182
—online portals 197–199
—participants 182–190
inter-bank market 4, 5, 7, 36, 37, 52, 54, 76, 77, 87, 105, 181–200, 214, 232
interest accrued overnight *see* rollover
interest rates and FX 92–94, 160, 166–167, 212–213, 214, 216, 218
intermediaries 69; *see also* brokers; online trading/margin FX providers
International Monetary Fund 9, 11, 20, 60, 61
intrinsic value 160
inverted charts *see* charts
investors in FX 64–65
Ireland 20
Italy 20

Japan 15, 185; *see also* Bank of Japan
Japanese yen (JPY)10, 23, 24, 64, 185
jaw-boning 56, 184
jobbing 55

law of one price 160–161
leverage 74–75, 188
liquidity 25, 27, 28–29, 65, 72, 77, 78, 85, 207
long position 32–33
Long-Term Capital Management 188
long-term charts 125–132

majors 26–27
Malaysia currency controls 101
Malaysian ringgit (MYR) 64, 65, 101
managed float 10, 184–185
margin 74–75
market makers 190–192
—pricing 71, 72, 190–192
markets 104–105
market segments 4–5
mean reversion strategy 201, 207–209
media reporting, local 48–49
Mexican peso (MXN) 28
momentum indicators 119
momentum oscillator indicators 142–144
monetary policy 14, 92–94, 169–170
money management 2, 231–239
MACD (moving average convergence indicators) 144
moving averages 140–142, 158

natural disasters *see* environment and FX
NDFs (non-deliverable forward markets) 53, 54
New Zealand 95, 104, 153
New Zealand dollar (NZD) 10, 28, 96, 103, 185
Norway 95
Norwegian krone (NOK) 28

offer quotes 5–6
oil crisis 11
online trading 194–199
online trading/margin provider 4, 52, 58, 65, 69–78
—access to other markets 81
—brokers 34–35, 70
—charting service 81
—counterparties 5, 73, 86
—choosing 71–84
—margin and leverage 74–75
—pairs available 81
—platforms 71, 78–80
—pricing model 71–73
—profits 84–87

—questions to ask 83–84
—regulatory environment 81–83
—size and backing 73–74
—spread width 77–78
—trade sizes 76–77
—terminology 39
open positions, risk management for 236–239
options market 52, 53–55
option strategies 3, 219–230
—Greek measures 221
—long call 222–223
—long put 224
—long straddle 227
—long strangle 228
—multiple 227
—short call 224–226
—short put 226
—short straddle 229
—short strangle 229–230
—types 219, 230
OTC markets 3, 4, 197

pairs, currency 15, 16, 24–26, 28, 42, 43, 48–49
—liquidity 28, 40, 78
—long and short positions 32–33
—most traded 26–26
participants, FX market 51–67
phone trading 80
pips 33–36, 40
fractions of 33–35, 36
pivot points 210–211
platforms, retail trading 71, 78–80, 194–195, 254–255; *see also* online trading/margin provider
Plaza Accord 56
politics, influence on FX markets 101–103
Portugal 20
PMI (purchasing managers index) and FX 110
PPI (producer price index), influence on FX markets 109–110
price discovery 69, 190–192
price maker 31–32, 37, 38, 57
price taker 31–32, 57
printing money *see* quantitative easing
products 52; *see also* spot; forwards; options
profit/loss 43, 44–45, 46
purchasing power parity (PPP) 161

quantitative easing 56, 170
quantitative policy 170–171
Quantum Fund 64
quotations, price 32–33
—components 38–39
—conventions 41–42
—direct 42–43
—indirect 42–43
—reasons for different 5–6
quoted currency *see* terms currency

range trading strategies 203–204
reason for FX trading 51
regulation of FX trading 73, 74, 81–83
Relative Strength Index (RSI) 143–144, 158
Reserve Bank of Australia 7, 10, 18, 21, 26, 93, 106, 169, 184, 189
Reserve Bank of New Zealand 106
retail sales and FX 109, 173–174
retail traders 4, 5, 34, 58–59
—calculating profit/loss 43, 44–45
—contract size 43
—costs 58–59
—online 31–32, 36, 37, 69–78
—Muslim 46
—no-swap accounts 46
—platforms/providers 4, 32, 37, 69–87

retail traders *(Cont'd)*
—price maker 31–32
—prices 52–53
—price taker 31–32, 39, 57
—spreads 58–59
Reuters (broker) 34–35, 191, 194
risk 55
—calculator 239
—managing 70, 86, 186–187, 218, 231–239, 245
—managing open positions 236–239
rollover (swap) 46, 84–85, 213
Russia 11, 95

scratch a trade 40
short-date transactions 53
short position 32–33
short-term charts 121–124
slippage 205, 206–207
Smithsonian Agreement 9
social trading networks 258–259
social unrest, influence on FX markets 103–104
Soros, George 64
South Africa 95
sovereign wealth funds 59–60
Spain 20
speculators 64–65
spot FX 33, 34, 35, 52–53, 54, 76, 96, 193, 213, 214–216
spreads *see* bid/ask, spreads
squaring up 55
Standard & Poor's 20, 98
State Administration of Foreign Exchange (SAFE) (China) 16
stop-loss orders 204, 205, 206–207, 238
straddling the market 204–207
straight through pricing (STP) 37, 71, 72, 78
straight through processing 197
strategies for FX trading 201–230; *see also* breakout strategies; carry trades; forward points strategies; forward rolls strategies; Greek measures; mean reversion strategies; options; pivot points; range trading strategies; trend following strategies
supernationals and FX 60–61
supply and demand, influence on FX markets 89–113
swap *see* roll-over
swap, FX 53
swap lines of credit 18
Swedish krona (SEK) 28
Swiss franc (CHF) 23, 24, 26, 27, 28

taking the offer 38
technical analysis for FX 115–158; see also Bollinger Bands; candlestick charts; chart patterns; Ichimoku Kinko Hyo charts; long-term charts; MACD (moving average convergence indicators); momentum oscillator indicators; retracements; short-term charts; support and resistance; trend following indicators; trend lines
—assumptions behind 120–121
—defined 115–120
—indicators 118–120
—trends 119, 121–123, 125–129
—using 150–158
—types of 121–132
technology, influence of 1, 197, 253–260; *see also* online trading; online trading/margin provider
terms (quoted) currency 41–42
terms of trade, influence on FX markets 95–97
Thai baht (THB) 64, 65
thirds 27
ticket fee 32, 41, 46
time zones 28–29, 46, 106, 153–155
today plus two *see* spot market

trade and FX 92, 171
trading, choice of currencies 27–29
transnational corporations 61–62
trends, following 152–153, 156; *see also* technical analysis
trend following indicators 139–142
— momentum oscillator 142–144
— moving averages 140–142
— strategies 202–203
2 per cent rule *see* fixed fractional method

unemployment *see* employment
unison movement of currencies 150–151
United Kingdom 14, 82; *see also* Great British pound
United States 17–19, 74, 83, 92, 98, 104–105, 109–110, 111
US dollar (USD) 9, 10, 15, 20, 23, 24, 25–26, 42–43, 89, 150

verbal trades 39
volatility in FX 18–19, 28–29, 53, 207, 241–242, 243
volume of FX trades 6–7, 18–19, 24, 25, 63, 106, 157
VPS (virtual private server) 256

wholesale FX market *see* inter-bank market
war, influence on FX markets 101–103
wealth creation and protection 245–251
wholesale participants, clients of 57–65
World Bank 9, 11, 60, 61
World Federation of Exchanges 7

%b 209

The foreign exchange market is dynamic and changing rapidly. To keep up to date with the latest developments you may like to visit the websites or Twitter accounts of the authors of this book:

Alex Douglas:

Website <www.alexdouglas.com>
Twitter @AlexDouglasFX

Larry Lovrencic:

Website <www.ichimokucharts.com>
Twitter @ichimokucharts.

Peter Pontikis:

Email peter.pontikis@gmail.com

Printed in Australia
11 Feb 2025
LP041382

9 780730 376521